Sappho in Early Modern England

THE CHICAGO SERIES ON
SEXUALITY, HISTORY, AND SOCIETY

Edited by John C. Fout

Also in the series

$\mathscr{S}$APPHO
in Early Modern England

Female Same–Sex Literary Erotics
1550 – 1714

Harriette Andreadis

THE UNIVERSITY OF CHICAGO PRESS
CHICAGO AND LONDON

HARRIETTE ANDREADIS
is associate professor of English at
Texas A&M University.

The University of Chicago Press, Chicago 60637
The University of Chicago Press, Ltd., London
© 2001 by The University of Chicago
All rights reserved. Published 2001
Printed in the United States of America
10 09 08 07 06 05 04 03 02 01   1 2 3 4 5

ISBN: 0-226-02008-8 (cloth)
ISBN: 0-226-02009-6 (paper)

Library of Congress Cataloging-in-Publication Data

Andreadis, Harriette
    Sappho in early modern England : female same-sex literary erotics, 1550 –1714 / Harriette Andreadis.
      p.   cm.—(Chicago series on sexuality, history, and society)
    Includes bibliographical references and index.
    ISBN 0-226-02008-8 (alk. paper)—ISBN 0-226-02009-6 (pbk. : alk. paper)
    1. English literature—Early modern, 1500 –1700—History and criticism.   2. Homosexuality and literature—England—History.   3. English literature—Women authors—History and criticism. 4. English literature—18th century—History and criticism.   5. Lesbians' writings, English—History and criticism.   6. Erotic literature, English—History and criticism.   7. Women and literature— England—History.   8. English literature—Greek influences.   9. Lesbians in literature.   10. Sappho— Influence.   11. Sex in literature.
    I. Title.   II. Series.
    PR428.H66 A54   2001
    820.9'3538'086643—dc21   00-012562

Parts of chapters 1, 2, 3, and 4 were published in earlier versions and appear here by permission of the publishers: "Theorizing Early Modern Lesbianisms: Invisible Borders, Ambiguous Demarcations," in *Virtual Gender: Fantasies of Subjectivity and Embodiment,* edited by Mary Ann O'Farrell and Lynne Vallone, 125–46 (Ann Arbor: University of Michigan Press, 1999); "Sappho in Early Modern England: A Study in Sexual Reputation," in *Re-Reading Sappho: Reception and Transmission,* edited by Ellen Greene, 105– 21 (Berkeley: University of California Press, 1997); "The Sapphic-Platonics of Katherine Philips (1631– 1664)," *Signs: A Journal of Women in Culture and Society* 15, no. 1 (autumn 1989): 34– 60; "The Erotics of Female Friendship in Early Modern England," in *Maids and Mistresses, Cousins and Queens: Women's Alliances in Early Modern England,* edited by Susan Frye and Karen Robertson, 241–58 (Oxford: Oxford University Press, 1999); © 1999 by Oxford University Press, Inc.; used by permission of Oxford University Press, Inc.

For Demetra
(1946–1994)

Contents

CHAPTER IV

DOUBLING DISCOURSES IN AN
EROTICS OF FEMALE FRIENDSHIP

101

CHAPTER V

CONFIGURATIONS OF DESIRE:
THE TURN OF THE CENTURY AT COURT

151

Illustrations

Preface

This project takes its title from the iconic status that Sappho and the Sapphic tradition have assumed throughout Western history into the present with respect to female literary creativity and, more particularly, in relation to female same-sex erotic love. While I devote a chapter to representations of Sappho in early modern England and pursue her influence as an ideal figure, "the tenth Muse," inevitably invoked by women writers, I call her forth here as the embodiment of female lyricism and of the erotic bonds between women, the subject of this book.

My goal in this project has been to explore how female same-sex erotic relations might have been enacted and articulated in early modern England. Because substantial historical documentation of same-sex behaviors between women during this period has yet to be discovered and amassed, I have located manifestations of a female same-sex erotics in discourse by men and women and have attempted to chart the trajectory of sexual knowledge from continental translations into the vernacular. Needless to say, the evidence gleaned from these mostly textual sources can give us information primarily only about literate persons, and so I have perforce concentrated in my analyses on the discourse of literate persons of the middling or "better sort" rather than on those who have left no direct record of their passing through the discursive world; however, it is my most passionate hope that future historians will succeed in bringing to light evidence of the discursive and real lives of ordinary English women before 1714.

In the chapters that follow, I examine the theoretical and practical difficulties involved in trying to recover the lives and experiences of early modern women, not least among which are those of overcoming our own mental dispositions—our *mentalité*—and the issues of nomenclature that are their baggage. Because the modern system of binary sexual identities that was to establish heterosexuality and homosexuality as separate and mutually exclusive identities did not become a dominant ideology until sometime during the eighteenth century, the historical moments just before its consolidation are an ideal, and challenging, environment in which to examine its emergence. The system of binary sexualities was developing as a discursive formulation between about 1650 and the beginning of the eighteenth century, when what had been tacit sexual knowledge was becoming more available for discussion, yet simultaneously being un-named. It is my intention here to describe the dissemination of knowledge about female same-sex erotic relations and to suggest the ways in which women participated in and managed their same-sex erotic affections.

I describe the historical process in which an eroticized discourse of intimate relations evolved among literate women, most often in the guise of patronage or friendship poetry. This was a mostly poetic discourse of female same-sex intimacy that developed apart from the more explicitly sexualized discourses of male-authored and male-read anatomies, travel narratives, advice manuals, and so on, and from a purposefully transgressive writing by women around the mid–seventeenth century and after. In demonstrating the historical trajectory of the discourses of female same-sex relations in sixteenth- and seventeenth-century England, I examine representations of Sappho's tribadism in mostly male-authored texts, in the tradition of an eroticized poetry of female friendship initiated by the poems of Katherine Philips after the Restoration, and in the work of a few women—like Aphra Behn, Margaret Cavendish, and Delarivier Man-ley—willing to write knowingly and transgressively without actually us-ing the vocabulary of public denunciation. Finally, I examine the court of Queen Anne to show how the discourses of female same-sex relations were responding to an emerging ideology of binary sexualities. By the be-ginning of the eighteenth century, imputations of female same-sex rela-tions were coming to be used as instruments of social control, to silence female erotic expression, and to enforce a sexual imperative that was grad-ually moving toward the notion of the exclusivity of sexual orientations and binary, heteronormative sexual identities.

This project is, then, about the dissonance between the fixed categories according to which Western cultures increasingly seem to have defined sexual relations and the fluidity of the erotic desires and understandings experienced by individuals. Once societies become conscious of sexual possibilities in arenas not previously named, as they had not been throughout all segments of early modern English society, avenues become available for the demarcation of cognitive and sexual boundaries and a policing, and silencing, of sexual borderlands becomes possible. A silenc-ing of the relations between women had not yet taken place in early mod-ern England because the sexual borderlands demarcating transgression had yet to be defined. I try to locate and describe the historical trajectory of the silencing that took place—and that has been in force until very re-cently in Anglophone and other cultures—as knowledge of transgressive

sexuality between women was circulated throughout an increasingly literate and urbanized society in which print culture was ever more rapidly being disseminated. In this way, I hope to provide a fresh perspective for
viewing the complexly nuanced interactions between individual erotic experiencings and the social and literary discourses that facilitate or inhibit
their expression.

Although they are only breath,
the words which I command
are immortal.
—Σαπφώ—

Fig. 1

Young Woman with Stylet, Called Sappho, Römisches Wandgemälde, 1.Jh.n.Chr.,
Pompeji Neapel, Museo Nazionale Archeologico.

CHAPTER I

AN EROTICS
OF UNNAMING

Recovering the Past: Problems of Identity

LITTLE IS GENERALLY KNOWN with certainty about the history of female same-sex erotics and the ways in which it might have been constructed throughout early modern Europe. There is, however, a textual history reaching back to classical times that identifies and describes tribadism and tribades as a class of sexually transgressive and socially ostracized females; yet apart from the existence of these demonized transgressors, our understanding of the construction of female erotic relations continues to be underexamined and undertheorized. It is my contention that early modern English women from the ostensibly respectable classes who might have transgressed into territories of physical intimacy would almost certainly not have defined themselves and their behaviors in the terms offered by then-available publicly circulated vocabularies, nor in fact would they have been likely to name themselves or their behaviors in ways that they and their culture would have understood as transgressive. I believe that women of the "middling sort"[1] who wished to retain social status, which more often than not would have included heterosexual marriage and children, used strategies of silence about sexual practice that allowed them both to acknowledge their erotic desires and to evade opprobrium. Literature by women in England during the early modern period,

before about 1700, often suggests the manner of these evasions and suggests the ways in which a female same-sex erotics, what I call "an erotics
of unnaming," might have been constructed quite apart from the public,
male-generated discourse of transgression.

The project of recovering early modern understandings of female
same-sex erotics is complicated by our working description of early modern constructions of identity and by our struggles to refrain from imposing upon them our own notions of selfhood. Recent scholarship has made
it apparent that the modern subject or "self" understood as individual
identity and characterized by, among other qualities, unity, interiority,
self-consciousness, autonomy, and coherence was not fully formulated
before the eighteenth century, though it was certainly in the process of
developing during the late sixteenth and early seventeenth centuries. As
Catherine Belsey's work in the drama demonstrates, the notion of a subject that included interiority was emerging only in a halting fashion during this earlier historical moment in England:

> [T]he unified subject of liberal humanism is a product of the second half
> of the seventeenth century, an effect of the revolution. Broadly this seems
> to me to be so. Liberal humanism, locating agency and meaning in the
> unified human subject, becomes an orthodoxy at the moment when the
> bourgeoisie is installed as the ruling class. Signifying practice, however,
> is not so well ordered as to wait for the execution of Charles I in 1649 be-
> fore proclaiming the existence of interiority, the inalienable and unalter-
> able property of the individual, which precedes and determines speech
> and action.[2]

In contrast to our own, early modern constructions of identity seem generally to have been determined by external or social attributes—the sum
of a constellation of characteristics such as class, sex, occupation, familial,
regional (e.g., urban/rural, north/south) and national origins, as well as
religious and political affiliations. An even relatively subjective personal
identity was not, then, analogous to what we now experience as gendered
selves constructed by an individualist psychology. With this difference in
mind, readings of early modern texts in search of "lesbian community"
seem manifestly absurd, though understandable in light of the contested
social positions of sexual minorities in the twentieth century and their attempts to move from marginality into a social mainstream, so-called.

In discussing the social genesis of the self, the philosopher Charles
Taylor notes that "conversation partners [are] essential to . . . achieving
self-definition" and remarks that "[a] self exists only within . . . 'webs of
interlocution,'" a point also made by Regenia Gagnier: "'the self' is not

an autonomous introspectible state—a Cogito or a unique point of view—but is instead dependent upon intersubjectivity, or the intersubjective nature of language and culture."[3] This philosophical perspective on the nature of the constructed self—that the self exists only intersubjectively—can be most useful in our efforts to comprehend early modern understandings of the nature of identity. With respect to female same-sex erotic transgression during the early modern period in England, we will find that an identity defined by specific behaviors indeed had been distinguished by the language community; however, it was, as we shall see, an identity characterized primarily by its alterity, by its "otherness," and, consequently, by its foreignness and its un-Englishness.

The problem is not, then, that there was no distinguishable category for female same-sex erotics. The problem is rather how women who might have chosen or been drawn into intense emotional and erotic connections with other women would have thought about those relations if (a) these women were not included in the mostly male language community that was aware of same-sex transgressive sexuality, or if (b) these women were aware of transgressive identities yet did not associate their own feelings or behaviors with those identities, or even if (c) these women were aware of transgressive identities yet rejected the possibilities of their own connection with those identified as "other."

On Naming Female Same-Sex Behaviors

The then-available signifiers for female same-sex transgressivity were, as is now generally known, the nouns "tribade" and "tribadism," which were used in conformity with classical precedent throughout the early modern period to describe the activities of women who engaged in sexual activity, as it was then understood, with other women.[4] More colloquially, "tribades" were also called "rubsters" in English and *"fricatrices"* or *"confricatrices"* after the French and Latin.[5] Like other terms we have become aware of—such as *"lollepot"* in seventeenth-century Dutch and "tommy" in eighteenth-century English, and like our modern American uses of "dyke" or "butch" and "femme" and their variants ("bull dyke," "diesel dyke," "bulldagger," "stone butch," etc.), or the early-twentieth-century use by the Bloomsbury Group of the more genteel "sapphist" or "sapph"—these terms operate in precise contexts and engage, at various times and in different places, nuances of disapprobation and reappropriation, or even of affirmation, that are marked by temporal, geographical, and social particulars. The realities represented by any given locution are not usually amenable to direct comparison with constructions of erotic behavior from another time, place, or social environment, so that we have to allow for the possibility that certain forms of erotic expression (e.g., oral-genital or manual-genital contact) between women might not have been considered sexual before the twentieth century within a masculinist sexual paradigm that reads and defines all erotic behaviors in terms of a heterosexual model.

Literally defined, then, a "tribade" was one who achieved sexual gratification by rubbing; in conjunction with this definition according to classical precedent, some early texts also mention that these women had preternaturally enlarged clitorises that they used "in the manner of a man." The enlarged clitoris and female appropriation of male sexual behaviors seem to have been an obsessive concern of anatomists and other male writers and are mentioned with nearly compulsive regularity whenever tribadism is the subject of discussion.[6] These persons were most often said to belong to the classical world or to be denizens of foreign lands, so their existence was consigned to exotic locales by travel narratives, as well as by medical and midwifery texts. Katharine Park has noted that the "projection of sexual irregularity onto the exoticized bodies of women of another race and continent was a familiar trope in early modern European topographical literature."[7] A notable example of such projections is the early 1585 translation into English of Nicolas de Nicolay's French account of his travels into Turkey, especially his description of the customs of women at the baths:

> [S]omtimes they do go 10. or 12. of them together, & somtimes more in a company aswel Turks as Grecians, & do familiarly wash one another, wherby it commeth to passe that amongst the women of Levan[t], ther is very great amity proceding only through the frequentation & resort to the bathes: yea & somtimes become so feruently in loue the one of the other as if it were with men, in such sort that perceiuing some maiden or woman of excellent beauty they wil not ceaste [*sic*] vntil they haue found means to bath with them, & to handle & grope them euery where at their pleasures, so ful they are of luxuriousnes & feminine wantonnes: Euen as in times past wer the Tribades, of the number wherof was Sapho the Lesbian which transferred the loue wherwith she pursued a 100. women or maidens vpon her only friend Phaon.[8]

The salient features of the exoticizing discourse used to describe female same-sex relations are all present here: the "luxuriousnes & feminine wantonnes" that leads these women to "become so feruently in loue the one of the other *as if it were with men*" [my emphasis]; the naming of "Tribades" in association with ancient Greece; and the use of Sappho as an icon of originary female sexual transgressiveness.

Jane Sharp's later observations, in *The Midwives Book* (1671), more explicitly identify the means of achieving sexual pleasure as well as the homology commonly understood to obtain between the clitoris and the male organ. Sharp's midwifery text reiterates in English ideas readily available in earlier anatomy and medical texts:

> [C]ommonly it [the clitoris] is but a small sprout, lying close hid under the wings, and not easily felt, yet sometimes it grows so long that it hangs forth at the slit like a yard [penis], and will swell and stand stiff if it be provoked, and some lewd women have endeavored to use it as men do theirs. In the Indies and Egypt they are frequent, but I never heard but of one in this country: if there be any, they will do what they can for shame to keep it close.[9]

These "lewd women" and their transgressions are located here at a safe remove from everyday English life, the Indies and Egypt having replaced Turkey as the "oriental" sites of luxury. It is noteworthy that toward the end of the seventeenth century, in this text intended for women and female midwives, Sharp avoids naming the transgressive women in question even though names (e.g., "tribades") were readily available. Sharp's reluctance to name may have been occasioned by the female readership of her book and an unwillingness to circulate a name perhaps otherwise unavailable to them. Or it may be part of the phenomenon, which I elaborate in chapter 2 of this study, in which women who could be identified as engaging in the particularly "lewd" acts of tribadism were regarded with increasing condemnation as we move from the sixteenth into the seventeenth century, so that dissemination of knowledge about their activities became more widespread at the same time that it began to be suppressed.

A comparison between another travel report and periodical accounts of transgressing females, both contemporary with de Nicolay's narrative, and an early-eighteenth-century letter by a noblewoman describing her travels in the Levant underlines the changes that were taking place in this simultaneously exoticizing and information-disseminating discourse in the vernacular. Ogier Ghislain de Busbecq's [Augerius Gislenius Busbequius] *Travels into Turkey* was initially published in Latin in 1589[10] and reprinted many times in various languages into the nineteenth century; it was first "Englished" somewhat more than a century later, in a London edition in 1694, following an Oxford Latin edition in 1660, and was commonly cited in conjunction with female same-sex relations. De Busbecq describes the relations between husbands and wives in Turkey, providing substantial detail about household arrangements in which, for example, Saturday nights are reserved for wives while husbands may use concubines on other nights, wives may divorce husbands "if they offer to abuse them against Nature,[11] (a Crime usual among them)," and husbands jealously set eunuchs to guard their wives:

> [N]ot ſuch as have only their Stones [testicles] taken out, but ſuch whoſe Yards [penises] are alſo impaired; becauſe otherwiſe they think, ſuch as loſt their Stones only may deſire the uſe of a Woman, tho' not for Generation, yet for Pleaſure. (sig. I7)

In this context, and as part of their bodily fastidiousness, women are sent to public baths, where erotic activity between them is indulged:

> ... ordinarily the VVomen bathe by themſelves, Bond and Free together; ſo that you ſhall many times ſee young Maids, exceeding beautiful, gathered from all Parts of the VVorld, expoſed Naked to the view of other VVomen, who thereupon fall in Love with them, as young Men do with us, at the ſight of Virgins.
>
> By this you may gueſs, what their ſtrict VVatch over Females comes to, and how 'tis not enough to avoid the Company of an Adulterous Man, for the *Females* burn in Love one towards another [*mulieres inter ſe amant:* women love among themselves]; and the Pandareſſes to ſuch refined Loves [*nefariorum amorum:* execrable or abominable loves] are the Baths; and, therefore, ſome *Turks* will deny their VVives the uſe of their publick Baths, but they cannot do it altogether, becauſe their Law allows them. But theſe Offences happen among the Ordinary ſort; the richer ſort of Perſons have Baths at home. ... (sig. I7–I7ᵛ)[12]

De Busbecq concludes his account of the baths by telling the story of an "old Woman" who falls in love with the daughter of a poor man, crossdresses as a wealthy man, and persuades the father to marry her to the girl. When she is discovered and taken to the authorities, her response restating the force of her love is ridiculed and she is ordered to be drowned. De Busbecq provides this conclusion: "[T]he Turks make no noiſe when *ſecret* Offences are committed by them, that they may not open the Mouths of Scandal and Reproach; but *open* and *manifeſt* ones they puniſh moſt ſeverely" (sig. I8). This should be familiar as a sort of sixteenth-century "don't ask, don't tell" policy. As these passages testify, female same-sex erotic transgression continued to be "othered," to be displaced to foreign countries with strange customs, in other words, to be orientalized, at the end of the seventeenth century in England. It was in this way

that English readers, both women and men, could continue a safely vicarious, and therefore virtuous, enjoyment of such stories. The Turkish
women described here—apart from the cross-dressing "old Woman" who
transgresses by appropriating male prerogatives—are presented as "respectable" women living within the parameters of a heterosexual econ-
omy, *except* at the baths, a protected female space; de Busbecq goes so far
as to emphasize that these women are "among the Ordinary ſort" insofar
as "the richer ſort of Perſons have Baths at home." These women of the
"Ordinary ſort" are neither named nor virulently condemned as tribades:
their behavior is clearly disapproved but only mildly condemned, perhaps
as a point of class snobbery, by both the European narrator and the English translator. De Busbecq's main point, apart from the description of
aberrant behaviors, is his sympathy with the attempts of Turkish men to
control their wives. The "old Woman," on the other hand, having abandoned all proprieties to indulge an exclusive passion, is said to have a
"beaſtly Love," "ſo notorious a Beſtiality, and ſo filthy a Fact" as to have
suffered for the "wild Amours" she would not disavow (sig. I8). This is a
cautionary tale. While the narrator displays an amused if disapproving indulgence at the excesses of ordinarily respectable married women at the
baths, he strongly condemns the openly unrepentant transgressiveness of
the "old Woman" who crosses class and generational as well as gender
boundaries. The behavior itself—that is, the precise nature of the transgressive sexual acts involved—is in neither instance described or named,
the presumption being that readers would recognize its nature; by 1694 in
England they would have done so. By the time translation into the vernacular was achieved, there was no need to name behaviors known and
recognizable. Further, the respectable married women in de Busbecq's
account do not conform to the conventional parameters of tribadism:
they are said to be in love, albeit abominably, rather than to abuse their
clitorises or to use prostheses. They are therefore distinguishable from
tribades, whereas the "old Woman" cross-dresses and achieves the male
prerogative of marriage with a woman. Neither case of exoticized female
erotics described in this travel narrative conforms nicely to the classically
derived notions of the transgressions of tribades as the English understood them at this historical moment.

The continued prurient interest on the part of the English in the exoticizing of female same-sex behavior, in its vernacular dissemination,
and in the failure to make an explicit association with tribadism is evidenced repeatedly in narratives from this period near the very end of the
seventeenth century. We have only to peruse *The Gentleman's Journal,* a

London literary and cultural periodical published by Peter Anthony Motteux that includes gossip and curiosities; there we find the story of another
female husband (this time displaced to Italy rather than to an "oriental"
locale),[13] "An Account of a Young Hermaphrodite,"[14] and an account of
the discovery of an heroic Englishwoman cross-dressed as a (male) soldier on the Continent discovered "playing with another of her sex." There
is scandal in each instance and punishment in the last, but in no case is
tribadism named, thereby shadowing the classical connection with explicitly named transgressing women. The cross-dressed soldier is, in fact,
introduced to illustrate the heroism of the English, even Englishwomen;
this heroism, however, is demonstrated on the Continent rather than in
London, though "[s]everal others are still living, and some of them in this
Town, who have serv'd whole Campaigns, and fought stroke by stroke by
the most manly Soldiers."[15] In this context, the young woman's sexuality
is presented with a certain matter-of-fact equanimity, perhaps indicating
some tolerance among sophisticated persons for the sexual foibles even of
Englishwomen, as long as they are not actually visible at home.

An account by a noblewoman of the women at the baths in Turkey
bears scrutiny as an example of the marked changes in discourse about
female same-sex erotics that had taken place since the sixteenth century;
by the second decade of the eighteenth century, tribades and tribadic behaviors continued to be described in English discourse but were not being actually named, in effect suggesting that what was no longer being
named no longer was in need of explicit identification. Lady Mary Wortley Montagu included the following eroticized and exoticized description
in a letter from Adrianople to a female friend, "To Lady ———," on
April 1, 1717:

> I was in my travelling Habit. . . . The first sofas were cover'd with Cush-
> ions and rich Carpets, on which sat the Ladys, and on the 2nd their slaves
> behind 'em, but without any distinction of rank by their dress, all being
> in the state of nature, that is, in plain English, stark naked, without any
> Beauty or deffect conceal'd, yet there was not the least wanton smile or
> immodest Gesture amongst 'em. . . . There were many amongst them as
> exactly proportion'd as ever any Goddess was drawn by the pencil of
> Guido or Titian, and most of their skins shineingly white, only adorn'd
> by their Beautiful Hair divided into many tresses hanging on their shoul-
> ders. . . . I was here convinc'd of the Truth of a Refflexion that I had of-
> ten made, that if it was the fashion to go naked, the face would be hardly
> observ'd. I perceiv'd that the Ladys with the finest skins and most deli-
> cate shapes had the greatest share of my admiration, thô their faces were

sometimes less beautifull than those of their companions. . . . ['T]is the Women's coffee house, where all the news of the Town is told, Scandal invented, etc. They generally take this Diversion once a week, and stay there at least 4 or 5 hours. . . . The Lady that seem'd the most consider-able amongst them . . . would fain have undress'd me for the bath. I ex-cus'd my selfe with some difficulty, they being all so earnest in perswad-ing me. I was at last forc'd to open my skirt and shew them my stays, which satisfy'd 'em very well, for I saw they beleiv'd I was so lock'd up in that machine that it was not in my own power to open it, which con-trivance they attributed to my Husband.[16]

The salient points in this description are Montagu's observation of the loss of class distinction that occurs with nudity, her erotic and admiring focus on the women's bodies, and her own coy modesty in vicarious en-joyment, yet her simultaneous refusal to join the enticingly erotic mêlée. Her observation that "yet there was not the least wanton smile or im-modest Gesture amongst 'em" suggests rather pointedly what is not being said, what is unnamed: Montagu is fully aware of imputations of lascivi-ousness among women at the baths in Turkey; by noting its absence, she invokes its subtextual presence and then brings it into the text by refusing the seductive requests of the women to join them in removing her attire. Since Montagu is the foreigner here, and an English foreigner at that, fully clothed amidst these nude women from various social stations, she plays the role of colonial observer, luxuriating in the fulfillment of her erotic gaze as she retains her armor against theirs. Thus her unwillingness to take off her "travelling Habit" to join them as an equal (i.e., to allow nakedness to make her as vulnerable to the others' gazes as they are to hers) makes it improbable that they would reveal their erotic secrets to her; she undoubtedly realizes this, for it is the unexpressed motive for her reluctance to join them. In refusing to join them naked, she refuses their unstated offer of a mutually erotic participation and retains her status as colonial observer. By 1717, then, Montagu was undoubtedly familiar with accounts of female sexual immodesty in Turkish baths, as presumably her reader was as well, and employed their by now conventionally exoticizing discourse. What was known and acknowledged, even among women who cherished their modesty and social status and who would earlier have been sheltered from such sexual knowledge, no longer needed to be named. Here the prospect of female same-sex sexual encounters is both erotically fascinating and clearly refused, mentioned only to be denied.

An even later, and frequently cited, example of the persistence of ideas about transgressing women, particularly their association with Sappho and their exoticizing, or "othering," is to be found in the anonymous mid-eighteenth-century *Satan's Harvest Home* (1749):

> *Sappho,* as she was one of the wittiest Women that ever the World bred, so she thought with Reason, it would be expected she should make some Additions to a *Science* in which Womankind had been so successful: What does she do then? Not content with our Sex, begins *Amours* with her own, and teaches the Female World a new Sort of Sin, call'd the *Flats,* that was follow'd not only in Lucian's Time, but is practis'd frequently in *Turkey,* as well as at *Twickenham* at this Day.[17]

As this passage demonstrates, an acknowledgment of the existence of transgressive women closer to home takes place as we move further into the eighteenth century, and a more elaborate and more native discourse of identification is being used, the slangy game of "Flats" that presumably refers to a rubbing without benefit of male protuberance or supplementation. By 1781 "tommy" may have been the colloquial analogue for "molly," slang for an effeminate male homosexual, at least in London.[18]

In contrast to our limited information about female same-sex erotic relations, a great deal more is generally known about male sexuality and the traditions of male-male sexual relations since ancient times, no doubt because the lives of men are lived more publicly and documented more extensively. Thus we have available narrative accounts—though they are as yet partial and speculative—of the emergence of a sodomitical subculture that included "molly houses," or early gay bars, in late-seventeenth- and eighteenth-century England and Europe.[19] Whether there might have been a similarly emergent culture of female same-sex erotic activity is now being addressed with more careful historical analysis and from a more adequately theorized perspective than has previously been the case. Recently, Bernadette Brooten's *Love between Women: Early Christian Responses to Female Homoeroticism* furnishes a much-needed historical and theoretical bridge between our knowledge of female same-sex relations during classical times and the early modern period. Brooten's study provides the early cultural contexts of female homoeroticism in the transmission of Sappho, Greek erotic spells, astrological texts, medical treatments, and dream analyses, through Egypt from the Greeks into early Christian Roman times.[20] Though Brooten's extensive analysis in part 2 of Paul's Letter to the Romans I:18–32, patristic writings of the second and third centuries, and church sanctions of the fourth and fifth centuries is also highly informative, it is her account of the transmission of the classics into early Christian times that helps illuminate the complex sources of early modern female same-sex eroticism. As I have indicated and as we will see in more detail, it was classical sources and their translations that provided names and identities for transgressing women in early modern England.

Physical Intimacy and the Erotics of Unnaming

Evidence of these and other literary and textual sources now available to us demonstrates unambiguously that same-sex physical behaviors between women were known and feared by men. In some ways and at some times, this knowledge and fear were presumably communicated to women, though it may not always have been explicitly articulated or fully conscious, depending on class and other environmental or social factors. There is reason to believe, for instance, that as more women became literate and gained access to texts previously accessible only to men, they also gained access to a broader range of sexual information and understanding, despite efforts by men and by other women like Sharp to bowdlerize texts for women.[21] It is also apparent that these behaviors were considered transgressive and not desirable for women who might wish to maintain a respectable social standing, who might, in other words, wish to remain among "the better sort." What, then, of those women of the middling sort, or of even higher status, whose connections with other women must have transgressed into the territories of physical intimacy, whether genital or not? I use "must have" deliberately here to indicate that, like Terry Castle, I assume that individuals are inclined to use, and in fact do use, their bodies—both alone and with one another—in the great variety of ways available to them physiologically, however they might define, or avoid defining, or even avoid acknowledging, these uses.[22] In light of this assumption, it is not improbable that women of all classes and social strata, those who were willing to be ostracized as well as those who were not, performed acts that, were they to be named, would be considered transgressive—that is, not normative because not heterosexual—by others or by themselves.

How might those respectable women who transgressed into territories of physical intimacy have defined for themselves the nature of their erotic feelings and activities? What literary and social forms might their definitions have taken? Or, from another perspective, in the case of women to whose literary voices we do have access, we might ask: "What did these women who wrote in impassioned ways about/to/for other women actually *do* with each other?" These are questions to which we have no empirically definitive answers, yet informed hypotheses yield valuable perspectives and considerable information for understanding the period before the beginning of the eighteenth century, before about 1714 and the death of Queen Anne. Though in the future diaries or other similar artifacts might be found that describe actual instances of same-sex female sexuality and the relationships in which they thrived, or there may emerge cases of prosecution that describe in detail sexual acts between women, for the time being we are obliged to theorize without such corroborative evidence to verify the *facts* of women's relations.

A well-known, though rather late, exception to this dilemma is the case of Anne Lister (1791–1840). Her understanding of the construction of an identity outside the bounds established by a formally sanctioned social community might perhaps be useful in thinking about the ways in which some early modern women during the sixteenth, seventeenth, and earlier eighteenth centuries might have negotiated socially as well as personally unacceptable erotic feelings and desires. Lister's diaries offer a clear definition of the nature of sexual acts between women and her use of code to name her sexual behaviors (e.g., "kiss" = orgasm) is conclusive evidence of her consciousness of transgression; further, her persistently deliberate efforts to find sexual companionship firmly substantiate the circulation of consciously transgressive and coded erotic communication among women of "the better sort" by the beginning of the nineteenth century.[23] Anna Clark describes Lister as one of those "individuals [who] deliberately construct their own identities with three elements: their own temperaments and inherent desires; their material circumstances; and the cultural representations available to them."[24] Because material and social circumstances were particularly limiting to women in the early modern period, cultural representations of tribades and of tribadism would have made identifying with them unlikely, if not impossible, for any woman who did not court social ostracism, which would have meant the loss not only of social status but almost surely of the means of material survival as well.

Without naming, however, there is no point at which to establish a sequence of boundaries between affection, eroticism, and sexuality.[25] Without being named, *without being spoken*, certain otherwise transgressive acts might simply be understood by the individuals involved as physiological gestures embodying mutual feelings of friendship, love, and/or affection. That boundaries demarcating affection, eroticism, and sexuality were not clearly established—or even thought necessary—for most (surely sheltered) women of the middling or better sort and circumstances is what I want to suggest here through my exploration of the vocabulary that might or might not have been available to them. And yet, as Caroline Woodward has already noted of eighteenth-century women, their "silence . . . about their sexual lives may have been an effective strategic practice,"[26] allowing them to experience desire as they simultaneously evaded opprobrium. The behaviors underlying such a strategic evasion could not be called, or even said to be "like," lesbianism; but they could be called transgressive when or if they were identified as tribadism. Unnamed, though, particularly before about 1714, the behaviors that were identified with the transgressions of tribades would have been benign and would not have stigmatized the women who engaged in them, nor would they have caused them to self-identify as transgressive. An "erotics of unnaming" could thus serve as a socially strategic evasion of what would certainly have been a devastating social opprobrium. Because we cannot know for certain how such transgressing women might have described for themselves their same-sex erotic behavior, we can take note of the social constructs that developed to accommodate and perhaps to contain a constellation of passionate emotions and behaviors. It has become increasingly clear that the primary social framework that provided both erotic opportunities and discursive camouflage for women in the sixteenth and seventeenth centuries is that of "female friendship" and that it was followed in the eighteenth century by the rhetorical constructs of female "romantic" or "passionate" friendship.[27]

In the absence of visible subcultures identified as transgressive—such as those that congregated in eighteenth-century molly houses known to serve men interested in same-sex connections—traditional social structure is sufficiently variable to accommodate unacknowledged transgressions and unnamed non-normative behaviors.[28] Secure social status, particularly for women of the middling or better sort in early modern England, may be maintained by individuals through their refusal to make an association, in either language or consciousness, between their behavior and socially identified transgression. Everyone thus colludes in accepting as normative the dominant social structures and ideology. This collusion, exemplified here by the silencing (or "unnaming") of female sexualities, is simply part of the process whereby culture constructs and demarcates the acceptability of sexual and erotic relations within particular boundaries and individuals respond in complex ways that both court and avoid transgression of those boundaries.

The Demise of Tacit Knowledge

The emergence of the modern system of gender difference and a discourse of sexuality, both of which formerly were only tacit understandings and experiencings, separated themselves out from an unconscious social matrix during the eighteenth century. This shift was facilitated, as Michael McKeon's recent account demonstrates, by the decline of patriarchalism as tacit understanding. McKeon describes the process by which the assumptions of patriarchalism were of necessity brought to consciousness and separated out in "the emergence of modern patriarchy [which] is co-extensive with the emergence of gender difference."[29] In seeing Robert Filmer's *Patriarcha* as marking "not the triumphant ascendancy of patriarchal thought, but its demise as tacit knowledge, the fact that it is in crisis," McKeon argues that "the long-term and uneven shift from patriarchalism to modern patriarchy entailed a separation out of elements which had formerly been tacitly understood and experienced as parts of an integral whole—the cosmos, the social order, the family, economic production."[30]

McKeon's notion of tacit understanding is useful in suggesting how the sexual naming of female same-sex eroticism during this period is part of the broader social dismantling of knowledge not previously articulated or identified. Along with the emergence of the discourse of sexuality, then, the older system of the tacit knowledge of erotic practice gives way to naming as subcultures become known and as certain erotic activities are recognized as sexual rather than as part of a larger complex of behaviors earlier embedded in a social context of "friendship." This process has already been described in detail for male behaviors and subcultures. The process of beginning to distinguish sexuality from the erotics of friendship was one that also took place with respect to women's behaviors within female social structures. In the absence of a male organ (or "supplementation" by an ancillary appendage, be it a dildo, an enlarged clitoris, or other prosthetic device), sexuality between women was located below the threshold of visibility and was, and sometimes still is, hard to define. With the eventual naming of what had been only tacitly acknowledged, particular erotic behaviors like kissing, touching, manual stimulation, and the like would have been included in the range of activities now defined as sexual. No doubt this process occurred later for women than for men, whose more public display of same-sex sexual activities in parks and molly houses evidenced the behavior of a clearly established subculture by the later seventeenth century.[31]

As long as women acceded to male precedence and did not transgress by assuming male prerogatives (i.e., cross-dressing), there seems not to have been much reason to explore or to name what women might do with one another's bodies. Following the Restoration in England, however, and the more general social license openly indulged by various individuals, especially by members of the aristocracy, the demise of the tacit ironically may very well have become a means of repressing unwelcome female transgressivity. The effect of naming—and the more public the naming the more profound the effect—was to bring to the consciousness of individuals the connections between their behaviors and named transgressions. In this way, to name may be to inhibit and to constrain.

The Textual Dissemination of Sexual Knowledge

The history of the textual availability of a language for female sexuality bears out this speculation. Earlier, before the mid–sixteenth century, tribades and tribadism were described by men and knowledge of their existence was available only to men in the Latin texts published throughout early modern Europe. The language for identifying this behavior and the persons who engaged in it did not become available in English until the classics began to be translated from Latin into the European vernaculars, at which time this vocabulary also became available to educated women. As we have seen in the example of the passage from Jane Sharp's midwifery manual, the acquisition of knowledge and the displacement of tribades to exotic locales through a familiar trope were enabled simultaneously. This new availability of vocabulary and information probably occurred earlier and/or slightly differently in the continental vernacular languages, though the process of accessibility is likely to have been similar in England and in English. As Sharp's language suggests, an inhibition in the accounts of tribadism appears to have been taking place as an understanding of the possibilities for exotic transgressions led to the eventual identification and naming of those same behaviors closer to home. A developing consciousness of the demarcations separating transgressive from conforming behaviors may have provided the impetus for inhibition. Profound changes in the cultural understandings of same-sex sexual behaviors among women occur clearly in conjunction with the increasing availability of vernacular print cultures. Not coincidentally, or surprisingly, these changes are associated with literacy among the middling and better sort.

The aftermath of the dissemination of knowledge during the Renaissance and the increasingly open availability of sexual discussion following the Restoration permitted the intensification of public discourse about sexuality in general and female same-sex sexuality in particular. We find male concern with women's same-sex erotic relations to be a pervasive theme in English literature before the Restoration. The influence of Ovidian myth effected the transformations that we note so frequently in the drama of Shakespeare and Lyly, to mention only two of the most obvious instances, in which the resolution to the dilemma of two women in love is a sex change miraculously achieved in advance of the possibility of any real discomfort of sexuality between two women.[32] Following the Restoration, we note the emergence of the explicit idea of female same-sex relations in the writings of women willing to appear publicly transgressive and not loath to name or to play at transgression, as in Delarivier Manley's Cabal in her roman à clef *The New Atalantis* (1709), and in several of Aphra Behn's poems, most notably the female same-sex erotics in "To the Fair Clarinda, Who Made Love to Me, Imagined More than Woman," and the transgressive female sexual agency in "The Disappointment" and "On Her Loving Two Equally." This phenomenon seems to mark a major break with the past and a movement into new forms of erotic and sexual understanding.

The consequence of an accelerated dissemination of sexual knowledge about female same-sex relations in a variety of texts, then, created a coherent verbal construct and began to make possible a codification of certain behaviors as transgressive and as violations of social norms in a way both more concrete and far-reaching than could have been accomplished simply by an oral/aural tradition. The increasing employment of the vernacular for literary purposes and the development of a vernacular print culture no doubt contributed to the shaping of transgressive identities that could elicit general assent.

Splitting Discourses

We can recognize in the latter half of the seventeenth century a splitting off of discourses from one another, a divergence of the discourses that name transgressiveness from those that do not. For instance, in the sixteenth century, transgressive female same-sex relations were clearly named in Latin and so were readily accessible to educated male readers of Latin before the translation of reference works and the like into the European vernaculars. In spite of the availability of this sexual knowledge in Latin medical and other texts, a process of the "unnaming" of female sexuality was simultaneously taking place in the real world of male medical manipulations of the female body. From ancient times and into the twentieth century, male physicians followed Galen's recommendations for female genital massage to relieve the symptoms of hysteria through what was known as the "hysterical paroxysm," recognized only in the twentieth century as female orgasm. During the early modern period, physicians gave midwives explicit directions for massage—including digital penetration—yet this activity was not recognized as sexual.[33] This medical production of orgasm for centuries facilitated male treatment of a fictitious malady and gave permission for women to achieve sexual satisfaction through the ministrations of women subservient to themselves. Physicians also recommended that midwives perform other manual manipulations to assist in the delivery of pregnant women; Thomas Raynalde in 1554 suggested various unguents to prepare the birth canal—he was especially fond of "the oyl of white Lillies"—and encouraged midwives that

> yf neceʃʃitie require it, let not the Mydwyfe be afrayed ne aʃhamed to handle the places [i.e., privy parts], and to relaxe and looʃe the ʃtraightes (for ʃo muche as ʃhall lye in her) for that ʃhal helpe wel to the more expedite and quicke labour.[34]

It is safe to say that the individuals involved were unlikely to have understood these socially legitimated behaviors as in any way partaking of tribadism. Thus, while the dissemination of sexual knowledge was gaining momentum in some quarters, a synchronous "unnaming" of female sexual experience persisted.

Later, at the end of the seventeenth century, the language of women willing to be transgressive continued to name transgressiveness, albeit at times more coyly and covertly, as in the case of Manley's Cabal. However, throughout the seventeenth century, the middling sort of "respectable" women—who were becoming educated and for whom texts were being made available in the vernacular (though often bowdlerized)—would have wanted to retain their status and to gain patronage as poets; to do so, they used the eroticized and romantic discourses of a heterosexual pastoralism to describe relations and behaviors that might have been identified as transgressive.

Since I have been most concerned with the poetic expressions of same-sex erotics between women during the early modern period, I have argued that insofar as poetry is a vehicle for the expression of impassioned feeling between literate Englishwomen, we can describe that poetry as an erotically charged communication of same-sex intimacy, yet an intimacy that often seems to reach beyond conventional notions of acceptability within, say, the context of friendship. In a number of instances, most notably that of Katherine Philips, sufficient biographical evidence exists to suggest that these poetic intimacies were genuinely felt representations of actual experience. The availability and the use of secondary biographical materials in any attempt to speculate about what these women did or felt is critical. Nevertheless, such materials still do not tell us unambiguously how these women—intelligent, literate, educated, materially reasonably comfortable—might have regarded, or even named, themselves. It seems doubtful that they would have wanted to categorize themselves as the infamous tribades they might have been made aware of in translations of the classics or in other contemporary texts. Since their experience of a same-sex erotics would not have been congruent with then-available descriptions of tribadism as defined by transgressive behaviors, their experience would have remained unnamed, and certainly unacknowledged in its possible transgression.

In order to account for the indications of same-sex erotics we encounter in women's literary productions, especially in their use of the conventions of heterosexual poetry and in their assertions of chaste love, we should note that within a context of patriarchal definitions of sexuality, female same-sex eroticism *is* chaste insofar as it does not emulate male penetrative behavior—that is, insofar as it does not involve the use of phallic prostheses or preternaturally enlarged clitorises. This is an idea very much at variance with modern understandings, both secular and religious, of "chastity"; nevertheless, there is reason to believe that this indeed was the case during the early modern period and before in Europe, as it continues today to be a prevailing notion about female sexuality in many non-Western cultures.[35] "Respectable" women, as the writers I will discuss generally regarded themselves, were likely to have looked on tribades (if they had heard of such women) as exotic, transgressive, and very much removed from themselves and their own understandings of their behaviors. If, as a function of their impassioned feelings for one another, they happened also to explore one another's bodies, they were not likely to have *named* their behaviors using a language then understood as sexual. For example, manual stimulation, oral contact (cunnilingus), and other erotic expressions need not be, and often are not, considered sexual in contexts defined by a masculine sexual paradigm.[36] Women may have been able to retain their "respectability" by living in conformity with prevailing social constructs that demanded marriage and children while also giving expression to their feelings for other women through the conventions of "chaste" romantic friendships, especially by the eighteenth century. The literary shape taken by a same-sex erotics between women was most frequently a poetic one, though it is being increasingly recognized that the prose literature of female community produced by women during the late seventeenth and eighteenth centuries is rich with erotic subtexts. Recent studies of Jane Barker's *A Patch-Work Screen for the Ladies* (1723) and Sarah Scott's *Millenium Hall* (1762) draw attention to the ways in which a female same-sex erotics was coming to be constructed and expressed, even before the later-eighteenth-century formulation of "romantic friendship,"[37] through literary representations of accepted structures of celibacy, contemplation, and female community, which all have a common source in the long European traditions of single-sex religious communities. The real tensions seem to me to have occurred later when the passionate romantic attachments of "friends" came into conflict with the demands of social conformity, as they did most famously in the case of the 1778 elopement of the Ladies of Llangollen.[38]

Reading the Past: A Language of Erotic Ellipsis

Reconstructing an accurate and adequately nuanced history of female same-sex erotics in early modern England requires the dismantling of binary understandings of sexuality and the disruption of genitally inflected notions of eroticism.[39] Until now, attempts to create "cultural narratives" of lesbianism—attempts, that is, to establish a historical "tradition" of lesbian identity by lesbian literary critics and historians—have tended to reinscribe contemporary paradigms by reading earlier literature—for the most part of the eighteenth and nineteenth centuries—through the lens of the identity politics of the last quarter of the twentieth century. My own vantage point with respect to this critical tendency is aptly summarized by Sally O'Driscoll, who writes that it is impossible to posit "a transhistorical or transcultural Lesbian Self" and that, despite an awareness of lesbian erotic practice, "evidence [before 1900] of what would now be termed lesbian sexual acts did not produce the equivalent of a twentieth-century lesbian identity."[40] My project extends backward into the earlier periods in England the assumptions of O'Driscoll's "outlaw reading" of Eliza Haywood's mid-eighteenth-century novel *La Belle Assemblée*.

Critics trying to establish a historical "tradition" of lesbian identity often reveal through their vocabularies the difficulties implicit in their efforts. For example, rather than problematize the notion of "lesbian" itself, one literary critic not wanting actually to attribute "lesbianism" to an earlier period has used the phrase "lesbian-like"[41] to describe behavior and identity that seem to be recognizable or familiar to a twentieth-century reader. Another reader, taking her cue from the use of "protofeminist," describes as "protolesbian" identities we believe we recognize.[42] This precarious precipice of neologisms is generated by the powerful desire to discover the antecedents of current paradigms. Anna Clark's conclusions about the early-nineteenth-century erotic life of Anne Lister (1791–1840) with other women exemplifies the conflation of scholarly analysis with modern identity politics and with the continuing vigor of 1970s ideas of "woman-identified women":

> Anne Lister was not able to create a lesbian network, let alone a subculture, because of her chronic concealment, and duplicity tangled her love relationships into webs of deceit and competition. Romanticism justified her lesbianism as part of her nature, but its focus on the unique individual also hampered her ability to support other lesbians. Meeting the masculine and learned Miss Pickford helped Anne realize that there were other women such as herself in the world, but her scornful treatment of her friend prevented them from developing more solidarity.[43]

Notions of "network," "support," and "solidarity" operate here to evoke modern lesbian-feminist paradigms of "community" and lesbian relations and thus to create normative expectations for the past. Elaine Hobby, like Clark and others, uses an unproblematized "lesbian" in her description of Katherine Philips and remarks that "the lesbian community then, as now, had its divisions,"[44] revealing that an unexamined and certainly misleading assumption is the foundation of her otherwise more nuanced historical understanding. In effect, a terminology that is not problematized attributes to an earlier era the relatively recent notion of "lesbian" identity and assumes its transhistorical presence.[45]

Gesturing toward an unambiguous history with which modern individuals can identify, lesbian academics have too often replicated what Jennifer Terry has described as "the 'hidden from history' model which launched the field of women's history in its early days."[46] In *The Apparitional Lesbian*, Terry Castle marshals an explicit rationale for the essentialism that drives efforts to recover lesbian cultural narratives. Her arguments for a pre-1900 "libidinal self-awareness" and her efforts to "'recarnalize' matters" outside the fashionable parameters of queer theory and the new postmodern paradigms bring a certain panache, not to mention seductiveness, to essentialist readings:

> And indeed, I still maintain, if in ordinary speech I say, "I am a lesbian," the meaning is instantly (even dangerously) clear: I am a woman whose primary emotional and erotic allegiance is to my own sex. Usage both confers and delimits meaning: the word is part of a "language game," as Wittgenstein might say, in which we all know the rules.[47]

But it hardly resolves the problems of historical, social, or geographical particularity either in the present or before 1850.

This approach, usually less eloquently articulated, appears to serve the interests of lesbigay rights agendas, but eventually undermines them by not offering a more nuanced view of the past. Lesbians especially have been vulnerable to the intellectual simplifications of identity politics since Adrienne Rich's "lesbian continuum" posited a de-eroticized lesbian identity that supplied cultural feminism with an intellectual framework.[48] "Queer theory,"[49] on the other hand, has tended to elide the particularities of identity politics under an umbrella term that purports to include practices that transgress heteronormativity; but while "queer theory" may seem to argue for the social constructedness of the broad spectrum of variant sexualities and genders, it does not customarily take into account the complex historical situatedness and evolution of ideas about the body and sexuality before about 1850.[50] If then we are to arrive at a nuanced reconstruction of our antecedents, the dual projects of *theorizing* the historical nature and understandings of female same-sex relations and of *recovering* historical materials that address the existence of female same-sex erotics must proceed in tandem, and they must do so with a clear sense of the problems inherent in current theories that cannot accommodate the particulars of a historicized understanding.

Until recently, Lillian Faderman's path-breaking 1981 study, *Surpassing the Love of Men,* set the evasive tone for the critical work that followed. Her discussions of Montaigne's idealized views of friendship in the *Apology to Raymond Sebond* and of the poetry of Katherine Philips are good examples of readings that strain to ignore or to redefine the erotics of particular texts, and to expunge from them any hints of corporeality.[51] Although lesbian scholars, grateful to Faderman for having introduced the subject of female same-sex erotics before 1800, now have been correcting and complicating her perspective, a number of heterosexual critics (both female and feminist) have perpetuated Faderman's reluctance to affirm the presence of a non-normative female same-sex erotics. The remarks of the editors of one anthology of early women poets that Katherine Philips "is chiefly important for her exaltation of Platonic friendship between women" and that "some of her champions choose to ignore her own stipulation that such friendship be free from carnal interest"[52] gloss over both the traditionally multivalent implications of the Renaissance rhetoric of friendship and the complexities of defining carnality during the early modern period.

Much of the textual material about female same-sex behaviors that was eventually available in England was continental because these behaviors were more generally known, prosecuted, and openly named earlier on the Continent than they were in England.[53] Because many instances of same-sex sexual transgression mentioned and repeated in these early modern textual sources (including prosecutorial records) concern women who cross-dressed or lived what we might understand as transgendered lives, recent scholars sometimes have conflated the issue of same-sex eroticism with issues of transvestism. But despite the perceived identity between sexuality and gender roles raised by cross-dressed persons during the early modern period, the actual occurrence of a connection between transgressive sexuality and gender role seems not to have been usual and is misleading as an index of sexual behavior. Instances of transvestism, because they do not necessarily involve motives for erotic transgression, prove to be a blind alley for the recovery of early modern constructions of female sexuality in England.[54] Further, an emphasis on cross-dressing women tends to focus on the liminal and the grotesque, on the socially marginal, thereby valorizing the exception insofar as it places the marginal at the center and refocuses concern away from the majority or the general run of women. The continuities and complexly signifying practices of other more generally sanctioned social forms, particularly those of female friendship, are thus obscured and the perhaps more common indications of female same-sex erotics are overlooked.

Additional possibilities of how same-sex eroticism might have been enacted in the larger context of social conformity and class distinction need to be considered. The complex interplay between individual behavior and social demand that takes place as women negotiate their relations with one another in the environments of patriarchy demands more scholarly attention. How women poets of the sixteenth, seventeenth, and even eighteenth centuries gave their feelings for one another verbal form is an expression of their cultural embeddedness in historically variable understandings and definitions of erotic behavior. And it is almost certain that those understandings and definitions were not uniform throughout English society, but varied according to social class (e.g., aristocratic vs. gentry vs. middling vs. laboring classes) and geographic location (e.g., urban vs. rural). Certain behaviors, both physical and verbal, that may seem to us similar to what we are accustomed to defining as "lesbian" may have been a tacitly accepted cultural element in certain segments of society, especially before the introduction of a Latinate sexual terminology by anatomy and medical texts, as well as by translations of the classics, in the late sixteenth century, and may not necessarily have been recognized as transgressive.[55]

I explore some of the implications of this theoretical perspective in my work on Katherine Philips and other women writers of this period in chapters 3 and 4 of this study, "An Emerging Sapphic Discourse: The Legacy of Katherine Philips" and "Doubling Discourses in an Erotics of Female Friendship." I believe that while it may be impossible to know for certain what these women actually "did" physically, it is important to recognize their erotic uses of conventional heterosexual rhetoric in their addresses to one another and to acknowledge the possibilities for erotic behaviors that they may not have recognized or named as sexual, but that may have motivated their poetic expressions of passion for one another. It is in the context of these understandings that we can discuss the nature of the erotic friendship poetry by women in the sixteenth, seventeenth, and early eighteenth centuries, and recognize the ways in which it develops a strategy I term a "shadowed language of erotic ellipsis" to express a possibly transgressive content. This process of an erotics of unnaming has already been noted many times in twentieth-century lesbian writing, both in poetry and prose, a primary example being the coded erotic writing of Gertrude Stein. We might want to acknowledge that the elliptical expression of erotic feeling in women's writing may, as a tradition, begin in English in the early modern period just before the Restoration—and long before any construction of a "lesbian" identity as we know it—with the friendship poems of Katherine Philips.

If we are to recover the constructions of earlier historical moments, then, we must continually keep in mind the dissonance between the fixed categories according to which Western cultures increasingly seem to have defined sexual relations and the fluidity of the erotic desires and understandings experienced by individuals. Once individuals become conscious of sexual possibilities in arenas not previously named, avenues become available for the demarcation of cognitive and sexual boundaries and a policing, and silencing, of sexual borderlands becomes possible. In early modern England, a silencing of the relations between women had not yet taken place because the sexual borderlands demarcating transgression had yet to be defined. My project in the chapters that follow is to locate and to describe the historical movement toward the silencing that took place as knowledge of transgressive sexuality between women became widespread throughout an increasingly literate and urbanized English society in which print culture was ever more rapidly being disseminated.

Fig. 2

Sappho at the Leucadian Rock, in Wye Saltonstall, trans., *Ovid's Heroical Epiſtles,* 5th ed. (London, 1663). This engraving of Sappho's impending plunge from the rock at Leucas illustrates the monitory purpose of Saltonstall's translation addressed "To the Vertuous Ladies, and Gentlewomen of England."

CHAPTER II

REPRESENTING SAPPHO:
EARLY MODERN PUBLIC
DISCOURSE

TO EXPLORE FURTHER the publicly circulated discourse about female same-sex sexuality, I examine here contemporary representations of the mythologized reputation of Sappho, who became for the English, as she was for the French and other Europeans, "the original poet of female desire."[1] She also came to be portrayed as the originary embodiment of same-sex female desire; for many modern readers and writers, the Sapphic corpus still represents Sappho as an icon for lesbian visibility and female community.[2] Though Joan DeJean, in her influential book on Sappho, has indicated that English texts on Sappho merely mimic French views of Sappho of a half-century earlier,[3] a closer examination of sixteenth- and seventeenth-century texts available in England reveals that the English rediscovery of Sappho did not wait for the French translations of Anne Le Fèvre Dacier and the turn of the eighteenth century. The complexities of Sappho's sexuality as they were represented in the ancient world were indeed disseminated and elaborated in England well before the Sapphic fictions of Addison and Pope in the eighteenth century.[4] Sappho's passionate involvements with other women were, in fact, well known to those able to read Latin, if not always to those who could not.

My investigations indicate that there were three primary modes of representing Sappho in early modern England: she was portrayed as a mythologized figure who acts the suicidal abandoned woman in the Ovidian tale of Sappho and Phaon; she was used as the first example of female poetic excellence, most often with a disclaimer of any sexuality (or what Abraham Cowley called "ill manners"[5]); and she was presented as an early exemplar of "unnatural" or monstrous sexuality. In this chapter, I describe in detail each of these modes of figuring Sappho in a variety of sixteenth- and seventeenth-century texts before going on to examine their implications for the vernacular discourse(s) about female same-sex eroticism (or sapphism) and their relations to representations of other transgressing classical women in early modern England. Although I have used these three modes as a means of organizing this discussion, it is important to keep in mind that modes of representing Sappho were not always discrete but rather functioned in ways that were interconnected and overlapping.

Suppressing Sappho's Tribadism: The Myth of Sappho and Phaon

The myth of Sappho and Phaon was given currency by Ovid's rewriting of Sappho's sexual reputation in the *Heroïdes,* following the reputedly scurrilous example of a number of Attic comedians, including Menander, who portrayed her as sexually dissolute. Ovid's shaping of the myth— through his appropriation of Sappho's voice and his ventriloquizing of her grief—seems to have provided a nexus for representing the destruction of Sappho's power as a poet/artist and for her reduction to the status of a tribade debilitated by unrequited heterosexual passion. The Athenian comedians, for reasons that are not clear in part because their plays are no longer extant, had conflated the real person of Sappho with a myth about the ferryman Phaon (also known as Phaethon)[6] and the goddess Aphrodite. They presumably created the myth later elaborated and perpetuated by Ovid, who echoed the language of Sappho's poetry to accentuate the pathos of her circumstances when he shaped his tale. Ovid's Sappho has rejected her female companions and, overwhelmed by grief, laments her unrequited passion for the much younger Phaon; in despair at his rejection, she ends her life by leaping to her death at sea from the White Rock of Leucas. Ovid's fictionalized representation of Sappho gained currency throughout early modern Europe in edition after edition of the *Heroïdes.*

The complexities of Ovid's stance toward Sappho in the fifteenth epistle have already been examined in depth by Howard Jacobson, Florence Verducci, and Joan DeJean.[7] For the purposes of this study, it is sufficient to recognize in the text Ovid's deep ambivalence in representing Sappho: the epistle conveys simultaneously a resentful, grudging admiration toward his influential female precursor and a misogynist eagerness to obliterate her preeminence as a rival poet. Consequently, in Ovid's reconfiguration of the myth, Sappho is seduced away both from her art and from her female companions by a self-destructive heterosexual obsession and finally commits suicide. As Gregory Nagy observes, the original Phaethon myth was suffused with overtones of death and rebirth and of the relation of the sun god to the sea;[8] the absence of these elements from the Ovidian version diminishes the myth and, by extension, the significance of this representation of Sappho's suffering.

Commentators in the many early modern editions of the *Heroïdes* were not shy in glossing Sappho's farewell to her women friends, nor were they overscrupulous in describing her presumed erotic activities in the brief biographies that accompanied their commentaries. Their accounts perpetuated the view of the eleventh-century lexicon known as the *Suda* that Sappho's relations with her friends were transgressive: "Sodales ejus & amicæ fuerunt tres, Atthis, Teleſippa, Megara: cum quibus etiam turpem conſuetudinem habuiſſe dicebatur." [Her friends and companions were three, Atthis, Teleſippa, Megara: with whom she is said even to have had shameful habits, or intimacies.][9] The nature of these "shameful habits, or intimacies" as same-sex sexual transgressions is clearly articulated here for readers aware of such behaviors. As early as the *Suda,* then, classical representations of Sappho's relations with other women had become integrated into the Western literary tradition. In keeping with this tradition, a series of Venetian editions of the *Heroïdes,* beginning with those of 1482, 1492, 1495, and 1499, and followed by subsequent continental editions well into the sixteenth century, reproduces the Latin commentary of Domitius Calderinus [Domizio Calderino, 1447–1478], which includes the following remarks:

> Erynna was the concubine (*concubina*) of Sappho. . . . [He gives the names of three of her friends (*amicas*)] who it is said she used libidinously (*ad libidinem*). . . . Ovid indicates that her poems were lascivious (*lasciva*). . . . [S]he did not fail to love [them] in the manner of a man, but was with other women a tribade, this is abusing (*insultando*) them by rubbing, for tribein [Greek] is to rub, which we say according to Juvenal and

Martial, and she was named by Horace *mascula Sappho*. . . . (sig. N1 in both editions)

The language of lust, *"concubina," "ad libidinem," "lasciva,"* leaves little to be inferred. Domitius also draws a clear distinction between acts of penetrative sexuality, "in the manner of a man," and tribadism, "rubbing," identifying both as aspects of the same transgressiveness. Further, Horace's well-known epithet *"mascula Sappho"* is here clearly associated with her sexuality rather than with her poetic gifts. Thus there is no question that Sappho's tribadism was an integral part of her representation in Europe at this early date. Similarly, the first Latin edition of the *Heroïdes* published in England, in 1583, somewhat abbreviates the fullness of detail in the Venetian editions, but retains enough of it to convey the crucial point of her tribadism, maintaining the definition of *tribas* and interpreting the Horatian epithet as referring to Sappho's same-sex erotic stance ("In XXI. Epistolam Argumentum," sig. H14 –H14ᵛ).

Sappho's presumed erotic connections with women were thus implicated in Ovid's representation of her as driven and destroyed by an unrequited heterosexual passion. She was punished for her aberrant erotic tastes as well as for the threatening and dangerous (to men) power of her art. This construction of her "life" was available to educated sixteenth-century English readers of Latin. This construction was also available, though less explicitly, to a wider English audience in the translation of Ovid's text, published in 1567 by George Turberville, without gloss and without an additionally appended "life" of Sappho:

> Pyrino is forgot,
> ne Dryads doe delite
> My fancie: Lesbian Lasses eke
> are now forgotten quite.
> Not Amython I force,
> nor Cyndo passing fine:
> Nor Atthis, as she did of yore,
> allures these eyes of mine.
> Ne yet a hundreth mo
> whom (shame ylayd aside)
> I fancide erste: thou all that love
> from them to thee hast wride.
>
> (sig. O5ᵛ)

In these lines, Sappho forgets the female companions Pyrino, Amython, Cyndo, and Atthis, who no longer allure "these eyes of mine." Phaon has

seduced her love from them and from "a hundreth mo / whom . . . / I fan-
cide erste." She has "ylayd aside" the lascivious "shame" of her love for
hundreds of women for him. Further on, Sappho laments the silencing of
her poetic music, yet asks the "Lesbian Lasses" who were its subject to return no more, for they have caused her disgrace, "for cause I looved you
sore / [you] Breede my defame":

> My lowring Lute laments for wo,
> my Harpe with doole is dombe.
> Ye Lesbian Lasses all
> that border on the Lake:
> And ye that of the Aeolian towne
> your names are thought to take,
> Ye Lesbian Lasses (that
> for cause I looved you sore
> Breede my defame) unto my Harpe
> I charge you come no more.
>
> (sig. P4)

Early in the next century, Wye Saltonstall's 1636 translation for "the Vertuous Ladies and Gentlewomen of England" modified both these passages in such a way as to undercut their explicit references to Sappho's
erotic activities with her own sex. Compare his bowdlerized translation
with Turberville's earlier one:

> I hate Amythone, and Cyndus white,
> And Atthis is not pleasant in my sight.
> And many others that were lov'd of me,
> But now I have plac'd all my love on thee.
>
> (sig. L6)

Saltonstall compresses the more elaborately stated forgettings of these
lines in Turberville to a simpler expression of a turning away from her female companions toward Phaon. Saltonstall's Sappho, unlike Turberville's, does not admit to having had her fancy delighted by her companions, nor to having forced Amython, nor to having had her eyes allured
by Atthis. The "hundreth mo" have become "many others" and a love that
Phaon "wride" from them—that is, "wried" or diverted, with the suggestion of contortion or twisting—is now less violently "plac'd" in him.
Saltonstall renders the second passage as follows:

> Yea, Lesbian Nymphs that mariage do desire,
> Yea, Nymphs so called from the Lesbian Lyre.

Ye Lesbyan Nymphs whose love advanc'd my fame:
Come not to heare my Harpe, or Lyrick straine.
For that sweet vaine I had in former time,
My Phaon took away, who is not mine.

(sig. L8)

In Saltonstall's later version, Sappho's rejection of the "Lesbian Nymphs" is emphatic, even a bit contemptuous, while the nature of her love for women might not be apparent to those not already familiar with her reputation; further, the nymphs not only fail to reciprocate her love but desire marriage with men. Underlined here as well is the connection between Sappho's excessive and futile passion for Phaon and the precipitous decline of her artistic powers. This is a pathetic Sappho indeed, having lost the "sweet vaine" of her "Lyrick straine" for a Phaon who abandoned her. Saltonstall seems to have been sufficiently aware of the erotic implications of Ovid's representation of Sappho's relations with her companions that he reconfigured his own Sapphic voice so as to modify those improprieties in a manner suitable to the "Vertuous Ladies" to whom he was addressing his text.

Three years after the publication of Saltonstall's text, John Sherburne's 1639 translation gives us a lasciviously heterosexual Sappho. References to her same-sex erotic partners are in some ways less explicit than those of Turberville, but also rather less evasive than in Saltonstall's "Ladies'" version:

Vile's *Amython*, vile *Cydno*. [*sic*] too the white,
Vile *Althis*, once most gratefull in my sight,
And hundreds more with whom my sins are knowne.

(sig. G9ᵛ)

In addition to disgust with her former friends and erotic partners as the consequence of her newfound and self-destructive heterosexual passion, this Sappho is burdened by what we might term tribadic promiscuity, a male fantasy of hedonistic and exotic pleasures with "hundreds more," "sins" she must regret and expiate through heterosexual suffering. Sherburne's Sappho has been, perhaps, suspiciously Christianized (i.e., "sins" have replaced "crimes") by a discourse that echoes the orientalizing and "othering" of tribadism to Middle Eastern locales during this period.[10]

Contemporary with Saltonstall and Sherburne's Ovidian translations are the two English editions of Thomas Heywood's compendium of famous women, *GYNAIKEION: or Nine Bookes of Various History Concern-*

inge Women . . . , published in 1624 and again in 1657.[11] Like Saltonstall, Heywood was writing exempla for women; but he provides in addition a biographical account from standard sources and furnishes his readers with an especially harsh representation of the consequences to Sappho of her excessive passion for Phaon. Having commented in his introduction to his female readers that we cannot know virtue without vice, Heywood adds:

> I wish you all to striue, that the beautie of your mindes may still exceede that of your bodies . . . and as the higher powers haue bestowed on you fairenesse aboue man, to equall that excellencie of iudgement and wisedome in which man claimes iustly a prioritie before you, so it is both behoouefull and becomming your Sex, that your outward perfections should altogether aime at the inward pulchritude of the mind; since the first is accidentall and casuall, the last stable and permanent. (sig. P4ᵛ; 164)

To this moralizing end, he provides a rich compilation of accounts of women. In "The Fifth Booke . . . Intreating of Amazons: and other Women famous either for Valour, or for Beautie," Heywood's portrait of strong women presents the Amazons, Joan of Arc, and others as brave and valiant, and as partaking of masculine qualities (sig. X5ᵛ–X6; 238–39). Yet a kind of misogyny clearly emerges as the Amazons become an object lesson in romantic failure and the miseries of unfulfilled sexuality; he describes "[a] law among the Amazons":

> To incourage their valour, and that there should be no coward amongst them, they haue a law, That no Virgin shall be capable of a husband, or enter into familiar congresse with man, before she hath brought from the field, the head of an enemie slaine with her owne hand; which hath beene the cause that so many of them haue died old wrinkled beldames, that neuer knew what belonged to the interchange of carnall societie. (sig. V4; 223)

It is in this context that Heywood presents Sappho. Unlike the other English translators of the Ovidian epistle, he compiles all the conventionally repeated elements of her biography, managing to add his own garbled turn to the traditionally doubled Sapphos (the one a poet, the second a strumpet) that he appropriates from the *Suda* via Gyraldus.[12] Following his biographical description, he quotes Ovid's epistle from Sappho to Phaon in its entirety, presumably in his own translation, including accounts of her relations with other women:

> The Pirhian gyrle, nor the Methimnian lasse
> Now please me; not the Lesbians who surpasse.

Vil's Amithon, vile Cidno too, the faire,
So Atthis that did once appeare most rare,
And hundreds more, with whom my sinn's not small:
Wretch, thou alone inioyest the loues of all.

(sig. Ll 3; 389)

Heywood's translation, like Sherburne's, is fairly explicit about Sappho's relations with her female companions, also imputing to her a pronounced hedonism and tribadic promiscuity ("And hundreds more"), as well as Christianizing her moral failure ("with whom my sinn's not small"). Heywood, however, also adds a unique twist of punishing anguish to the Ovidian account that seems not to appear in any other translation: the implication of "Wretch, thou alone inioyest the loues of all" seems to be that Phaon, who is addressed directly, now enjoys Sappho's former companions, driving her to a frenzy of jealous distraction. The extreme pathos of her loss of poetic powers, as well as the hope of love, follows:

My Verse is of her first power destitute,
Silent's my Quill, my Harpe with sorrow mute.
You Lesbian Matrons, and you Lesbian young,
Whose names haue to my Lyre beene oft times sung.
You for whose loues my fame hath suffred wrong,
No more in troopes vnto my Musicke throng,
Phaon hath stole all that you nam'd Diuine,
I was (O wretch) about to call him mine.

(sig. Ll 5; 393)

A pitiful Sappho has thus lost her audience as well as her lover and her song. Heywood's description of her death is of a richly deserved punishment:

From that Rocke, ſhee caſt her ſelfe headlong into the Sea, and ſo periſhed. For prepoſterous and forbidden Luxuries which were imputed vnto her, *Horace* calls her *Maſcula Sapho;* yet many are of opinion, this to be the ſame whom *Plato* tearmes the Wiſe . . . (sig. Ll 5ᵛ; 394)

The "yet" on which this sentence turns curiously suggests an attempt to disengage the two Sapphos, the poet from the whore, and creates confusion; it perhaps also reveals Heywood's considerable ambivalence about acknowledging that "the tenth Muse" might have embodied trespass along with wisdom and a divine poetic voice. While not indicating the precise nature of these "prepoſterous and forbidden Luxuries"—which would have been known to any male readers—and while partly obscuring the nature of Sappho's transgressions, Heywood makes clear to his female readers that this is forbidden territory whose boundaries are crossed only at a devastatingly high cost.

These examples suggest that as Ovid's epistle of Sappho to Phaon began to reach a larger reading audience in English translation, the clearly delineated tribadism familiar to those who could read Latin was reconfigured in favor of a representation of the preeminent female poet as creatively and emotionally debilitated, sacrificing herself on the altar of passion for a man. Apart from what this might suggest about patriarchalism in early modern England, it does seem to indicate that there was sufficient consciousness about female same-sex eroticism and a reasonably clear understanding of the meaning of tribadism, at least among educated males, that discourse in the vernacular was being inhibited, particularly when it was addressed or made available to respectable women. Where Ovid's epistle is concerned, the representation of Sappho as a model of behavior was clearly in need of reconfiguration. In contrast to the relatively straightforward presentation of Sappho's putative tribadism by sixteenth-century Latin commentators, seventeenth-century translators are more self-consciously ambiguous in their handling of the complexities of her erotic behaviors.

As it made its way into the vernacular, into the drama and popular romance of the seventeenth century, the story of Sappho and Phaon failed to maintain the complexly misogynistic elements of the Ovidian epistle or the Renaissance humanists' "'defamation of Sappho,'"[13] or even to hint at Sappho's love for women and the erotically transgressive nature of her poetry. In his late-sixteenth-century mythological court play *Sapho and Phao* (1584), John Lyly uses the figure of Sappho as an "Empress" who represents Elizabeth I, at least in part: in this version, Sappho turns the tables on Phao (who serves, presumably, as a suitor to Elizabeth), by rejecting *his* love and taking control of Cupid and Venus. Far from succumbing to love for Phao, Lyly's Sappho emerges triumphant over the potentially disruptive powers of Venus and Cupid. There is perhaps an oblique suggestion—though not in a manner inappropriate in a compliment to Elizabeth—that she might have preferred the company of members of her own sex. Here, as Janel Mueller has suggested,[14] Lyly is in all probability drawing plot complications from Sappho's prayer-poem, the ode to Aphrodite, to structure his dramatic situation until its "reversing dénouement." Lyly uses a version of the familiarly mythical name of Phaon, but for all practical purposes ignores the substance of Ovid's epistle.[15]

That a bowdlerized narrative of Sappho and Phaon had a wide currency is demonstrated by its presence in the 1601 English translation, by Phile-mon Holland, of Pliny's (ca. 23–79 C.E.) encyclopedic compendium of natural lore, *Historie of the World; or, The Natural History,* which was a widely distributed and popularly known standard reference work in early modern England. Pliny's account of Sappho and Phaon appears in his de-scription of the herb white eryngion (i.e., mandrake root),[16] "the reason (men say) that ladie *Sappho* was so enamoured upon the yong knight *Phao* of Lesbos" (sig. L6). In this attribution of the motive for Sappho's infat-uation to the magic properties of an herb, Pliny neatly dispenses with the entire mythic superstructure of goddesses and rocks and seas and relieves Sappho of responsibility for her lovesickness while displacing the lovers from a classical into a chivalric world of "ladie" and "yong knight." Hol-land's translation thus disseminated to seventeenth-century English read-ers a paradigmatically Englished version of Ovid's myth.

A later English version of the myth appears as a digression in William Bosworth's 1651 romance, *The chaſt and loſt lovers . . . Arcadius and Sepha.* This mid-seventeenth-century version bears very little resemblance to any Latin sources, to Lyly's play, or to any of Sappho's then-known works. It is sheer fantasy in an outmoded Elizabethan vein, except that Bos-worth—unlike Lyly or Holland's translation of Pliny—retains Sappho's status as an artist. In Bosworth's version, Phaon is a knight, complete with shield and sword, come to Lesbos to renew his patrimony. A young Sap-pho (in Ovid she is well past her prime) falls in love with him; he does not return her love but, for reasons not clearly explained in the text, kills him-self. Sappho then drowns herself in a stream and is mourned by yet an-other knight. Thus has the drama of the Leucadian Rock degenerated: Lesbos has been domesticated, complete with a romantic grotto and stream. Gone are Sappho's Ovidian monologue of lovelorn despair and any hint of sexual transformation or loss of artistic capacities. Bosworth's digression is a genteel exemplum of thwarted lovers.

These contemporary versions of the Sappho and Phaon myth thus do not with any consistency adhere to the conventional Ovidian scenario and Sappho's tribadic excesses. What remain are the mythologized names with some characteristics of Sappho's fame intact and some semblance of a narrative of love.

The historical trajectory of Ovid's attempted defamation of Sappho is demonstrated as well by the fate of his well-known reference to her in the *Tristia,* written in exile, lamenting that he has been punished for his sex-ual escapades while others, among whom is Sappho, have not: "Lesbia quid docuit Sappho, nisi amare puellas?" [What did Lesbian Sappho teach the girls if not love?] (Cambridge 1638, sig. B8). Early modern English translations of this Ovidian passage, whose erotic implications are clear enough in Latin and in any literal translation, are initially faithful in their rendering of the original but later begin to obscure Sappho's progressively more problematic relations with her own sex. In 1572 Thomas Churchyard translated this line as "What hath dame *Sapho Lesbia* learnde, but maydens fayre to love" (sig. B6), and in 1633 Wye Saltonstall translated it as "And *Sappho* doth instruct mayds how to love" (sig. D3); both these translations retain the possibility of erotic connection between Sappho and young women, though it is muted in Saltonstall's translation. But Zachary Catlin's rendering into English, in 1639, as "What taught the *Lesbian Sappho* but to love?" (sig. C8) entirely ruptures the continuity of these lines with the tradition of a tribadic Sappho; her companions have disappeared. By mid–seventeenth century, then, "puellas" is finally eliminated and Sappho's tribadism is obliterated from the English Ovid. In this passage, we see again that by the mid–seventeenth century in England the treatment of Sappho's tribadism has become increasingly self-conscious and ambiguous when it is not altogether obliterated.

These modifications in the presentation of Sappho in English texts make clear that the imputation of tribadism to her and her association with female same-sex erotic relations were progressively suppressed. There were no doubt several reasons for this change. But the most important were, first, the fact of the availability of English texts to women, for whom such sexual knowledge was deemed inappropriate, and, second, a more generalized discomfort at disseminating this knowledge beyond the elite circles of educated men who read Latin.

Sappho as Originary Icon of Female Poetic Excellence

That Sappho's preeminence in the world of letters was generally acknowledged in the ancient world is also evidenced by the numerous surviving encomia to her. In his *Rhetoric*, Aristotle points out that "[e]verybody honors the wise . . . and the Mytilineans honored Sappho although she was a woman."[17] Though her works were lost during the depredations of the early Christians and it was left to the late nineteenth and twentieth centuries to recover fragments of her poems in papyri abandoned in ancient refuse heaps, two of her poems and a number of fragments were preserved in Renaissance Europe. The French led in the recovery of her work when in 1566 the great printer Henri Estienne (Henricus Stephanus) published the two odes preserved in their entirety by Dionysius of Hali-carnassus and by Longinus, as well as all known fragments, in his second edition of the Greek lyric poets (sig. C1ff.).[18] The English were much later in publishing Sappho's known poems—in contrast to Ovid's account of her—only in 1695 including both odes in a Latin/Greek edition of the *Odes of Anacreon* published in London. No doubt, before the end of the seventeenth century, those English speakers who wanted to read her in Greek could obtain a French edition, or they could read the French trans-lations of the odes that had become available.

A portion of Sappho's work became well known, as did the fact that both odes addressed love between women, the ode to Aphrodite and *Phainetai moi,* in which the speaker's passion for her beloved is triangu-lated through a man.[19] Despite the ambiguities of her sexual reputation, Sappho became the one figure associated with female poetic excellence; she was the sole ancient model to which contemporary women writers might compare themselves and to whom they might be compared. Plato had called her "the tenth Muse," and that epithet became more or less in-evitably, and conventionally, attached to her name in literary circles; even those not familiar with her surviving poems no doubt knew of her iconic status as the first and preeminent female poet.

In the latter half of the seventeenth century in England, Sappho's name was used to apostrophize female poets, often with a disclaimer about their sexuality or erotic proclivities. This was, at least at first, almost certainly a fashionable echo of Mme. de Scudéry's having styled herself the second Sappho and having rewritten her own fiction of Sappho in book 10 of *Artamène ou le Grand Cyrus* (1649–53), which included an acknowledgment—albeit subtle—of Sappho's erotic interest in women. In the seventeenth century, male contemporaries referred to Katherine Philips, who was also an admirer of Mme. de Scudéry, as "the new Sap-pho," making certain always to emphasize Philips's exemplary virtue. Philips's friend the poet Abraham Cowley writes:

> They talk of *Sappho,* but, alas! the shame
> Ill Manners soil the lustre of her fame.
> Orinda's [Philips's nom de plume] inward Vertue is so bright,
> That, like a Lantern's fair enclosed light,
> It through the Paper shines where she doth write.[20]

The compliment was later taken over, without the sexual disclaimer, by women writers who used it among themselves, and it became almost de rigueur in the commendatory poems introducing volumes of poetry by women writers, as an examination of the work of Anne Killigrew, Jane Barker, or Anne Finch, countess of Winchelsea, reveals. Delarivier Manley and Catharine Trotter, as well as other female dramatists, use Sappho as a literary icon to describe one another in the commendatory poems that preface their plays. For example, Mary Pix addressed Delarivier Manley on her play *The Royal Mischief* (1696) as "[l]ike Sappho Charming. . . ."[21] Sappho's literary reputation was, in this way, well established in seventeenth-century England, though often—especially when referred to by men—with an evident unease about her sexuality, with what nineteenth-century England was to name "sapphism," so that her poetic reputation was often confounded by her reputedly transgressive sexuality.

Sappho as Exemplar of Female Same-Sex Desire

Sappho was, then, already being used in early modern England as an Ovidian example of tribadism in literary discourse. She also became the most prominent exemplar of erotic behaviors between women in the nonliterary discourses and texts through which her erotic reputation was also circulated. Some brief mention of tribadism, often with Sappho as its exemplar, occurs in descriptions of the clitoris in medical texts and in the Latin anatomies available in England sometime around the mid–seventeenth century. However, during the mid–sixteenth century, female same-sex eroticism was clearly known and was a topic of some interest among educated males; for example, the 1562 edition of Fallopius and the 1595 edition of Laurentius convey the nature of knowledge about tribadism that was disseminated among male readers of Latin. These works also convey a sense of the characteristic tone of descriptions of the clitoris and of the context into which Sappho was to be integrated as more texts became available in the vernacular and as disapprobation came to be increasingly directed against what was understood as female same-sex sexuality.

Fallopius remarks, with some degree of clinical detachment, on the role of the clitoris in female same-sex relations:

> Auicen[na] . . . meminit cuiuſdam partis in pudendo muliebri ſitam, quam virgam vel albathara vocat. Hanc Albucaſis . . . tentiginem appellat, quae ſolet aliquando ad tantum incrementum peruenire, vt mulieres hanc habentes coeant cum aliis, veluti ſi viri eſſent. Partem hanc graeci κλητορίδα vocârunt, vnde verbum κλητορίζειν obſcænum diductum est. Anatomici verò nostri penitus neglexerunt, neque verbum quidem de ipſe faciunt. (sig. p4ᵛ)

[Avicenna makes mention of a certain member situated in the female genitalia which he calls *virga* or *albathara*. Albucasis calls this *tentigo*, which sometimes will increase to such a great size that women, while in this condition, have sex with each other just as if they were men. The Greeks call this member *clitoris*, from which the obscene word *clitorize* is derived. Our anatomical writers have completely neglected this and do not even have a word for it.]

Fallopius evokes the authority of Avicenna and Albucasis to name the clitoris and to locate the transgressiveness of female same-sex behaviors in the way in which they imitate heterosexual relations ("veluti ſi viri eſſent" [as if they were men]) when their member increases to a great size. The Latin terminology he provides also describes the clitoris by way of analogy with the male organ: *tentigo* translates as "tenseness" or "lust" and was used in English throughout the seventeenth and eighteenth centuries to mean "an attack of priapism" or "an erection";[22] *virga* translates as "a root," "a twig," or "a sprout," suggesting the diminutive size of the clitoris in relation to the penis. The ancient Greek terminology Fallopius offers, *clitoris*, was ultimately to be the word appropriated into English, though *clitorize*, the "obscene" verb derived from it, seems not to have followed. Significantly, Fallopius underlines the failure of early modern anatomical writers to address the presence of this member capable of a masculinized tumescence: "Our anatomical writers have completely neglected this and do not even have a word for it." At the end of the sixteenth century, Laurentius quotes Fallopius and then, next to the marginal gloss "vſus clitoridis" [use of the clitoris] goes on to provide the language most commonly used to describe female same-sex behaviors:

Huius vſum agnoſcimus, vt perfricata torpentem excitet facultatem. Creſcit in quibuſdam tam importuné, vt extra rimam pendeat mentulæ inſtar, & eaſeſe mutuò fricent mulieres, quas propterea tribades ſeu fricatrices dicunt. (sigs. Ll 4ᵛ–Mm1)

[I have become aware of the use of this (clitoris), whereby after being rubbed all over it excites the sluggish faculty. It increases in some people to such an inappropriate extent that it hangs outside the fissure the same as a penis; women then often engage in mutual rubbing, such women accordingly called *tribades* or *fricatrices*.]

Just over thirty years after Fallopius had noted the neglect of the clitoris by early modern anatomists, Laurentius not only gives a precise description of how tumescence is achieved and of its homology with the male organ, but he also provides a more extensive and contemporary vocabulary for those who use the engorged clitoris inappropriately. He makes clear that the Greek *tribades* and the Latin *fricatrices* were used interchangeably to describe women who enacted these behaviors, described—and under-stood—primarily as mutual "rubbing" ("eaſeſe mutuò fricent mulieres" [women mutually rub each other]) of an enlarged member. Laurentius elaborates on Fallopius's brief "ad tantum incrementum peruenire" [to in-crease to such a great size] with the more explicitly detailed "Creſcit in quibuſdam tam importuné, vt extra rimam pendeat mentulæ inſtar" [it in-creases in some people to such an inappropriate extent that it hangs out-side the fissure the same as a penis].

Later, in the seventeenth century, anatomies in English tend to devote more space to their descriptions of the clitoris in order to add additional commentary of a judgmental nature. In 1615 Helkiah Crooke in his En-glish anatomy repeats the commentaries of his Greek and Latin prede-cessors; next to the marginal gloss "*Tribades odioſæ feminæ*" [Tribades, hateful women], he remarks:

> [A]lthough for the moſt part it [the clitoris] hath but a ſmall production hidden vnder the *Nymphes* and hard to be felt but with curioſity, yet ſometimes it groweth to ſuch a length that it hangeth without the cleft like a mans member, eſpecially when it is fretted with the touch of the cloathes, and ſo ſtrutteth and groweth to a rigiditie as doth the yarde of a man. And this part it is which thoſe wicked women doe abuſe called *Tribades* (often mentioned by many authours, and in ſome ſtates worthily puniſhed) to their mutuall and vnnaturall luſtes. (sig. Y5ᵛ)

Quite apparent in Crooke's description are both the contemporary ob-session with the homologies between the clitoris and the "yarde"—per-haps bred by anxiety but also reflective of the more pervasive tendency to read male and female anatomies as homologous[23]—and a growing con-tempt for female same-sex eroticism, the two no doubt interconnected. What had earlier seemed merely clinical and somewhat disapproving de-scriptions, now become in English rather heavy-handed condemnations: tribades are now "hateful," "wicked women" "worthily punished" for their "unnatural lusts."

The 1634 translation of the anatomy of Ambroise Paré by Thomas Johnson makes the usual references to earlier authorities, especially to Re-aldo Columbo and to Fallopius, and provides a narrowed vocabulary for identifying the clitoris, but emphasizes the Greek verb as "that infamous word . . . (which signifies impudently to handle that part)." As oppro-brium is transferred from the action of handling the clitoris to the clitoris itself—"an obscene part"—readers who want to know more are coyly referred to the original sources:

> *Columbus* cals it *Tentigo, Fallopius Cleitoris,* whence proceeds that infamous word *Cleitorizein,* (which ſigniſies impudently to handle that part.) But becauſe it is an obſcene part, let thoſe which deſire to know more of it, reade the Authors which I cited. (sig. M5ᵛ)

The text thus avoids naming female same-sex sexuality in English. That the terms of description used for the clitoris remain remarkably consistent, with authors echoing their predecessors, is evidenced repeatedly over a quite long period of time. Alexander Read's comments in his 1642 *The Manuall of the Anatomy* are characteristic:

> [The] Clytoris . . . is a nervous and hard body: within, full of a black and ſpongious matter, as the laterall ligaments of the yard. . . . And as it doth repreſent the prick of a man, ſo it ſuffereth erection, and falling; It may be called a woman's prick. In some women it hath been as big as a mans. (sig. F5ᵛ–F6)

As the mid–seventeenth century approaches and anatomical texts are translated into the vernacular or written directly in English, "clitoris"—often accompanied by "tentigo"—becomes the more or less stable signifier of a female organ seen in terms of male anatomy as "a woman's prick." During the first half of the seventeenth century, as Johnson's translation of Paré and Read's English anatomy demonstrate, explicit description of female same-sex behavior appears to have been suppressed. We might speculate that between the explicitness of Crooke's 1615 text and the later evasiveness of Johnson's 1634 translation and Read's 1642 anatomy, an awareness of the possibility of women readers as audience for these texts may have encouraged a change in judgments of how much knowledge it was appropriate to circulate.

The anatomical connection with Sappho is made rather later, toward the middle of the seventeenth century, as prurient interest in the clitoris evidently increased and as circulation of sexual knowledge in the vernacular expanded. From the relatively brief period toward the beginning of the century when there was an inhibition of explicit description in English of female same-sex sexuality accompanying definitions of the clitoris, midcentury brought an elaborated account of female same-sex behaviors for circulation in the vernacular. In 1653 the Swedish anatomist Thomas Bartholin revised, expanded, and translated into English his father's 1633 Latin anatomy of the human body. The Latin of Caspar

Bartholin clearly describes contemporary understanding of female same-sex sexual activity, but does not include the anecdotal embellishments and example of Sappho added by the younger Bartholin twenty years later in the English translation. The entry "Of the Clitoris" includes engravings of that part, with explicit comparisons to the penis, or "yard," and the following description:

> The Greeks call it *clitoris,* others name it *Tentigo,* others the womans Yard or Prick: both because it resembles a Mans Yard, in Situation, Substance, Composition, Repletion, with Spirits and Erection. And Also because it hath somewhat like the Nut and Fore-skin of a Mans Yard, and in some Women it grows as big as the Yard of a man: so that some women abuse the same, and make use thereof in place of a mans Yard, exercising carnal Copulation one with another, and they are termed *Confricatrices* Rubsters. Which lascivious Practice is said to have been invented by Philaenis and Sappho, the Greek Poetress, is reported to have practised the same. And of these I conceive the Apostle Paul speaks in the I. of *Romans* 26. And therefore this part is called *Contemptus virorum* the Contempt of Mankind. (sig. Z2–Z2ᵛ)

Thus a connection is incontrovertibly made between Sappho and the specific behaviors of tribadism, which here appear to include penetration (i.e., "carnal Copulation") along with rubbing. He also introduces the colloquial "Rubsters" as a literal translation of *Confricatrices,* with which it is in apposition.[24] He goes on to say that an unusually large clitoris is "praeternatural and monstrous" and comments further that "the more this part encreases, the more does it hinder a man in his business" (sig. Aa1). The androcentrism of Bartholin's commentary and his thinly disguised prurience may be too obvious to need commentary, yet it is important to underline the particular form they take here: male anxiety is expressed not only in the presence of the female assumption of male sexual prerogative (i.e., "make use thereof in place of a mans Yard"), but also in the prospective thwarting of his own perceived prerogatives and just deserts (i.e., being "hinder[ed] . . . in his business"). Indeed, as we have seen, these anxieties and the androcentrism and prurience to which they give rise typify contemporary accounts.[25] Bartholin's description of the clitoris, including his incorporation of Sappho as the icon of tribadism, subsequently furnished a model for the semipornographic medical treatises that were to follow in the eighteenth century.[26] Bartholin's account of the clitoris thus suggests to us the language through which what since the late nineteenth century has been called lesbianism, with Sappho as its leading exemplar, originally entered cultural consciousness in the vernacular.

Other Transgressing Classical Women

While Sappho was clearly the primary and most prominent exemplar of female same-sex relations, other well-known women from the classical period were also singled out as secondary icons of tribadic promiscuity. Most notable among these secondary figures was the Leucadian Philaenis mentioned by Bartholin, appropriately enough associated with the location of Sappho's mythic humiliation and suicide, though anachronistically so, because her dates are later than Sappho's. Very little is known about Philaenis: the sources of early modern knowledge of her appear to have been *The Greek Anthology* and two lewdly misogynistic epigrams by Martial. The first of Martial's epigrams opens, "Pedicat pueros tribas Philaenis / et tentigine saevior mariti / undenas dolat in die puellas" (67, bk. 7). [That tribade Philaenis sodomizes boys, and with more rage than a husband in his stiffened lust, she works eleven girls roughly every day]; the second reads, "Ipsarum tribadum tribas, Philaeni, / recte, quam futuis, vocas amicam" (70, bk. 7). [You, Philaenis, tribade to tribades, rightly call friend her whom you f**k.][27] The transgression in these lines is located clearly in Martial's projected fantasy of Philaenis's appropriation of male sexual prerogatives in penetrating both boys and girls . . . like a husband. It is useful to note that at least for the Romans "tribadism" and "tribades" appear to have included a range of sexual acts, not simply the "rubbing" originally referred to in Greek. Thomas Heywood, in his *GYNAIKEION*, provides a comparatively less explicit account of Philaenis for his female readers:

> Philenis was a strumpet of Leucadia, her Verses were as impurely wanton as her life was immodest and vnchast: . . . Shee was the first that deuised kataklysis [a sexual act possibly incorporating purging or douching] in the Veneriall Trade, and left certaine bookes behind her of Veneriall Copulation. This you may reade in Gyraldus in 30. *Dialog. Histor. Poet.* . . . [28]

Heywood's Philaenis is a wanton with men and follows in the classical tradition of her association with a manual of sexual positions. Heywood gives his source in Gyraldus, but he must have been aware that few of his female readers would, or could, seek out the original. There they would have found a clear reference to Martial's Philaenis, though not an elaborated description of her transgressive behaviors: "Alteram Philænem Tribadem lacerat Martialis." [Martial tears to pieces another Philaenis Tribade.][29] More particular knowledge of her activities would appear to have been reserved for male readers of Martial's Latin.

Gyraldus and Heywood also mention Elephantis, another writer of a classical sex manual whom Philaenis was said to emulate; she is not explicitly associated with tribadism except insofar as her writings suggest "beastly and preposterous Luxuries,"[30] an evidently coded and repeated reference by Heywood either to sodomy or to tribadism, or to both. Another woman transgressing with her own sex is to be found in Martial's epigram 90, book 1, a virulent attack on one Bassa, who uses women like a man; his description of Bassa's exploits echoes his account of Philaenis in its focus on the female assumption of male penetrative prerogatives and in its contemptuous tone.[31] Clearly, there were abundant examples of female same-sex transgressors available to male readers, who often, like Heywood, functioned as gatekeepers of sexual knowledge for literate women: the texts they produced manipulated women's access to the particulars of transgressive behaviors, and to transgressing figures like Sappho and Philaenis, through skillful translation and editing; they also shaped women's moral perspectives through condemnatory rhetoric and injunctions against sin.

Vernacular Discourses

The discourses used by men in the vernacular to describe female same-sex erotic behaviors and the complex processes through which knowledge of these behaviors was circulated are illuminated by a comparison between references to and descriptions of these behaviors, with the occasional inclusion of Sappho, during two rough temporal spans: first, at the end of the sixteenth and beginning of the seventeenth centuries and, second, toward the end of the seventeenth century and into the early eighteenth century. A reference to the classically derived "tribade" early in the seventeenth century occurs in 1621, in a subsection of Robert Burton's great compendium *The Anatomy of Melancholy*, titled "How love tyrannizeth over men," in which he inveighs against "wenchers, gelded youths, debauchees, catamites, boy-things, pederasts, Sodomites, . . . Ganymedes, &c." among the companies of priests and of "self-defiling monks" that have "Spintrias [or those that seek out and invent new and monstrous actions of lust], Succubas, Ambubaias [or Dancing-Girls], and those wanton-loined womanlings, Tribadas, that fret each other by turns, and fulfill Venus, even among Eunuchs, with their artful secrets."[32] The *OED* lists the first occurrence of "tribade" in an English text in Ben Jonson's 1601 *Forest*, "Light Venus . . . with thy tribade trine [the Three Graces], invent new sports" (x. Præludium). Jonson again (before 1609) uses a reference to tribadism to condemn Cecelia Bulstrode's poetry writing and to underline the transgressiveness of female attempts at literary creativity: "What though with Tribade lust she force a Muse?" ("Epigram on the Court Pucell").[33] It is probable that the word had currency earlier than these usages indicate, if not in English printed texts, then almost certainly in speech and private writing among educated men.

Evidence for such an earlier use of this language can be found almost ten years before in an exchange of privately circulated verse letters, dated 1592 to 1594, between John Donne, then a student at Lincoln's Inn, and a Mr. T. W. (Thomas Woodward), a young man who seems to have been the object of his erotic attentions. Woodward responded to Donne's initial admiring verses about his poetic skill with a poem called "Thou sendst me prose"; it concludes with the following erotic metaphors:

> Have mercy on me and my sinfull Muse
> Which rub'd and tickled with thyne could not chuse
> But spend some of her pithe and yeild to bee
> One in that chaste and mistique tribadree.
> Bassaes adultery no fruit did leave,
> Nor theirs which their swolne thighs did nimbly weave,
> And with new armes and mouthes embrace and kis
> Though they had issue was not like to this.
> Thy Muse, Oh strange and holy Lecheree
> Beeing a Mayd still, gott this Song on mee.[34]

Here tribadism ("tribadree") is used to name the erotic play of their Muses: note "*rub'd* and *tickled*," "*spend* some of her *pithe* and *yeild*" (my emphasis), all of which have explicit sexual referents. The "tribadree" of their Muses, then, is "chaste" (i.e., absent a male member and "issue") and so "mistique." The eroticism of "tribadree" continues in the next lines with the use of Bassa's well-known adultery with other women and with the powerful images of bodies entwined, particularly the lust conveyed by "their swolne thighs." The point being made is that of the sterility of tribadism, the lack of issue in the relations between two women, which is made to contrast nicely with the "strange and holy Lecheree" of Donne's Muse, "Beeing a Mayd still," begetting this poem on Woodward. Like Jonson's use of tribadism, it is associated with the erotics of creativity. It is not unwarranted, I believe, to conclude that many educated young men must have had a more than casual interest in the relations of women with one another. Here, the relations of tribadism seem to stand in for a more overt acknowledgment of the nature of the interest between these two young men, which is doubly displaced and distanced as their mutual interest in writing poetry is seen through the lens of a female same-sex erotics.

Indeed, like his friend and contemporary Ben Jonson, Donne retained an interest in the erotic relations of women with one another. In his erotic heroical epistle "Sapho to Philaenis," Donne assumes the voice of Sappho but plays changes on the Ovidian suffering lover, and on the form of the Ovidian heroical epistle generally, by anachronistically pairing Sappho with Philaenis to explore in detail the utopian dynamics of female desire.[35] Far from abandoning her female companions for an unresponsive male beloved, this Sappho takes pleasure in the physicality of a woman who mirrors her own desires; Phaon is left behind as Sappho turns to Philaenis. Yet, again, female same-sex love is associated with creativity; the poem opens:

> Where is that holy fire, which *Verse* is said
>> To have? is that inchanting force decai'd?
> *Verse* that drawes *Natures* workes, from *Natures* law,
>> Thee, her best worke, to her worke cannot draw.
> Have my teares quench'd my old *Poetique* fire;
>> Why quench'd they not as well, that of *desire*?[36]
>>>> (1–6)

Drawing a traditional distinction between the worlds of art and nature, this Sappho, like Ovid's, laments the loss of her poetic talent but makes clear that in this instance the power of nature has defeated the powers of art to represent "her best worke," her beloved Philaenis. Incorporating the elements of a triangulated erotics from the Sapphic fragment *Phainetai moi*, in which a jealous and grieving speaker observes her beloved with a man, Donne's Sappho articulates an eroticism of mutual passion by noting its absence in male-female connections:

> Plaies some soft boy with thee, oh there wants yet
>> A mutuall feeling which should sweeten it.
> His chinne, a thorny hairy unevennesse
>> Doth threaten, and some daily change possesse.
>>>> (31–34)

Further, the distinction made is not only between heterosexual congress and female same-sex relations, but also between relations with a boy and with an adult male past puberty. Donne may be alluding here to the topos

that appears frequently in Latin homoerotic poetry of the inappropriateness of boys as objects of desire once they have reached puberty, that is,
once they have developed beards and pubic hair ("a thorny hairy uneven-
nesse / Doth threaten")[37] and the ability to procreate:

> Thy body is a naturall *Paradise,*
>   In whose selfe, unmanur'd, all pleasure lies,
> Nor needs *perfection;* why shouldst thou than
>   Admit the tillage of a harsh rough man?
> Men leave behinde them that which their sin showes,
>   And are as theeves trac'd, which rob when it snows.
> But of our dallyance no more signes there are,
>   Then *fishes* leave in streames, or *Birds* in aire.
> And betweene us all sweetnesse may be had;
>   All, all that *Nature* yields, or *Art* can adde.
>
>   (35–44)

In these lines, Donne reverses the traditional injunction to procreate and
thwarts the convention of sterility in "single-blessednesse" or in same-sex
relations. Sappho sings of the Edenic perfections of female embodiment
in averring that "[t]hy body is a naturall *Paradise,*" needing no "tillage of
a harsh rough man." The absence of possibilities for procreation creates
possibilities for an infinite variety of natural bodily pleasures and "all
sweetnesse": "All, all that *Nature* yields, or *Art* can adde." In the lines
that follow, Sappho describes their bodily touchings, part by part, anato-
mizing her lover as in a blason. The poem concludes with Sappho's
loving wishes for the well-being of her beloved, whom she asks to "cure
this loving madness, and restore / Me to mee; thee, my *halfe,* my *all,* my
more" (57–58).

This rewriting of Ovid's heroical epistle and Donne's adaptation of the
Sapphic voice of the *Phainetai moi* fragment seem to me an entirely positive portrait of female same-sex erotic desire. Donne is as interested in exploring the varieties of sexual experience, at least poetically, as he is in reshaping the poetic conventions of the Ovidian heroical epistle. We might
speculate whether Donne's sexual experiences might not have included
male homoerotic friendships that contributed to an imaginative curiosity
about the dynamics of a female same-sex erotics. In any case, we must
conclude that discourse about female same-sex relations had entered the
vernacular speech of educated men by the late sixteenth and early seventeenth centuries, though it was not to be more widely current until the
later seventeenth century.

While "tribade" in its various grammatical forms was used among educated men in Latin as well as in privately circulated texts and certainly in
conversation, other words were no doubt used in the conversation of less
elite environments. This is suggested by the surfacing of the vocabulary
we have seen in Thomas Bartholin's anatomy just after midcentury (1653):
"[T]hey are termed *Confricatrices* Rubsters," words that Terry Castle
might call part of a "whole slangy mob" of synonyms for sexual transgressors. The form that may have been more common was the Latin-derived
"fricatrice," which we have already seen in the 1595 Latin edition of Laurentius, and which according to the *OED* makes its first vernacular appearance in 1605 in Jonson's *Volpone:* "[A patron] To a lewd harlot, a base
fricatrice" (iv.ii). Like "tribade," *"fricatrice"* refers specifically to rubbing,
as Bartholin's use of its cognate *"confricatrice"* in apposition to "rubsters"
indicates. But *"fricatrice"* may have been more common as a street epithet,
as its early appearance in the theater suggests. "Ingle" and "catamite,"
male analogues for *"fricatrice,"* make their appearance in the drama in the
late 1590s; their printed reappearance together much later in the early
eighteenth century in, according to the *OED*, Motteux's 1708 *Rabelais*
("Ingles, Fricatrices, He-Whores" [v.v.165]), in a combination that points
to the use of *"fricatrice"* as a further denigration of sodomites, indicates the
continued vernacular circulation of this epithet throughout the seventeenth century.

Printed occurrences of *"fricatrice"* between Jonson's theatrical reference
in 1605 and Bartholin's 1653 anatomical use have not yet come to light.
This does not mean that other examples may not become known, but it
does suggest that they are likely to have been very rare in print until later
in the seventeenth century, when there was an increased circulation of the
language of female sexual transgression. An instructive comparison may
be drawn between Donne's "Sapho to Philaenis" and a poem by Edward
Howard, "Fricatrices: or a She upon a She," which was included in a 1673
volume of poems and essays.[38] In this poem, Howard uses the language
that by this time had made its way more generally throughout all levels of
society: he reiterates and specifically details the obsessive male fantasy of
female desire as heterosexually imitative and in need of a male member.
The poem opens with a statement of the lack encountered by two women
seeking to play a "Tickling game," "something like" the game of Venus:

> Two Females meeting, found a sportful way
> Without Man's help a Tickling game to play.
> They cozen'd Venus, yet consented so

> That something like it they resolv'd to do.
> What Nature to their aid did next present,
> We must suppose was short of their intent.

We must infer that the unnamed bodily part presented by nature and "short of their intent" was a clitoris *not* preternaturally enlarged. Howard goes on to describe a frustrating and frustrated struggle to accomplish the impossible:

> The Fairest then lay down; the other strove
> Manhood to act with Female power and love.
> Their nimble heat dissolv'd the active dew,
> Which from their Pearls within its moisture drew.
> But soon their pleasures were deceiv'd, to finde
> The one Thing wanted to which both had minde.
> Like Vessels that no Rigging want, or Gale,
> Ply here, and there, for want of a Top-sail.

Again, physiological absence and lack are paramount: the metaphor of ships without sails, tossed hither and yon, neatly captures the purpose-lessness attributed by the speaker to the women's efforts. Striving unsuccessfully to perform "Manhood," their exertions dissipate the signs of the excitement "Which from their Pearls within its moisture drew." They argue who should be the top, who bottom:

> One said she was the Woman; t'other swore
> She ought to be the man, and she the Whore.
> Who upper lay, the under now would be;
> But which should be the Woman, can't agree:
> At last, at their mistake they yield to smile,
> And grant Loves pleasures nothing can beguile.
> A Man they wanted, and a Man would have,
> Since he the Dildo has which Nature gave.[39]

And so the poem concludes with a good-humored gesture: having acknowledged their mistake, the women resolve to find a man, whether one for each or one for both of them remains an open question. The crucial point for the speaker is that the women "grant Loves pleasures nothing can beguile." This line apparently turns on the meaning of "nothing" or "no thing," in all probability—like "naught" or "O"—a slang term for the female genitals.[40] Thus, our *fricatrices* are constrained to admit that their inferior (in both senses) parts cannot "beguile" "Loves pleasures," do not have the power to give real satisfaction. Only nature's "Dildo," the penis, can do that. So, the relations between two women can merely counterfeit the "real" thing.

Whereas Donne's exploration of female eroticism is both a literary and a personally passionate expression of interest in the permutations of love, Howard's rhyming couplets are finally an excoriation, albeit a seemingly lighthearted one, of women who would seek pleasure with one another. Further, Howard's disdain refuses the elevating and distancing effects that Donne's invocation of Sappho and Philaenis confers on his subject. By 1673, then, we may infer that women who sought same-sex erotic satisfaction were commonly enough known and named and frequently enough discussed in the vernacular to have been regarded as objects of derision or, in the case of Howard, as humorously inadequate. If the condescension of Howard's rhyming couplets can be taken as in any way representing contemporary cultural attitudes, by the later seventeenth century men appear to have been sufficiently threatened by the prospect that women might attempt to satisfy one another without benefit of male intervention that they articulated the primacy of the phallus at the same time that they offered provocative descriptions of women's erotic activities.

These examples from a wide range of printed sources spanning the years from the late 1500s to the late 1600s furnish evidence that an early modern analogue to lesbianism as we know it, with Sappho as its chief exemplar, had entered vernacular discourse in England by the middle of the seventeenth century. Until the mid–seventeenth century, "tribade" was the term most commonly used by educated males; simultaneously, a different and more negative colloquially descriptive vocabulary began to predominate: *"fricatrice"* and its variant *"confricatrices"*—a pseudo-Latinate nonce word—became, literally, the English "rubsters," an epithet that eventually in the eighteenth century yielded to "tommies," perhaps as an analogue for the male homosexual "mollies." [41]

My reading of these materials therefore confirms that there was a change in discourse about female same-sex eroticism in England in or around the mid–seventeenth century. The language of literature and respectable society became more evasive as the existence of female same-sex sexuality was increasingly acknowledged by other dimensions of public discourse, often with Sappho as primary icon and embodiment of transgression.

Although there has been some contention about the shifts, both discursive and behavioral, in the understanding of male same-sex eroticism, my analysis seems to confirm with regard to women the hypothesis initially proposed by Mary McIntosh in 1968. Using a structuralist functionalist approach, McIntosh argues that a specific male homosexual *role*—as distinguished from merely homosexual *behavior*—of the effeminate sodomite emerged under the particular historical circumstances of the late seventeenth century, a role that "keeps the bulk of society pure in rather the same way that the similar treatment of some kinds of criminal helps keep the rest of society law abiding."[42] In concurring with McIntosh's chronology, Alan Bray uses the evidence of legal theory and of court cases to demonstrate that an identifiable male homosexual *subculture*—at least in London, if not in other provincial English cities—crystallized and took recognizable shape some time after the mid-1600s and by the close of the seventeenth century. Bray's evidence suggests that before the mid-1600s,

> [s]o long as homosexuality was expressed through established social institutions, in normal times the courts were not concerned with it; and generally this meant patriarchal institutions—the household, the educational system, homosexual prostitution and the like. . . . Despite the contrary impression given by legal theorists, so long as homosexual activity did not disturb the peace or the social order, and in particular so long as it was consistent with patriarchal mores [i.e., as long as it did not interfere with marriage and the production of progeny], it was largely in practice ignored.[43]

That is to say, from the close of the Middle Ages to the mid-1600s, homosexual behavior was "not socialized to any significant degree at all" and did not coalesce into "a specifically homosexual world, a society within a society" made up of molly houses and other casual meeting places, until some time later, between the mid-1600s and the turn of the eighteenth century.[44] Before about the mid–seventeenth century, then, before the apparent emergence of a social role within an identifiable subculture, the Elizabethans had "the unwelcome difficulty . . . in drawing a dividing line between those gestures of closeness among men that they desired so much [in 'the orderly relationship of friendship'] and those they feared" in "the profoundly disturbing image of the sodomite, that enemy not only of nature but of the order of society and the proper kinds and divisions within it."[45]

We may speculate that an analogous female homosexual subculture might also have emerged in or around the same period in London. Its visibility, or rumors of its existence, might have precipitated the evasiveness and eventual silence of the more private discourse of "respectable" society, as well as the transgressiveness and prurience we have observed in other quarters with respect to public discourse about erotic relations between women. As several recent scholars have observed, attempts to define "lesbian" seem inevitably to founder on the Scylla of essentialist, transhistorical meanings and the Charybdis of feminist controversies between a "lesbian continuum" of romantic friendship and the necessary sexualizing of female erotic relations; definitional impasses are no longer surprising, are in fact to be expected, in lesbian theoretical writing.[46] It does seem clear, however, that the public discourse of transgressive female same-sex relations in early modern England was increasingly relegated to medical and other texts that could provoke and satisfy pruriently misogynist interests, as well as to the writings of women willing or able to be unconventional.

With the approach of the eighteenth century, the definition of female same-sex relations seems to have become even more narrowly focused on a specific set of forbidden sexual behaviors. On the one hand, discursive representations of transgressive female sexuality continued in the eighteenth century to employ Sappho as their vehicle, as witnessed by Alexander Pope's 1712 translation of Ovid's epistle "Sapho to Phaon" or Nicholas Venette's 1750 manual *Conjugal Love; or, The Pleasures of the Marriage Bed;* yet, on the other hand, this forbidden sexuality seems to have been increasingly circumscribed and split off from representations and understandings of the relations between "respectable" women.[47] This splitting off, or bifurcation, of discourses creates a space for the development, in the mid– to later eighteenth century, of the language of female romantic friendship as the dominant discourse defining "virtuous" female friends.[48] That the relations between "respectable" women might be highly eroticized, might even partake of behaviors not defined as sexual because not modeled on valorized male penetrative action, would have been of little import. For those who were defined as transgressing were ever more conclusively ostracized and relegated to a liminal existence in a subculture that would also ensure the acceptability of those women not so relegated.

Fig. 3

Frontispiece engraving of Katherine Philips by Faithorne, in Katherine Philips,
Poems (London, 1667). This bust of Philips appears in the posthumous edition of her
poetry and has been widely circulated. By permission of the Folger Shakespeare Library.

CHAPTER III

AN EMERGING SAPPHIC DISCOURSE: THE LEGACY OF KATHERINE PHILIPS

THE VARIETY OF WOMEN'S affective relations with one another, and the possibilities for their eroticizing, becomes clear as we read their literary productions during this period of changing sexual understandings.[1] Against a cultural backdrop of more widely disseminated knowledge of female same-sex behaviors and the increasing suppression, or unnaming, of references to these behaviors in texts addressed to women or accessible to women, literate women were writing and circulating manuscripts among their intimates in literary circles and at court. Like men, women addressed poetry and other literary efforts to one another as well as to the men in their social circles; and like their male peers, women wrote in the variety of styles and explored the range of themes that were then culturally available to them. From among the styles and themes that were the vehicles of expression, of most concern here are women's articulations of same-sex erotic affectivity and the literary forms that served as their vehicles in a culture in which the discourse for describing female same-sex relations was both well known and increasingly circumscribed by selective silences.

The life and work of Katherine Philips are of singular importance for understanding the discursive terrain women were obliged to negotiate if they wished to write their loves within the parameters of social acceptability during the complex historical moment of the English mid–seventeenth century. It was she who established and made permissible for the women writers who followed her not only a female writing persona, but also an apparently chaste language of passionate female friendship whose veiled and shadowed subtext is inescapably erotic.

Philips's reputation during the seventeenth century was based on a privately circulated group of poems addressed to her intimate women friends and chronicling in some detail her emotional relations with them. Her other poems were for the most part occasional or moral-philosophical exercises in what we now consider the traditional, and rather undistinguished, mode of the seventeenth century; elegies, encomia, political poems, verse essays on friendship, poems of personal retirement and contemplation, and a journey poem are characteristic.[2] Despite Philips's bourgeois background, her great charm and cultivated feminine modesty gained her admittance, after the Restoration, to the best literary and court circles. She came to be identified with Orinda, her poetic pseudonym, and was extravagantly praised by her male contemporaries: Abraham Cowley, the earl of Roscommon (Wentworth Dillon), Jeremy Taylor, and John Dryden.[3] Laudatory references continued into the eighteenth century, particularly by women writers who, responding to male commentary on the proper female poetic persona, saw in Philips a model of success to be emulated.[4] Later, even John Keats referred to her as the female standard of excellence toward which all other women writers ought to aspire.

But throughout the nineteenth century and for the better part of the twentieth, the acclaim Philips garnered from her contemporaries was drastically diminished: she was regarded either as a minor Caroline poet who kept alive the traditions of the cavalier poets through the years of the Interregnum or as a writer of embarrassingly emotional poems to other women.[5] At best, she was categorized as the poetic model for a late-seventeenth- and eighteenth-century female "school of Orinda"[6] or as an influence on particular male poets. At worst, she was accused of versifying gossip.[7] More recently, however, in the last decade of the twentieth century, feminist scholars have recognized her unique contributions to women's writing and to the cultural history of women's relations. And they have attended to her work in a less perfunctory fashion. Lillian Faderman, the first feminist critic to address sympathetically the eroticism of Philips's poems to her female friends, opened up a discussion of that subject while at the same time denying its historical presence as a viable, or even thinkable, sexual reality.[8] Subsequently, the very qualities that caused unease for earlier critics motivated lesbian feminist readers to assimilate Philips's work into a late-twentieth-century lesbian aesthetic; unfortunately, this critical trajectory has sometimes failed to situate Philips's poetry in an appropriately nuanced historical context.[9] Several younger scholars have attempted to rectify these difficulties, with varying degrees of success; while offering readings that both accept and struggle with the historicity of Philips's erotics, they still leave unresolved the issue of her relation to the various erotic discourses that were circulating in early modern England.[10]

An examination of the materials of Philips's life and work reveals a woman whose emotional focus was primarily on other women and whose passionate involvement with them guided much of her life and inspired her most esteemed poems. Philips's original and unusual use of literary conventions accounts for the acclaim she was accorded by her contemporaries; her unique manipulation of the conventions of male poetic discourse, of the argumentative texture of John Donne, of the language of the cavaliers, and of the tradition of platonic love became the means by which she expressed her same-sex affective impulses in an acceptable form. Philips's contribution was to appropriate the cavalier conventions of platonic heterosexual love, with their originally platonic and male homoerotic feeling,[11] and to use those conventions and that discourse to describe her relations with women. While homoerotic male poetic discourse in the form of male friendship poetry was by no means unusual during the Renaissance and early seventeenth century, Philips's is the earliest printed example of a woman's poetic expression in English of intense same-sex love between women.

The poems that brought her acclaim, and that still are considered her best work, established a "society of friendship" that used, superficially, the rhetorical conventions of the cavalier poets and of French *préciosité*. In her attempt to create an ideal "society" of friends, in her use of pastoral nicknames for her friends, in her reading of Italian and French romances, and in her attraction to the idea of platonic love, Philips embraced current literary and courtly fashions.[12] To see her work merely as an example of *préciosité* does not, however, do justice to the breadth of interests and influences her work reveals. Moreover, though she uses its superficial trappings, her poetic language does not fit the *précieux* prescription for periphrasis, tortured hyperbole, or excessive imagery. Instead, a disinterested reading of Philips's works suggests a more judicious view than has been offered by literary critics: like others among her contemporaries, most notably Abraham Cowley, one of her admirers, she moved in the course of her literary career—as did a number of male poets—from the private, contemplative, metaphysical mode of her poetry during the Interregnum to a more public neoclassical style during the Restoration.[13] Her earlier work is composed for the most part of the platonic love lyrics to her female friends that initially won her praise; but later, during and after the Restoration, she turned to longer poems on public themes and to translations of Corneille. Certainly Philips was ambitious and certainly her work was embedded in the traditions, culture, and fashions of her time. Yet it would be more accurate to say that the forms she used coincided with and appropriated literary fashion rather than that she wrote as she did only because she courted poetic success. The evidence of her life indicates that the forms she used also fulfilled important personal needs.

Philips used the conventions of her time to express in her own poetry a desexualized—though passionate and eroticized—version of platonic love in the love of same-sex friendship. I wish to draw here the fine distinction between a generalized erotic and emotional passion—what Ruth Perry has called "libidinous energy"[14]—and the narrowly focused genital, particularly male genital, definition of sexuality that was pervasive in early modern England.[15] In Philips's poetry, friendship between women is infused with the passionate intensity and rhetoric of heterosexual love as it was understood by seventeenth-century male poets. The major influence on her friendship poems may not be the cavaliers or *préciosité* but John Donne and the metaphysical conceit, for the intensity of her friendship feelings is expressed through echoes of Donne's early seduction poems.[16] Not only does Philips echo the language and imagery of male love poetry, but she also often assumes the active subject position vis-à-vis her female friends that we usually associate with an importunate male suitor/lover.

A reading of her poems addressed to Rosania, her pseudoclassical name for her school friend Mary Aubrey, and to Lucasia, Anne Owen, who replaced Rosania in Philips's affections after Rosania's marriage, reveals the intensity of Philips's emotions and her unique use of convention as a vehicle to express her intimate feelings. "To my Lucasia, in defence of declared friendship," one of Philips's best-known and most admired poems, is typical of her work: she appropriates both the sentiments of metaphysical platonism and the form of male poetic discourse to shape her passion. Stanzas 8 through 12 are especially clear in illustrating her rhetorical choices:

> Although we know we love, yet while our soule
> Is thus imprison'd by the flesh we wear,

> There's no way left that bondage to controule,
>   But to convey transactions through the Eare.
>
> Nay, though we read our passions in the Ey,
>   It will obleige and please to tell them too:
> Such joys as these by motion multiply,
>   Were't but to find that our souls told us true.
>
> Beleive not then, that being now secure
>   Of either's heart, we have no more to doe:
> The Sphaeres themselves by motion do endure,
>   And they move on by Circulation too.
>
> And as a River, when it once has pay'd
>   The tribute which it to the Ocean ow's,
> Stops not, but turns, and having curl'd and play'd
>   On its own waves, the shore it overflows:
>
> So the Soul's motion does not end in bliss,
>   But on her self she scatters and dilates,
> And on the Object doubles, till by this
>   She finds new Joys, which that reflux creates.[17]

Evident here is the manner in which Philips channels a passionate emotional intensity into acceptable metaphysical images and argument. The platonic union of souls, the eyes as vehicles of the spirit, and the analogy between the movement of human hearts and the circulation of the spheres were stocks in trade of the male discourse of metaphysical passion for women. Here, a female poetic voice uses these conventional images to address her intensely beloved female friend, assuming the posture of the active, seducing lover who extols love's pleasures. In her invocation to her beloved to speak their love, she adds to these images the particularly female and subliminally erotic analogy of a river's flow, which captures the rhythms of female sexual passion. Further, we might read the opening image of the ear, with its vaginal-like folds and secret channel, as erotically receiving the sounds of passionate declaration: the "bondage" of the flesh is controlled by "convey[ing] transactions through the Eare," so that "though we read our passions in the Ey, / It will obleige and please to tell them too." Read this way, the poetry that *tells* her love is itself unmistakably a form of lovemaking.

Philips's use of Donne, rather than the lesser cavalier poets, is apparent not only in the echoes of his particular images but also more precisely in the force of her argumentative stance, in the relentless development of thought through the manipulation of conceit. "To My excellent Lucasia, on our Friendship," again echoes Donne:

> I did not live untill this time
>   Crown'd my felicity,
> When I could say without a crime,
>   I am not Thine, but Thee.
> This Carkasse breath'd, and walk'd, and slept,
>   So that the world believ'd
> There was a soule the motions kept;
>   But they were all deceiv'd.
> For as a watch by art is wound
>   To motion, such was mine:
> But never had Orinda found
>   A Soule till she found thine;
> Which now inspires, cures and supply's,
>   And guides my darken'd brest:
> For thou art all that I can prize,
>   My Joy, my Life, my rest.
> Nor Bridegroomes nor crown'd conqu'rour's mirth
>   To mine compar'd can be:
> They have but pieces of this Earth,
>   I've all the world in thee.
> Then let our fame still light and shine,
>   (And no bold feare controule)
> As innocent as our design,
>   Immortall as our Soule.
>
> (no. 36, 121–22)

In the extravagant intensity of the conceit of the watch in this poem, Philips's discourse reaches beyond the merely conventional image of "two friends 'mingling souls.'"[18] Except that these poems are addressed to a woman, they could have been written by a man to his (female) lover. Clearly, the discourse used by Philips is both male and heterosexual with Philips herself assuming a role analogous to that of the pursuing male.

"To My excellent Lucasia" adumbrates Donne's imagery as well as the intellectual form of his metaphysical poetic. The union of lover and beloved, the soullessness of the "Carkasse" before discovery of the

beloved, the negative comparison of the condition of the beloved to more
worldly joys ("Nor Bridegroomes nor crown'd conqu'rour's mirth") to enforce the sacredness of the relation, and the insistence on the "innocent . . . design" of their love are also integral to Donne's love poetry.

"Friendship in Emblem, or the Seale, to my dearest Lucasia" perhaps
most obviously draws on Donne in its use of the compass image from "A
Valediction: Forbidding Mourning." Here again, the crucial element that
distinguishes her source as Donne rather than the cavaliers is the sustained force of her intellectual argument in developing the conceit. Stanzas 6 through 13 illustrate this clearly:

> The compasses that stand above
> Express this great immortall Love;
> For friends, like them, can prove this true,
> They are, and yet they are not, two.
>
> And in their posture is express'd
> Friendship's exalted interest:
> Each follows where the other Leanes,
> And what each does, the other meanes.
>
> And as when one foot does stand fast,
> And t'other circles seeks to cast,
> The steddy part does regulate
> And make the wanderer's motion streight:
> So friends are onely Two in this,
> T'reclaime each other when they misse:
> For whosoe're will grossely fall,
> Can never be a friend at all.
>
> And as that usefull instrument
> For even lines was ever meant;
> So friendship from good = angells springs,
> To teach the world heroique things.
>
> As these are found out in design
> To rule and measure every line;
> So friendship governs actions best,
> Prescribing Law to all the rest.
>
> And as in nature nothing's set
> So Just as lines and numbers mett;

So compasses for these being made,
Doe friendship's harmony perswade.

And like to them, so friends may own
Extension, not division:
Their points, like bodys, separate;
But head, like soules, knows no such fate.

(no. 29, 106–8)

The conceit of the compass, an emblem of constancy, as used by Donne to explore the meaning of his approaching absence from his wife, is present here as silent counterpoint throughout Philips's poem.[19] Her use of the same conceit—and it is her most obvious echo of Donne—to describe her passionate friendship for Lucasia is played against the unvoiced text of Donne's poem, which reverberates through it and underlines its platonism as well as its eroticism. Philips, then, relies on her audience's knowledge of Donne's "Valediction" to add force to her themes as well as to render them acceptably transparent, that is, not disquieting because familiar.

These are only a few examples of Philips's assimilation of Donne and the metaphysical mode of argument. A reading of all of her poems to her female intimates yields others. It is the intense, passionate quality of her feeling, the emotional tension inherent in the argument of the conceit, that distinguishes these poems from her other poetic efforts. She appropriated a male heterosexual poetic discourse, with its platonism, its implicit eroticism, and its impassioned argument via conceits, rather than the less intense, more distant tone of the male friendship poetry of her contemporaries because this discourse suited the deeply intimate nature of the emotions she sought to chart and for which she sought a vehicle.

Literatures and Traditions of Friendship

A variety of literatures and traditions of friendship make up the complex cultural matrix from which Philips's poetic voice emerged. A possible antecedent for the passionate expression we note in Philips's friendship poems is one that she is unlikely to have known: Poem XLIX in a collection of Middle Scots poetry, *The Maitland Quarto Manuscript* (1586),[20] describes the impassioned friendship of the female speaker for another woman. Tradition attributes to Mary Maitland, daughter of Sir Richard

Maitland, the compilation, if not the transcription, of the manuscript; she has also been said to be the author of Poem XLIX, even though there is no evidence that would confirm her authorship. Whoever its author, this early poem in many ways foreshadows the female desire spoken by Philips. The writer of Poem XLIX voices a number of the traditional motifs associated with ideal friendship during the Renaissance; but it is highly unusual—even unheard of—for the ideals of friendship to be associated with women, let alone expressed by one woman toward another. The writer's sexual identity is not revealed until the middle of the poem, in the sixth of twelve stanzas, when she finally articulates her desire for the fortune to shape-shift ("Wald michtie Ioue grant me the hap" [Would mighty Jove grant me the fortune]) so that, like Iphis in Ovid's tale of Iphis and Ianthe,[21] she can become a man to marry her beloved friend. By invoking as models the erotically charged friendships of such famous male couples as Achilles and Patroclus and David and Jonathan, as well as the fidelity of the biblical Naomi and Ruth and of the Homeric Penelope and Ulysses, the speaker has prepared us to include her own passionate "amitie" within the parameters established by these famous models. Implicit in the poem are two transgressions: first, her articulation of the possibilities of passionate friendship between women; second, her acknowledgment of the eroticism of this "perfyte amitie" that will be maintained "for euer."

The significance of Poem XLIX in *The Maitland Quarto Manuscript* is that it tells us of a same-sex female erotic passion that was seeking expression in the vernacular in the British Isles, quite apart from the language associated with tribadism and overt sexual transgressions. Rather, before 1586, this discourse of female same-sex eroticism was already seeking to model itself on heroic cultural figures, on the ideals of male friendship, and on biblical precedent for love between women. It also demonstrates the speaking persona's assumption of an active—that is, male—subject position in relation to the female friend she courts, and so acknowledges the unspoken erotic desires that drive the poem itself. It is impossible to know whether this poem is an isolated expression of female same-sex desire, whether it might in fact have been written by a man ventriloquizing a female voice (as did Donne in "Sapho to Philaenis"), or whether it might be the lone surviving representative of many more poems and poets seeking poetic forms to express their passions. Whether or not this poem or others like it might have been known to the mid–seventeenth century, its existence forces us to recognize that a vernacular discourse of eroticism different from the discourses of overt transgression was thought of and already circulating in Britain by the late sixteenth century, well before Philips's efforts to develop a means of expression for her own passionate attachment to other women.

Philips is far more likely to have been familiar with contemporary literatures and traditions of male friendship, both visual and verbal, though it is unclear to what extent she may have been acquainted at first hand with earlier Renaissance models. But the emblems that circulated in emblem books and were available for reinterpretation and recirculation certainly demonstrate the currency of earlier models throughout the early modern period. An especially pertinent emblem for the understanding of Philips's poetry and other seventeenth-century statements on friendship is one found in the very popular *Emblemata* of Andrea Alciati. The caption for Alciati's tripartite emblem is *"Amicitia etiam poſt mortem durans,"* or "Friendship lasting even beyond death," a sentiment Alciati would have found both in *The Greek Anthology* and in Erasmus's *Copia*.[22] Below the caption is a woodcut of a vine clinging to an elm, and below that a poem that reads as follows:

> Arentum ſenio, nudam quoque frondibus ulmum,
>   Complexa eſt uiridi uitis opaca coma.
> Agnoſcitq[ue] uices naturæ: & grata parenti
>   Officii reddit mutua iura ſuo.
> Exemploq[ue] monet, tales nos quarere amicos,
>   Quos nequid diſiungat fœdere ſumma dies.

[A vine shady with green foliage embraced an elm tree that was dried up with age and bare of leaves. The vine recognises the changes wrought by nature and, ever grateful, renders to the one that reared it the duty it owes in return. By the example it offers, the vine tells us to seek friends of such a sort that not even our final day will uncouple them from the bond of friendship.][23]

Variations of Alciati's motifs are to be found in a number of other emblem collections, notably the *Symbola et Emblemata* of Joachim Camerarius. The caption over the woodcut, "Amicvs post Mortem" [Friend after Death], is elaborated by two lines below the picture of a vine clinging to an elm, "Quamlibet arenti vitis tamen hæret in ulmo: Sic quoq[ue] post mortem verus amicus amat." [Howsoever the parched vine still clings to the elm: So too loves the true friend after death.][24] The visual and verbal elements that made up the complex of ideas called friendship thus have a long and recognizably stable continuity that was part of a shared cultural heritage, repeatedly shaped and reshaped to various ends, not only on the Continent but in England as well.

Like these friendship emblems, Michel de Montaigne's well-known essay "De l'amitié" [On Friendship], in his *Essais,* was translated into English in 1603 by John Florio and continued to be reprinted throughout the early seventeenth century. Despite the wide circulation of these ideas, we cannot be certain that Philips actually read the essay.[25] However, she would certainly have been aware of the model of male friendship that was kept vital in England during the reign of James I by Florio's translation and by elaborations of and variations on that model circulated later at the court of Charles I; these models of friendship were integral to contemporary ideologies of male-male relations, both social and literary.

The model of male friendship circulated in Florio's Montaigne, as Jeffrey Masten has shown, uses the language of sexual "enjoyment" to circle back and to "describe its supposed opposite, friendly love"; insofar as Florio's Montaigne rejects "Greeke licence" (i.e., pederasty) and perpetuates the ancient misogynistic notion that women are incapable of true friendship, "what appears to be the strict separation of friendship and sexuality . . . then, is instead a refusal of relations founded in 'disparitie': of gender, of age, or of 'office'" with the consequence that "Renaissance friendship texts inscribe an erotics of similitude that goes far beyond the modern conception of mere sameness of sex."[26] In other words, while forbidding pederasty, a relation of "disparitie," Montaigne valorizes here an erotics of friendship between male equals that, in a hierarchy of relations, is more to be valued than relations between men and women, which are relations of disparity because of the lower status of women and the inevitable intervention of "lust."

Richard Brathwait's popular conduct book *The English Gentleman* also includes a substantial chapter on the conduct of male friendship. *The English Gentleman* was published in 1630, in 1633, and again in 1641, when it was bound together with Brathwait's conduct book for women, *The English Gentlewoman,* originally published in 1631. *The English Gentleman* is, as its title indicates, a class-inflected gathering of prescriptive advice, "*Containing* Sundry excellent *Rules* or exquiſite *Obſervations,* tending to Direction of every *Gentleman,* of ſelecter ranke and *qualitie;* How to demeane or accommodate himſelfe in the manage of publicke or private affaires." It is no accident, I believe, that Brathwait's presentation of his materials—particularly the title page and the "Draught" of the frontispiece—echoes the visual cues and organization by topic of the emblem books that had become such familiar didactic devices to seventeenth-century readers. By appropriating an emblem book–like visual introduction to his eight vernacular essays, Brathwait reshaped the moral didacticism of the emblem tradition to appeal to a class of gentlemen, or would-be gentlemen, who did not necessarily read Latin; thus, in his own account of relations between men, he fused the visual immediacy of the emblem tradition with the values of Florio's Montaigne in the essay on friendship.

This reshaping is illustrated as follows: among the eight allegorical figures of virtue represented on the frontispiece of Brathwait's volume, surrounding the central figure of a gentleman, is that of "Acquaintance," elaborated in a long section on male-male friendships and their importance for a life of gentlemanly civility. The "Draught of the *Frontiſpiece*," a sheet that folds out from the volume's binding to explicate the allegorical figures opposite, provides this account of the two entwined and dancing male figures that represent acquaintance: "ACQUAINTANCE is in two bodies individually incorporated, and no leſſe ſelfly than ſociably united: two Twins cannot be more naturally neere, than theſe be affectionately deere; which they expreſſe in hugging one another, and ſhewing the conſenting Conſort of their minde, by the mutuall interchoice of their Motto; *Certus amor morum eſt* [a secure love is a virtue]." [27] The intimacy of this description, with its idyllic vision of incorporation, union, twinning, hugging, and the "conſenting Conſort" of one mind, is an argument for fusion, for a oneness of spirit and soul allegorically represented by the embrace of the two dancing male figures. The bond is an erotic one in the sense that it engages the male friends fully in an intense union of bodies and souls that had not yet in 1630 come to be associated with sodomitical transgressions because it was a bond of equals in every respect. [28]

Brathwait elaborates his description of the bond of friendship by giving many examples of false as well as of true friendship. His statement of the importance of male friendship to the conduct of a gentleman's life is, then, part of the discourse that was widely circulated and provided the rationale for bonds of intimacy between men:

> Here ſee apparent arguments of true love, mixed with a noble and hero-ick temper: for *friends* are to be tried in extremities, either in matters of ſtate or life: in ſtate, by releeving their wants; in life, by engaging themſelves to all extremes, rather than they will ſuffer their *friend* to periſh. . . . ſo amongſt men, *friendſhip* multiplieth joyes, and divideth griefs. (Ii1ᵛ–Ii2)

Fig. 4

"Acquaintance," from title page of Richard Brathwait, *The English Gentleman* (London, 1630). This woodcut of two men dancing from the title page of Brathwait's volume illustrates one of the major topical divisions of the volume, "Acquaintance," on friendship between men. The other divisions are Recreation, Moderation, Education, Disposition, and Youth. By permission of the Folger Shakespeare Library.

A gentlewoman, or any literate woman for that matter, seeking analogous sanction for her own passionate attachment to another woman would have found none in the long tradition of classical male friendships. Nor would she have found a section in the first edition, in 1631, of Brathwait's *The English Gentlewoman*, the companion volume to *The English*

Gentleman. The omission is striking because the section on male friendship in the first conduct book takes up seventy-one pages.[29] To have no analogous section in the companion volume—and it did indeed become a companion through the inclusion of both books in one volume in 1641—speaks more loudly through silence than any more pointed statement about the unworthiness of women as friends could have done.[30]

An exception, and perhaps a harbinger of eventual change in ideas about women's capacities for friendship, is offered by Sir Kenelm Digby (1603–1665), gentleman of the bedchamber to Charles I, prolific author of scientific and philosophical works, and older contemporary of Philips. In his *Private Memoirs,* written just before the 1632 edition of Florio's Montaigne and the publication of Brathwait's conduct books, Digby devotes considerable space to a generalized discussion of friendship that introduces his description of his future wife, the exceptional woman who will create with him "the perfect friendship and noble love of two generous persons."[31] He gives a relatively lengthy account of why such marriages are extremely rare:

[T]he main defect . . . is oftentimes on the woman's part, through the weakness of that sex, which is seldom, and almost but by miracle, capable of so divine a thing as an assured constant friendship, mingled with the fervent heat of love and affection. . . .

And, besides, because that in exact friendship, the wills of the two friends ought to be so drowned in one another, like two flames which are joined, that they become but one, which cannot be unless the faculties of the understanding be equal, they guiding the actions of a regulated will, it cometh to pass, for the most part, that this halteth on the woman's side, whose notions are not usually so high and elevated as men's; and so it seldom happeneth that there is that society between them in the highest and deepest speculations of the mind, which are consequently the most pleasing, as is requisite in a perfect friendship. Which reasons have moved some to place the possibility of such friendship only between man and man; but, certainly, if they had considered how thus they leave out one half of man, and indeed the first motive of affection, being that the understanding can judge only of what is represented to it by the senses, whose objects are corporeal, they would not have concluded their proposition so definitely but that they would have left this exception, to wit, unless a masculine and heroic soul can be found informing the body of a beautiful and fair woman, so to make the blessing of friendship full on every side by an entire and general communication.

If, then, I should be asked where such an example might be found, I must confess that, besides this which I intend to speak of, I could urge none. . . .[32]

These quasi-autobiographical memoirs are likely to have circulated at court. But whether or not they actually did so, the ideas that inform them certainly must have been familiar at court in connection with Digby's prominence and reputation; these ideas are rather conventionally repeated from earlier literature, with the difference that Digby is at pains to make an exception for his wife. As the passage indicates, women were not considered capable of the steadfastness and intellectual equality necessary for friendship with one another or with men, and so the highest pleasures of friendship are reserved for the mutual loves of men for one another. Digby's use of the image of two flames becoming one is a traditional emblem of friendship that incorporates the notion of union with equality and a disciplined will: "[I]n exact friendship, the wills of the two friends ought to be so drowned in one another, like two flames which are joined, that they become but one, which cannot be unless the faculties of the understanding be equal, they guiding the actions of a regulated will." But the motivation for Digby's philosophical digression here is to create an exceptional space for Stelliana, his wife, née Lady Venetia Stanley;[33] he rejects those who "place the possibility of such friendship only between man and man" in order to embrace the "masculine and heroic soul . . . informing the body of a beautiful and fair woman," that is, his wife. How many of Digby's male contemporaries shared his view of female capabilities cannot, of course, be known, but it is perhaps possible that he gave some hope to women by articulating a view somewhat at variance with convention.

The painter Anthony Van Dyck, during the years that he spent in the 1630s at Charles I's court, was good friends with Sir Kenelm Digby[34] and conveyed in many of his portraits of the English nobility the generally accepted ideologies of friendship in England. Zirka Zaremba Filipczack points out that while other painters such as Raphael, Titian, Holbein, or Rubens had each produced at most two "friendship" portraits, Van Dyck "returned to this subject again and again, painting at least ten portraits that can be described as friendship portraits" for his English patrons, and "also an unprecedented type of friendship portrait, that of women."[35]

In portraits of two adult women, Van Dyck and his studio solved the problem of placement differently for women than for men. Because "the placement of figures in a double portrait . . . carried hierarchical significance . . . the less powerful person was usually placed at the other's left." Van Dyck, however, altered this delicate visual status cue so that, in the case of men, the more important position was given to the older man, regardless of rank, while in the case of women, "precedence went to the one who was married, or had been married longer," regardless of age or rank.[36] Thus, despite the innovativeness of Van Dyck's shaping of visual cues, his portraits of women friends, though unusual in themselves, nevertheless enforce the gender role parameters of marriage as the final determinants of status for women, with friendship a disposable relationship once marriage has taken place. Marriage, as Philips was to remind her friends, heralded the end of a passionate female bond.[37]

Apart from these examples of models that would have made up the cultural environment in which Philips matured, most of her reading appears to have been limited to her near contemporaries whose friendship poetry employs, instead of a Renaissance Platonic ideal, the Horatian ideal of civilized life and the Aristotelian notion of friendship[38] as the bond of the state to defend against the "cavalier winter."[39] Many of Philips's contemporaries frequently are more concerned to place friendship in the context of retirement to nature as an escape from the turmoil of the times than to explore the ecstasies and trials of intimacy through the language of Platonism. Theirs is often a generalized approach to the subject that is in contrast to Philips's more impassioned use of direct address and metaphysical conceit; her poetic discourse brings together the ideals of Horatian civility and Platonic eroticism using the passionate heterosexual modes of the metaphysicals.

A Life of Friendship

That Philips's friendship poems were not merely clever exercises in courtly convention by a woman seeking reputation and patronage (as were, perhaps, some of her Restoration poems addressed to royalty) is confirmed by the circumstances of Philips's life and letters. Born Katherine Fowler, the daughter of a prosperous London cloth merchant, in 1648 she married James Philips, whom she was to call Antenor in keeping with her penchant for devising pseudoclassical names for her intimates. She was sixteen; he was fifty-four. Clearly, in this marriage, probably arranged by her mother, she loved and respected her husband as she was socially and morally bound to do. Yet, clearly also, there was much physical and probably emotional distance between them. He lived on the remote west coast of Wales at Cardigan Priory, while she was attached to the intellectual and social amenities of London and took, or created, every opportunity to return to literary and court circles. Her politics were also different from his: she remained a royalist like her friends and courtly admirers, while he and her family were parliamentarians. This publicly recognized political difference at least once threatened his political career.[40]

Antenor's absence never evoked the same metaphysical anguish in Philips as did that of Rosania or Lucasia; she wrote of him most often in terms of her "duty." A telling contrast is that between the frequently unrestrained emotion in her many poems lamenting the absence of a female friend [41] and the relative coolness of her single poem to Antenor upon his absence and of her descriptions of her "duty" to Sir Charles Cotterell. On her immanent departure from Ireland and Lucasia, she wrote: "I have now no longer any pretence of Business to detain me, and a Storm must not keep me from ANTENOR and my Duty, lest I raise a greater within. But oh! that there were no Tempests but those of the Sea for me to suffer in parting with my dear LUCASIA!" (Letter 19, II:61). This passage succinctly points to a contrast that is apparent throughout Philips's writing; it juxtaposes, on the one hand, her feelings of obligation to her husband and, on the other, her passion for Lucasia. As to the rest of her immediate family, her son is mentioned only twice in her writings, both times in poems, one of them a particularly dull one about his death at the age of forty-one days; her daughter, who survived her, is never mentioned at all, either in her poems or in her letters.[42]

Having endured, in 1652, Mary Aubrey's (Rosania's) defection from their friendship into marriage, Philips wrote at least one poem on her "apostasy," and quickly replaced her with Anne Owen (Lucasia).[43] In 1662 Anne Owen, too, married; that Philips despised Owen's new husband, Marcus Trevor, added to her grief. Nevertheless, she accompanied the newlyweds to Dublin and stayed on for a year, ostensibly to conduct her husband's business (he was now in some financial and political distress owing to his parliamentarianism), to finish her translation of Corneille's *Pompey,* and to see it played at the Theatre Royal, Smock Alley, Dublin. She had also begun to develop aristocratic connections: the earl of Orrery offered her encouragement, she frequented the duke of Ormonde's salon, and she was becoming friendly with the countess of Cork.

She described her feelings to Sir Charles, whose suit to Anne Owen she had unsuccessfully encouraged, presumably in an attempt to keep Anne within her immediate social circle and in close geographical proximity: "I am much surpriz'd that she, who is so well-bred, and her Conversation every way so agreeable, can be so happy with him as she seems to be: for indeed she is nothing but Joy, and never so well pleas'd as in his Company; which makes me conclude, that she is either extremely chang'd, or has more of the dissembling Cunning of our Sex than I thought she had" (Letter 13, II:45).[44] She wrote repeatedly to Sir Charles of her grief and disappointment, not unmixed with bitterness, at the loss of her bond with Anne Owen. Her grief in these letters is as acute as the passion in the earlier poems is intense. From Dublin on July 30, 1662, she wrote:

> I now see by Experience that one may love too much, and offend more by a too fond Sincerity, than by a careless Indifferency, provided it be but handsomly varnish'd over with civil Respect. I find too there are few Friendships in the World Marriage-proof. . . . We may generally con- clude the Marriage of a Friend to be the Funeral of a Friendship. . . . Sometimes I think it is because we are in truth more ill-natur'd than we really take our selves to be; and more forgetful of past Offices of Friend- ship, when they are superseded by others of a fresher Date, which carry- ing with them the Plausibility of more Duty and Religion in the Knot that ties them, we persuade our selves will excuse us if the Heat and Zeal of our former Friendships decline and wear off into Lukewarmness and Indifferency: whereas there is indeed a certain secret Meanness in our Souls, which mercenarily inclines our Affections to those with whom we must necessarily be oblig'd for the most part to converse, and from whom we expect the chiefest outward Conveniencies. And thus we are apt to flatter our selves that we are constant and unchang'd in our Friend- ship, tho' we insensibly fall into Coldness and Estrangement. (Letter 13, II:42–45)

Her letters to Sir Charles during this period are full of disappointed idealism, of high-mindedness scorned. The scale of values Philips holds dear in these letters and in her poetry places the noble feelings of disin- terested friendship far above the frequently compromised and banal mo- tives of marriage and duty. Still, her notion of disinterested friendship is driven by intensely passionate commitment to the individual woman in question, so that when, in the usual course of things, her friend marries, her response is like that of a lover scorned. The feelings she expressed in her letters to Sir Charles concerning the defection of Anne Owen rever- berate from the poems she had written ten years earlier on the apostasy of Mary Aubrey:

> Lovely apostate! what was my offence?
> Or am I punish'd for obedience?
>
> . . . .
>
> For our twin-spirits did so long agree,
> You must undoe your self to ruine me.
>
> . . . .

> . . . Glorious Friendship, whence your honour springs,
> Ly's gasping in the croud of common things;
>
> . . . .
>
> For from my passion your last rigours grew,
> And you kill me, because I worshipp'd you.
>
>   ("*Injuria amici,*" no. 38, I:123–25)

Orinda's anger and resentment at being rejected here take a turn toward grief and contempt. In "For our twin-spirits did so long agree, / You must undoe your self to ruine me," Philips uses the image of the union of friends' souls to underline the violent, deathlike sundering of separation and the degradation of a "Friendship" that now "Ly's gasping in the croud of common things." Extreme distress is unmistakable in these lines and suggests the defeat that follows the loss of passionate intimacy: "And you kill me, because I worshipp'd you." Thus Philips reveals a covert, innate rebelliousness; she protests with chagrin Mary Aubrey's and Anne Owen's replacement of such romantic sentiments with ones more suitable to the exigencies of social and economic life.

Her last known passionate attachment seems to have been to Berenice, whom she knew at least since 1658, when she wrote begging her to come to Cardigan and console her for Lucasia's absence.[45] Philips evidently continued her correspondence with Berenice after returning from Ireland to her home at Cardigan Priory in Wales, because the last letter is dated from there a month before her death in London. The tone of the four letters to Berenice is a combination of nearly fawning supplication to a social superior and breathless passion, the two inextricably fused, as class difference imbues Philips's passion with an unmistakable frisson of anxious solicitousness:

> All that I can tell you of my Desires to see your Ladiship will be repetition, for I had with as much earnestness as I was capable of, Begg'd it then, and yet have so much of the Beggar in me, that I must redouble that importunity now, and tell you, That I Gasp for you with an impatience that is not to be imagin'd by any Soul wound up to a less concern in Friendship then yours is, and therefore I cannot hope to make others sensible of my vast desires to enjoy you, but I can safely appeal to your own Illustrious Heart, where I am sure of a Court of Equity to relieve me in all the Complaints and Suplications my Friendship can put up. (Letter III to Berenice, II:7–9)[46]

It is impossible to disentangle the elements of Orinda's passion for Berenice, complicated as their relationship was by social inequality and as our understanding of it is by an absence of any information external to the four letters. However, Philips's tone in these letters seems desperate beyond any conventional courtliness; she yearns to fill the void left by Lucasia's absence and eventual rejection. The excessiveness of her language here is a barometer of her frustrated passions.

After her success with *Pompey* on the Dublin stage, Philips found it difficult to remain immured at the Priory and finally was able to solicit an invitation from her friends and her husband's permission to return to London, where she died of smallpox at the age of thirty-one. A major change had taken place in Philips's life when the loss of her friendship with Lucasia was coincidentally accompanied by the foundering fortunes of her husband, which she attempted to remedy with the help of her well-placed friends. That she had not succeeded in doing so when she died suggests that the double blow she had suffered left her depressed (as the anxiety in her last letters to Sir Charles shows), weakened, and vulnerable to disease.

After the defection of Lucasia, she wrote no more of the poetry that had won her such high praise; instead, she poured her energies into using her court connections to gain patronage for herself and, probably unsuccessfully, preferment for Antenor. She wrote numerous poems to royalty, self-consciously addressing public themes, and increasingly fewer intimate poems to particular friends. Also, she vied with the male wits for recognition of her theatrical translations, which are still considered the best English versions of Corneille.[47] Philips's immersion in Corneille and the adoption of a more neoclassical style may have been politically expedient in the early 1660s, but at this time in Philips's life, Corneille's subordination of personal passion to duty and patriotism in the long speeches that she translated also must have appealed to her own need to control her disordered emotions.[48]

Her royalist sympathies throughout the Interregnum no doubt now enabled her to advance the interests of her parliamentarian husband as well as her own literary ambitions. Philip Webster Souers comments on the notable change in her poems and in her stance toward literary circles: "The Cult of Friendship may be said to have died with the marriage of its inspirer. All that remained was the empty shell, which, in this case, means the names, so that when, later, poems addressed to new friends appear, it must be kept in mind that the old fire is gone."[49] Souers's judgment is borne out by the poems Philips addressed to the Boyle sisters, daughters of the countess of Cork, a patron during Philips's stay in Ireland. Though she attempts to continue, or perhaps to revivify, the traditions of her cult of friendship by bestowing pastoral nicknames, Philips reveals in her later poems the conflict and ambivalence with which more intimate approaches to her social superiors are fraught. She confronts this problem of friendship with aristocratic women directly in "To Celimena" (1662–64), addressed to Lady Elizabeth Boyle; the eight-line poem concludes: "Wouldst thou depose thy Saint into thy Friend? / Equality in friendship is requir'd, / Which here were criminal to be desir'd" (no. 107, I:227). Her earlier passionate avowals of friendship have become reverential.[50]

The poems that made Orinda famous depended for their creation on Philips's personal affections. When the person to whom those affections were directed removed herself permanently from the sphere of Philips's life, the well of her unique creativity dried up, though she continued to refine her craft. Orinda may have sought other muses, such as Berenice, but if indeed she did, the quest seems to have been fruitless, or even half-hearted, given the severity of her loss and the need to turn her attention to the matter of her husband's (and her own) livelihood and economic well-being. That Philips was aware of the change in her interests and, indeed, undertook it deliberately, is poignantly obvious in her comments to Sir Charles from Dublin on May 2, 1663:

> I have us'd all the Arts that Diversion could afford me, to divide and cure a Passion that has met with so ill a Return, and am not a little oblig'd to my Lady CORK's Family for assisting me in that Intention: But oh! I begin already to dread what will become of me, when I return home, and am restor'd to the sight of those Places, where I have been so often blest with the Enjoyment of a Conversation in which I took so much Delight, and is now for ever ravish'd from me. (Letter 29, II:85)

She needed, however, to keep up appearances and, as Souers notes, did so in a perfunctory manner—conscious that impassioned friendship was incompatible with social advancement—by continuing to write poems to women that retained the form, if not the passion, of her earlier work.

This examination of Philips's life in conjunction with the friendship poems that initially won her praise confirms that her poems to Rosania and Lucasia were an honest expression of her love channeled into the already acceptable, even fashionable, mode of male-to-female poetic discourse of love. Once we understand that the feelings in these poems have biographical origins that are corroborated by Philips's letters to Sir Charles and Berenice, we can be certain that they also express a same-sex female erotics and have a place beside the long classical tradition of the literature of male love.

A Confluence of Traditions: Ideologies of Friendship, Sappho, and Orinda's Reputation

Philips's poetry paralleled rather than emulated much of the poetry of the male friendship tradition. It is distinguished from the poetry of her contemporaries in its personal intensity and in the metaphysical platonism she used to address female friendship. Male friendship literature[51] written in English before the 1580s, according to Stephen Latt, relies heavily on classical precedent and "tends to be unoriginal or, at best, a rehearsal of old commonplaces—without originality, without personal application."[52] In the 1580s, however, male friendship literature exhibited a movement "towards a more emotional expression of friendship,"[53] which appropriated the civilities of Horatian and Aristotelian ideals and which continued into the seventeenth century with the poems of Thomas Carew, James Howell, Richard Lovelace, and Henry Vaughan (who was also part of Orinda's circle of male literary friends). In describing the friendship literature of the years 1620–64, Latt notes a "gradual movement away from the public level of experience. With the pressures of the times, writers turned increasingly inward. The turmoil of dissension, the chaos of rebellion, and the catastrophe of regicide freed loyal monarchists to desert the public scene."[54] It was this escapism, particularly its use of pastoralism, that Philips infused with her more passionate intimacy.

Philips's awareness of the connection between her own feelings and the male tradition of friendship as we have seen it circulating in the culture surrounding her is manifest in her attempts to assure herself of the acceptability of her attachments by writing to Jeremy Taylor concerning the religious nature and limits of friendship. His answer to her, in "A Discourse of the Nature, Offices, and Measures, of Friendship, with Rules of Conducting It, in a Letter to the Most Ingenious and Excellent Mrs. Katharine Philips" (1657), cannot have been very satisfactory; his view is, as one might expect, rigorously androcentric in its treatment of women as friends only in relation to men: "A man is the best friend in trouble, but a woman may be equal to him in the days of joy: a woman can as well increase our comforts, but cannot so well lessen our sorrows."[55] Reaffirming traditional views, Taylor denied women's capacity for true friendship with men and ignored friendship between women.

Surely more satisfying to Philips must have been Francis Finch's treatise *Friendship* (1654), dedicated to Anne Owen (who apparently had suggested that he write it) as "D. Noble *Lucasia-Orinda*"; this dedication ac-

knowledges and graciously compliments the relationship so important to
Philips through an allegorical marriage of names and fusing of identities.
The headings under which Finch characterizes friendship anticipate the
ambiguities of the relation he describes: "[I]t hath a Uniting quality, it is
Secret, it is Virtuous."[56] That "it is Secret" suggests the deep intimacy of
the relationship and/or that something in the friendship might require
discretion, including his own in signing the discourse with his pseudonym, Palaemon, and in ensuring its extremely select distribution. The
paradoxical phrasing and circumlocution of his definition of friendship
point to a sense of perplexity about where, exactly, to draw a distinction
between the "Passions" of "Love" and "other Passions," presumably lustful ones, and whether indeed these are separable, and if so, how:

> Some have been so prodigall in their Encomiums and descriptions of
> Love, that they have not been content to keep the other Passions at a
> just distance and subjection, but have quite swallowed them up: and by
> making the objects of every Passion lovely in the eyes of that Passion
> whereby they are pursued, have taken away the proper name of that Pas-
> sion and anabaptised it Love. And thus the Extreams of a Passion which
> hardly avoid being vitious where the Passion itself is virtuous, must carry
> the plausible inscription of Love, though Love itself be brought into
> Detestation.[57]

Finch struggles here to avoid naming the passions that he describes as
"vitious," ones that should be kept "at a just distance and subjection,"
though they appear often to be confused with the expression of a more
virtuous passion: "must carry the plausible inscription of Love, though
Love itself be brought into Detestation." He moralizes that "the Ex-
treams of a Passion which hardly avoid being vitious where the Passion itself is virtuous" must be called "Love," though it demeans "Love" itself.
Does, then, this passionate friendship between women expressed by
Orinda threaten to take away "the proper name of that Passion" (i.e., the
lust of woman for woman, tribadism) and "anabaptise" it "Love"? It would
seem so, and Finch would seem to be cautioning "*Lucasia-Orinda*" against
that disreputable folly.

Finch's treatise situates Philips in a historical moment during which
cultural change is about to take place but has not yet become a reality.
While a public discourse of female same-sex trespass is available, it seems
not yet to have become entirely clear to individuals exactly whether,
when, and how it might overlap with the traditional ideologies of friendship familiar to them. It is this uncertainty, perceptible as a subtextual

uneasiness, that reappears throughout the middle decades of the seventeenth century.

The persistence of this anxiety about the overlap between friendship and transgressive eroticism emerges in comparisons between Philips and Sappho. Philips's control of male poetic idiom in the service of a same-sex female theme placed her clearly in a tradition whose only previous female exponent was Sappho and made comparisons inevitable. The admiration for Philips's work elicited by her daring manipulation of convention is apparent in the commendatory poems that introduce her poetry and in other contemporary comments that repeatedly praise her likeness to Sappho. Philips was evidently the first English poet to evoke that classical comparison and, until it later became a more conventional literary compliment, it was somewhat problematic because of Sappho's reputation for sexual transgression. Sappho's work was recognized as the highest literary achievement in lyric poetry by a woman and, although her subject matter was regarded as questionable, it was echoed by Orinda. Sir Charles wrote in the preface to the 1667 edition of Philips's poems: "We might well have call'd her the English *Sappho,* she of all the female Poets of former Ages, being for her Verses and her Vertues both, the most highly to be valued. . . . And for her Vertues, they as much surpass'd those of *Sappho* as the Theological do the Moral, (wherein yet *Orinda* was not her inferior)."[58] In making this comparison, Sir Charles distinguishes Orinda's Sappho-like poetic skills from her "Vertues" that "surpass'd those of *Sappho*" and thus distances Orinda from Sappho's tarnished moral reputation.

Philo-Philippa, "lover of Philips," the pseudonymous author of one of the commendatory poems for the 1667 volume, develops the gendered aspects of the comparison with Sappho. She writes:

> Ingage us unto Books, *Sappho* comes forth,
> Though not of *Hesiod's* age, of *Hesiod's* worth,
> If Souls no Sexes have, as 'tis confest,
> 'Tis not the he or she makes Poems best:
> Nor can men call these Verses Feminine,
> Be the sense vigorous and Masculine.[59]

Abraham Cowley, the author of *Davideis,* which takes for its subject one of the most prominent traditional models of male passionate friendship and contains at least one homoerotic passage, describes Philips's poetic art in similarly gendered terms. Typically androcentric assumptions underlie Cowley's praise of Philips's intellectual gifts:

'Tis solid, and 'tis manly all,
Or rather, 'tis Angelical:
    For, as in Angels, we
    Do in thy verses see
Both improv'd Sexes eminently meet;
They are than Man more strong, and
    more than Woman sweet.

Moreover, in the following passage he is at pains to describe Philips as a more virtuous Sappho, to distinguish her exemplary modesty and purity from the manners of her model:

They talk of *Sappho,* but, alas! the shame
Ill Manners soil the lustre of her fame.
Orinda's inward Vertue is so bright,
That, like a Lantern's fair enclosed light,
It through the Paper shines where she doth write.
Honour and Friendship, and the gen'rous scorn
    Of things for which we were not born,
(Things that can only by a fond disease,
Like that of Girles our vicious stomacks please)
Are the instructive subjects of her Pen.[60]

These lines evidence considerable anxiety lest Orinda be associated with the "shame" of "Ill Manners" that "soil[ed]" Sappho's fame, so that there is little doubt that Cowley refers to Sappho's reputed transgressions with women. Cowley underlines this reference by a further gesture to distance Orinda from Sappho's nonliterary reputation when he adds that Orinda writes with a "gen'rous scorn / Of things for which we were not born." Cowley's eagerness to deny the erotics of Philips's writing suggests that he fears the clarity of those erotics in her poems and their possible association with behaviors identified as transgressive.

Praise of Philips as the standard of female excellence and poetic skill continued through the seventeenth century and into the mid–eighteenth century. Her name continues to be linked with those of Aphra Behn (Astrea) and Sappho in many of the commendatory poems and epistles written by women that preface plays written by women for the London stage of Queen Anne; she became a model to be emulated and replaced. In 1696 Mary Pix addressed Delarivier Manley on "her Tragedy call'd *The Royal Mischief*": "Like *Sappho* Charming, like *Afra* Eloquent, / Like Chast *Orinda* sweetly Innocent."[61]

Orinda and Astrea became, as Nancy Cotton and Jane Spencer point out, the two ideals in a female tradition to which later women writers aspired.[62] Yet Sappho continued to provide the second figure in a separate dyad and continued to be linked with Orinda when the issue was female poetic genius, so that the comparison of Orinda to Sappho became increasingly conventional.[63] The tenacity of this association is apparent in these lines from John Duncombe's 1754 "The Feminiad: A Poem," which echo very clearly the sentiments expressed by Cowley almost a century earlier:

> Nor need we now from our own Britain rove
> In search of genius, to the Lesbian grove,
> Tho' Sappho there her tuneful lyre has strung,
> And amorous griefs in sweetest accents sung,
> Since her, in Charles's days, amidst a train
> Of shameless bards, licentious and profane,
> The chaste ORINDA rose; with purer light,
> Like modest Cynthia, beaming thro' the night:
> Fair Friendship's lustre, undisguis'd by art,
> Glows in her lines, and animates her heart;
> Friendship, that jewel, which, tho' all confess
> Its peerless value, yet how few possess![64]

Though, after this, Orinda's reputation seems to have declined, its particular characteristics were reclaimed intact when, in 1905, George Saintsbury wittily introduced her poetry as "her Sapphic-Platonics."[65]

These comparisons with Sappho are important both because they refer to the great classical female model of lyric poetry and because they explicitly indicate a similarity of subject matter. Even though Cowley and Duncombe acknowledged this similarity of subject matter, they were also, paradoxically, eager to dispel the erotic content implicit in the comparison by emphasizing Orinda's purity. What some might now call Sappho's bisexuality, to which Cowley and Duncombe allude, was also part of Sappho's legend for Orinda's contemporaries. That Sappho's reputation for erotic involvement was with women, as well as with men, was well known in the seventeenth century, having been conveyed by the long traditions of representation in Ovid's *Heroïdes* ("No more the *Lesbian* Dames my passion move, / Once the dear Objects of my guilty Love"), by Horace's references to *mascula Sappho* and Sappho's complaints about the young women of Lesbos, and by the ode preserved by Longinus from Sappho to a female lover.[66] Donne's explicit "Sapho to Philaenis" only perpetuated Sappho's reputation. These lines leave little to the imagination:

> And betweene us all sweetnesse may be had;
>   All, all that *Nature* yields, or Art can adde.
> My two lips, eyes, thighs, differ from thy two,
>   But so, as thine from one another doe;
> And, oh, no more; the likenesse being such,
>   Why should they not alike in all parts touch?
> Hand to strange hand, lippe to lippe none denies;
>   Why should they brest to brest, or thighs to thighs?
>
> (ll. 44–50)[67]

Pierre Bayle's *Dictionary* (1710), though somewhat later, also is unequivocal in its view of Sappho's erotic activities ("her Amorous Passion extended even to the Persons of her own Sex" and *"Sappho* always passed for a Famous *Tribas,*" or tribade), citing evidence that had been available much earlier, at least since the eleventh-century *Suda.*[68] The writers of contemporary encomia to Orinda thus understood the nature of allusions to Sappho but were eager to dispel any suggestions of unnatural sexuality. They wished to pay Katherine Philips the high compliment of comparing her to the great classical lyricist not only for her poetical voice, but also for her unique subject matter; at the same time, they wished to reconfirm her platonic purity. The encomium was appropriate and perhaps inevitable, if somewhat uncomfortable. Eventually, as it became more conventional, the comparison to Sappho was often used to suggest only literary accomplishment—until Saintsbury recalled its original significance. Between Saintsbury and the feminist movement of the late twentieth century, readers of Philips's work simply neglected or trivialized her considerable contribution to the history of poetic ideas: the recovery of the homoeroticism of Platonic ideals in a classical Sapphic context.

It was Philips's use of the conventions of male poetic discourse, particularly of the metaphysicals and the cavaliers, and her echoing of the literary tradition of male friendship, that sanctioned her unconventional subject and made it a novelty in her time. Because her discourse was familiar, her subject was acceptable. Without those conventions, and without Philips's modest and feminine demeanor in court circles and her presumed exemplary personal virtue, it seems unlikely that her poetry would have been praised as it was. The men who were her contemporaries accepted her ideals of passionate friendship between women and were persuaded to regard them as ennobling because they could recognize in their rhetorical strategies a parallel or analogue to their own Platonic ideals of heterosexual love and the love of male friendship.

While the poetic use of classical pastoral and friendship conventions tells us next to nothing about the actual circumstances of people's lives,[69] external sources in the form of letters in Philips's case indicate that the feelings expressed in her poems were more than conventional or courtly gestures. That her poetic model was Donne, and that she echoed his un-questioned male-female sexuality in the erotics of her own poems, only emphasizes the erotic nature of her passions. Her literary example of the use of recognized conventions as vehicles for a shadowed discourse of fe-male same-sex erotics initiated a tradition of published female friendship poetry whose parameters I attempt to define here.

Since Patrick Thomas's careful study of Philips's manuscripts and printed editions, a number of additional Philips manuscripts have come to light;[70] reconsideration of the major manuscripts confirms that Philips's reputation following her death was based on the presentation of her po-ems in the posthumous 1667 edition and its subsequent reprintings rather than on the manuscripts circulated during her lifetime. While it has been generally acknowledged that Philips's writing was edited, probably by Sir Charles Cotterell, to conform to a more conventional poetics, the pos-sible effect of the rearrangement of the poems—and therefore also the re-construction of the narrative trajectory presented in her manuscripts, or more precisely, its renarrativization—has recently been accorded much needed critical attention.[71] Notable among extant manuscripts is a manu-script book in which Philips made fair copies of her poems, arranging them so that she copied poems on one leaf only of each opening, and when she reached the last leaf turned the book over and continued copy-ing her poems onto the blank leaves on the opposite side of each opening. Thus, the manuscript book presents a more intimate account of Orinda's experience than do the 1664 and 1667 printed editions in which her ex-emplary status as a royalist and admired woman poet is highlighted by the commendatory poems and by the occasional and public poems to the king and queen that open the published volumes. The printed editions disperse the friendship poems that circulated in manuscript and so disrupt the nar-rative movement we might read in them of Orinda's courtship, joy in pas-sionate friendship, and then absence or rupture and final disappointment in intimacy.

However we interpret this important contrast between manuscripts and printed editions—whether we see it as a function of the symbolic values of friendship during a royalist exile, or as a change in response to an alteration in the cultural climate surrounding same-sex relations, or as a strategy for the furthering of literary reputation—several crucial issues bear on this change in emphasis from circulated manuscript to printed text. First, because Philips often relied on Sir Charles's literary judgment and because he was her literary executor, it is impossible to know whether she might have concurred with the rearrangement of the sequence of her poems in the 1667 edition. Further, her royalist sympathies and her joy at the return of the monarchy, her recent Dublin theatrical success with *Pompey,* her newfound connections with prominent aristocrats, her hopes of return to London, and her anticipation of earning a position for her husband to ease their financial distress would all have made desirable the shaping of an increasingly public persona had she lived. Finally, the contrast between the manuscripts' intimate narrative structure and the presentation of an iconic public figure in the printed editions speaks to us of the profound shift that was taking place from manuscript to print culture in England during these years: the change we note in Philips's texts from the intimacy of privately circulated or presentation manuscripts to the "packaging" of a public personage in a printed text is the perfect textbook illustration of this process.[72] Given the ways in which these personal, social, and cultural forces impinged on the transmission of Philips's texts, attempts to draw conclusions about the form taken by her poems through a close reading of their reorganization for the printed editions would seem rather perilous.

Despite the complexities of balancing these various considerations, we can still read the reconstructed narrative of the printed texts in light of the increasingly ambiguous, even problematic, status of Philips's passionate female friendships. That Philips's relations with other women were coming to be understood as liminal in ways that members of polite society were loath to mention is certainly acknowledged by Francis Finch (as Palaemon), by the commendatory verses of Abraham Cowley and Philo-Philippa, and finally by the persistently uneasy comparisons with Sappho.

Writers Transgressing: Margaret Cavendish and Aphra Behn

Several women, writing slightly later than Katherine Philips, were not as constrained as was Philips by considerations of social acceptance and literary ambition and were not reluctant to transgress conventional boundaries in depicting women's erotic relations and female sexual subjectivity.

Margaret Cavendish, duchess of Newcastle (1623–1673), was to some degree protected by her status as an aristocrat married to a powerful member of the court, while Aphra Behn (1640–1689), even younger and somewhat later, appears to have been an intrepid adventuress with little to lose but her reputation, though she complained openly about not being admired, as were men, for forays into sexual subject matter on the stage. Cavendish anticipates Behn when she explores the possibilities of a female same-sex erotics, teasingly approaching and then evading an explicit sexuality between women that is not named. Tribadism as such is simultaneously invoked and derailed as Cavendish punctuates her exploration by commentary on the opposition between natural and unnatural relations. Cavendish in her plays is explicit in pointing out the transgressiveness and physicality of the female same-sex relations she presents. In so doing, she identifies the sexual implications of the passionate friendships and erotic intimacies only hinted at in the idealized poetry of so many of her contemporaries. But then, Cavendish's are closet dramas, both literally and figuratively, in both the early modern and modern senses of that term.

Cavendish articulates in her drama the post-Restoration dilemmas created by circulating knowledge about tribadism and same-sex sexuality among women and the erotic distinctions that are evidently crystallizing in the society around her. *The Convent of Pleasure* (1668)[73]—perhaps now her best-known work apart from her early utopian science fiction narrative *The Blazing World*—goes well beyond the clever manipulations of cross-dressing and breeches parts with which we have become so familiar in early modern drama by men. In this play, Cavendish anticipates the ideal female communities that were to become so popular in the eighteenth century (e.g., that of Mary Astell) and plays with the conventions of female friendship and pastoralism in a play-within-the-play using cross-dressed couples. *The Convent of Pleasure* develops an especially witty, charming, and playfully satirical plot in which a group of women escapes from marriage into a convent and in which it is demonstrated that pleasure is gained rather than lost without men. In act 1, scene 2, Lady Happy, the instigator of the action, makes clear her intentions to Madam Mediator, who, as her name suggests, mediates between Lady Happy and the convent's women and the group of men who pursue them:

MEDIAT[OR]. In my opinion your Doctrine, and your Intention do not agree together.
L[ADY] HAPPY. Why?

MEDIAT[OR]. You intend to live incloister'd and retired from the World.

L[ADY] HAPPY. 'Tis true, but not from pleasures; for, I intend to incloister my self from the World, to enjoy pleasure, and not to bury my self from it; but to incloister my self from the incumbred cares and vexations, troubles and perturbance of the World.

MEDIAT[OR]. But if you incloister your self, How will you enjoy the company of Men, whose conversation is thought the greatest Pleasure?

L[ADY] HAPPY. Men are the only troublers of Women; for they only cross and oppose their sweet delights, and peaceable life; they cause their pains, but not their pleasures. Wherefore those Women that are poor, and have not means to buy delights, and maintain pleasures, are only fit for Men; for having not means to please themselves, they must serve only to please others; but those Women, where Fortune, Nature, and the gods are joined to make them happy, were mad to live with Men, who make the Female sex their slaves; but I will not be so inslaved, but will live retired from their Company. Wherefore, in order thereto, I will take so many Noble Persons of my own Sex, as my Estate will plentifully maintain, such whose Births are greater then their Fortunes, and are resolv'd to live a single life, and vow Virginity: with these I mean to live incloister'd with all the delights and pleasures that are allowable and lawful; My Cloister shall not be a Cloister of restraint, but a place for freedom, not to vex the Senses but to please them. (I.ii; sigs. B2ᵛ–C)

I have cited this exchange in its entirety in order to highlight Lady Happy's long monologue with its awareness of female economic limitation and social subordination in the patriarchal environments of early modern England.⁷⁴ Certainly Margaret Cavendish could afford to articulate such sentiments—and they were no doubt among the transgressions that drew down on her such epithets as "mad Madge"—from the safe vantage of her happy marriage to an approving spouse and her secure social status. Perhaps it is that very vantage that sharpened her understanding of women's status and allowed her to fantasize the paradoxical freedoms of female cloistered pleasures.

The action is set in motion by the arrival of "a great Foreign Princess" described by Madam Mediator to Lady Amorous as "a Princely brave Woman truly, of a Masculine Presence" (II.iii; sig. E1ᵛ). While the "real" sexual identity of the "Princess" is perhaps hinted at in this description, it is by no means made certain, so that the reader/audience is no more enlightened than are the players because there is none of the dramatic irony usually associated with theatrical cross-dressing. The "Princess" is therefore a princess until her unmasking in act 5, scene 1. This allows Cavendish to focus on the relations of friendship in Lady Happy's convent, so that these avowals take place and confirm a not very submerged subtext:

> PRIN[CESS]. I desire you would be my Mistress, and I your Servant; and upon this agreement of Friendship I desire you will grant me one Request.
>
> L[ADY] HAPPY. Any thing that is in my power to grant.
>
> PRIN[CESS]. Why then, I observing in your several Recreations, some of your Ladies do accoustre Themselves in Masculine-Habits, and act Lovers-parts; I desire you will give me leave to be sometimes so accoustred and act the part of your loving Servant. (III.i; sig. F2ᵛ)

This avowal of friendship entails cross-dressing, the eroticism of female masculinity, and the assumption of male/female roles in which the convent women court one another and play out their attractions in roles of submission and domination (i.e., master/mistress and servant). They then mutually declare their exclusive fidelity to one another, and Lady Happy remarks upon the chastity of female lovers: "More innocent Lovers never can there be, / Then my most Princely Lover, that's a She" (III.i; sig. G). There can be no mistaking the import of these lines: they again draw attention to the eroticism of female masculinity; they reassert the impossibility of unchastity between women; and they emphasize that women's erotic passion has its basis in emotional rather than sexual love.

Act 4, scene 1, opens with Lady Happy in the midst of a lovelorn quandary:

> *Enter Lady Happy drest as a Shepherdess; She walks very Melancholy, then speaks as to her self.*
>
> My Name is Happy, and so was my Condition, before I saw this Princess; but now I am like to be the most unhappy Maid alive: But why may not I love a Woman with the same affection I could a Man?
>
> > No, no, Nature is Nature, and still will be
> > The same she was from all Eternity.
> >   (IV.i; sig. I1ᵛ)

Lady Happy's lament—"But why may not I love a Woman with the same affection I could a Man?"—questions the nature and boundaries of erotic transgression. That questioning continues in the exchange that follows the "Princess's" entrance *"in Masculine Shepherd's Clothes"*:[75]

L[ADY] HAPPY. How can harmless Lovers please themselves?

PRIN[CESS]. Why very well, as, to discourse, imbrace and kiss, so mingle souls together.

L[ADY] HAPPY. But innocent Lovers do not use to kiss.

PRIN[CESS]. Not any act more frequent amongst us Women-kind; nay, it were a sin in friendship, should not we kiss: then let us not prove our selves Reprobates.

They imbrace and kiss, and hold each other in their Arms.

PRIN[CESS]. These my Imbraces though of a Femal kind,
    May be as fervent as a Masculine mind. (IV.i; sig. I2)

Cavendish evokes the familiar theme of friendship only to problematize it. The emblematic union of the souls of friends is here complicated by the presence of transgressively identified women (i.e., tribades) hovering in the background as Lady Happy attempts yet again to locate the boundary between friendship and transgression. Fortunately, act 5, scene 1, brings a swift resolution to this dilemma and the "Princess" is unmasked as a male interloper into the convent and a conveniently male-female marriage is solemnized.

After the unmasking of the "Princess" and just before the union of the happy, now differently sexed couple, however, Madam Mediator enters in act 5, scene 2, to explain the discovery of the deception to the men who have been wanting entry into the convent:

COURTLY. But could you never discover it? nor have no hint he was a Man?

M[ADAM] MEDIAT[OR]. No truly, only once I saw him kiss the Lady *Happy;* and you know Womens Kisses are unnatural, and me-thought they kissed with more alacrity then Women use, a kind of Titillation, and more Vigorous. (V.ii; sig. N1ᵛ)

Cavendish in these lines punctuates the earlier conversation between Lady Happy and the "Princess" with an unmistakable attribution of transgressiveness to the behavior Madam Mediator has witnessed. Cavendish's treatment of the erotic complications of a relation between two women, drawing as it does on the traditions of female friendship and the associations of all-female community in the myth of Diana and her nymphs, brings into sharp focus contemporary understandings of the boundaries between acceptable affections and transgressive behaviors. Cavendish obviously questions and manipulates those boundaries for our pleasure and thoughtful reconsideration; but she resolves their troublesomeness by concluding the drama with an overt, perhaps an excessively overt, gesture toward convention.[76] The unmasking that makes possible this assimilation to convention plays on the familiar Ovidian expedient of a sexual metamorphosis for one of the women that has its source in the tale of Iphis and Ianthe in book 9 of the *Metamorphoses*.[77] Cavendish surely asks us to question such a fortuitously simple, yet witty, solution to the more disturbing dilemma of serious passions between women.

Aphra Behn is perhaps the best known of early women writers of erotically transgressive texts. Both condemned and admired for her frank and often witty treatments of sexuality, she played an assertive Astrea to Philips's modest Orinda. "To the Fair Clarinda, Who Made Love to Me, Imagin'd More than Woman" is among Behn's best-known poems because it is one of her most frequently anthologized, along with "The Disappointment" (a witty pastoral narrative about premature ejaculation), "The Willing Mistress," and "On Her Loving Two Equally." In today's classrooms, these are the works through which students first encounter Behn, so that her reputation for immodest female transgressiveness has remained intact.

Though a number of critics read the female same-sex erotics of "To the Fair Clarinda" as "a panacea to lesbian desire,"[78] as though "lesbian desire" were transparently transhistorical, the construction of a female same-sex erotics during this historical moment shortly after the Restoration and the death of Katherine Philips was considerably more complex than such readings suggest. A few intrepid individuals like Behn and Cavendish, a self-styled eccentric, were creating a discourse of female same-sex erotics that was not in the least evasive but that also avoided identification with the vulgar and unnatural sexuality identified as tribadism. In other words, writers like Behn and Cavendish maneuvered—to their social detriment—in the narrow space between tribadism and "chaste" but passionate female friendship: while acknowledging the presence of erotic desire between women, they simultaneously failed to name it or to identify it with the derogated identity of tribades.

In 1688 Aphra Behn published a volume of poems, *Lycidas; or the Lover in Fashion,* many of which are obviously autobiographical. "To the Fair Clarinda" is, tellingly, the last poem:

> Fair lovely Maid, or if that title be
> Too weak, too Feminine for Nobler thee,
> Permit a Name that more Approaches Truth:
> And let me call thee, Lovely Charming Youth.

These opening lines immediately fulfill the promise of the title to imagine the woman who made love to her as "more than Woman," as a (male) youth, a clear reference to the penis or to a prosthesis, "*more* than Woman":

> This last will justifie my soft complaint,
> While that may serve to lessen my con[s]traint:
> And without Blushes I the Youth persue,
> When so much beauteous Woman is in view.

The attraction of imagining her female lover as male lies in the provocative nature of the beauty of woman combined with the speaker's lust for the penis. It also provides opportunity for the female speaker herself to assume the male role of pursuit "without Blushes," revealing another transgressive desire. Yet,

> Against thy Charms we struggle but in vain
> With thy deluding Form thou giv'st pain,
> While the bright Nymph betrays us to the Swain.
> In pity to our Sex sure thou wer't sent,
> That we might Love, and yet be Innocent

The speaker thus goes on to reveal frustration at the absence of a phallus, "With thy deluding Form thou giv'st pain," and yet she acknowledges the possibilities of a sexual love between women in which they remain innocent *because* of the absence of the male organ: "That we might Love, and yet be Innocent." Thus, innocence and chastity are retained *because* of a lack; in other words, Behn confirms that physicality between women doesn't *count* as sex. The speaker elaborates this point:

> For sure no Crime with thee we can commit;
> Or if we shou'd—thy Form excuses it.
> For who, that gathers fairest Flowers believes
> A Snake lies hid beneath the Fragrant Leaves.

Can the "Crime" here consist of colluding in one woman's assumption of male prerogatives with an engorged clitoris or a phallic prosthesis, the "Snake [that] lies hid beneath the Fragrant Leaves"? Ah, but her "Form excuses it." This, after all, is the behavior condemned by male railers against tribadism. The speaker brings the poem to its conclusion with this sestet separated by a space from the lines above:

> Thou beauteous Wonder of a different kind,
> Soft Cloris with the dear Alexis join'd;

When e'r the Manly part of thee, wou'd plead
Thou tempts us with the Image of the Maid,
Whil we the noblest Passions do extend
The Love to Hermes, Aphrodite the Friend.[79]

In summarizing the views of earlier critics, Ros Ballaster attempts to un-
ravel the ambiguities of this poem by speculating that these lines describe
a hermaphrodite and may lead us back to Behn's lover John Hoyle, "for
whom there is some evidence of homosexuality, although none of trans-
vestitism."[80] This is a seductive hypothesis, based on Behn's witty pun on
Hermes and Aphrodite, a split Herm/Aphrodite, in the last line, that certainly "encourages [the] reader to enjoy the play across both sexes and the
subversive power of the image of the hermaphrodite."[81] I would argue,
however, that what Behn describes here is, as the title tells us, a fantasy of
female same-sex physicality whose erotics are amplified by her female
lover's titillating assumption of the male sexual role; excitement is generated by the masculinity of femininity: "Soft Cloris with the dear Alexis
join'd; / When e'r the Manly part of thee, wou'd plead / Thou tempts us
with the Image of the Maid." Surely the greater subversion here is not in
an imagined hermaphrodite—though their vogue in medical texts and
other writings is undeniable—but in the startling female masculinity that
the poem presents to us. To the extent that Behn's "real" lover John Hoyle
is believed to have had sexual relations with other men, he might be said
to represent her desire for an ambiguously constructed masculinity, or
even perhaps for a feminine masculinity. So in this poem Behn describes
her desire (if we can conflate her with her speaker) for a masculinized
femininity—or female masculinity—and her understanding of the already nuanced erotics operating in the interstices between sex and gender.
Behn's transgression, then, is to explore in her poetry, if not in life, the
erotics made possible by the rich permutations of gender variation.

As this review of Margaret Cavendish and Aphra Behn makes clear, in
the twenty years between 1668 and 1688, some more daring women writers were examining the implications of their own growing awareness of
the transgressive possibilities implicit in passionate female friendships.
Behn and Cavendish both try to clear a path of understanding for a female erotics that is more than friendship and yet falls short of tribadism.
As in the tale of Iphis and Ianthe, Cavendish portrays the fulfillment of a
female same-sex erotics as thwarted, frustrated, and forbidden, but it is
nevertheless fully elaborated and completely experienced as a love passion
in *The Convent of Pleasure;* that is, it is acknowledged as experientially le-

gitimate. A generation later, Behn plays wittily with the implications of a more successful bodily fulfillment.

Writers Transgressing: Delarivier Manley

The writing of Delarivier Manley (1667/71–1724)[82] marks clearly a significant moment in the discourse of female erotics that I have been charting. The increasingly ambiguous status of Philips's passionate female friendships—that is, the ways in which her relations with other women were coming to be understood as liminal—foreshadowed the shifts in sexual understandings that would take place at the end of the seventeenth century. The modern system of binary sexual identities that was to establish heterosexuality and homosexuality as separate and mutually exclusive identities did not become a dominant ideology until sometime during the eighteenth century but was developing as a discursive formulation between about 1650 and the beginning of the eighteenth century, when what had been tacit sexual knowledge was becoming more available for discussion, yet simultaneously being unnamed.[83] Writing just as the eighteenth century was beginning, Manley articulated with precision—and in a sophisticated, knowing voice—the assumptions that informed sexual discourse during the transitional historical moments immediately prior to the consolidation of a dominant ideology of binary sexualities.

Manley was even less constrained by respect for social propriety or by the desire to appear virtuous than was either Aphra Behn or Margaret Cavendish. A theatrical career, the scandal of a bigamous marriage, and several shady sexual liaisons did not offer opportunities for claiming virtue or respectability; nor did her natal connections to the court through her father, a cavalier soldier and writer who served in various political capacities, help in this regard. Manley was self-dramatizing and seemingly unable to refrain from including snippets of her own life in the scandal fictions that made her as well as her subjects notorious.[84] Her best-known novel, and the one that contains her famous account of a group of women she identifies as "the new Cabal," is the roman à clef *The New Atalantis*—whose complete (and spoofing) title is *Secret Memoirs and Manners of Several Persons of Quality, of both Sexes. From the New Atalantis, an Island in the Mediterranean. Written Originally in Italian*—described by Rosalind Ballaster, her modern editor, as a "Tory-motivated exposé of the supposed secret lives of rich and powerful Whig peers and politicians of the reigns of the Stuart kings and queens from Charles II to Anne I."[85] Manley was arrested, along with her printer and publishers, following the publication of *The New Atalantis,* whose successfully salacious appeal is attested to by its seven editions between 1709 and 1736. Her account of the same-sex erotics of "the new Cabal" thus had an eager audience and was widely circulated.

In her account of "the new Cabal," Manley uses a discourse that clearly identifies, without ever naming, the transgressive behaviors of a group of aristocratic women; instead of using a public discourse that has been unnamed, she employs a strategy of innuendo and complicity with her readers. Through this mode of indirection, she articulates and questions the assumptions that have been driving sexual understandings during the last quarter or more of the seventeenth century. Manley's portrait of the Cabal is an ambivalent one that both condemns some among the rich and famous Whig aristocracy at the same time that it criticizes the social structures that constrain women; her representation of the Cabal "oscillates uneasily between satire and Utopia," as Ballaster notes.[86] The description of the Cabal opens with a series of questions that locates precisely the dilemma of women's erotic lives:

> [T]hese ladies are of the new Cabal, a sect (however innocent in it self) that does not fail from meeting its share of censure from the world. Alas! what can they do? How unfortunate are women? If they seek diversion out of themselves and include the other sex, they must be criminal? If in themselves (as those of the new Cabal), still they are criminal? Though censurers must carry their imaginations a much greater length than I am capable to do mine, to explain this hypothesis with success. They [the censurers] pretend to find in these the vices of old Rome revived.... (154)

Women who desire agency in shaping their erotic lives will be condemned whether they choose "diversion" with men or with their own sex, as do the women of the Cabal. The speaker's mockery here is focused on those who would censure the activities of "the new Cabal" as less than "innocent," as "criminal," as "the vices of old Rome revived." The speaker's coy stance of distance from the censurers, saying that they "must carry their imaginations a much greater length than I am capable to do mine," captures nicely the ethos that has allowed erotic relations between women to be unnamed, to include the intimacies of friendship, but *not* to preclude marriage because of the narrow definition of sexuality as possible only in the presence of a male organ. Manley also points up here the fluidity of erotic possibilities in a culture in which marriage is an arrangement of social convenience and necessity. Her description of female same-sex erotics continues in this vein, underlining a discourse of denial:

> The Cabal . . . have all the happiness in themselves! Two beautiful ladies joined in an excess of amity (no word is tender enough to express their new delight) innocently embrace! For how can they be guilty? They vow eternal tenderness, they exclude the men, and condition that they will always do so. What irregularity can there be in this? 'Tis true, some things may be strained a little too far, and that causes reflections to be cast upon the rest. . . . (154)[87]

The defining language in this passage is "joined in *an excess of amity . . . innocently* embrace" (my emphasis). "Amity" reappears in this novel as well as in other contexts as a word associated with the excessive passions of erotic friendship and was evidently used as a circumlocution to evade a less savory description of transgression.[88] Here, the speaker asks, what "irregularity" could there possibly be between two women alone? That "some things may be strained a little too far" among some (the tribades? the *fricatrices*? the *named* transgressors?) destroys the reputations of all, "causes reflections to be cast upon the rest." The passage goes on to describe the "enemies of the Cabal . . . who will not allow of innocency in any intimacies" and who are like those "detestable censurers" who condemned Socrates' scopophilic pleasure in young men:

> Such excursions as these have given occasion to the enemies of the Cabal to refine, as much as they please, upon the mysteries of it. There are, who will not allow of innocency in any intimacies, detestable censurers who, after the manner of the Athenians, will not believe so great a man as Socrates (him whom the oracle delivered to be the wisest of all men) could see every hour the beauty of an Alcibiades without taxing his sensibility. How did they recriminate for his affection, for his cares, his tenderness to the lovely youth? How have they delivered him down to posterity as blameable for too guilty a passion for his beautiful pupil?— Since then it is not the fate of even so wise a man to avoid the censure of the busy and the bold, care ought to be taken by others (less fortified against occasion of detraction, in declining such unaccountable intimacies) to prevent the ill-natured world's refining upon their mysterious innocence. (155)

Basically, how dare the censurers defile, "recriminate," tenderness and affection? Society has reached a pass wherein individuals must beware lest their "mysterious innocence" be condemned by an "ill-natured" world, lest their intimacies be deemed "unaccountable." The evasions built into this discourse that describes without naming are ones that were common parlance in a society that sought to describe what was recognized as transgressive without condemning actors who had social position and the power to retaliate. The targets of Manley's satire are women at the court of Queen Anne, particularly Anne and her favorites, about whose activities there was considerable gossip in London.

More specific descriptions of individuals involved and the manners—one might say, ethics—of the Cabal follow. A moralized perspective on marriage and relations between the sexes informs Manley's social satire:

> The persons who passed us in those three coaches were returning from one of their private, I was going to say silent, meetings, but far be it from me to detract from any of the attributes of the sex. The Lady L——[Margaret Sutton, Lady Lexington] and her daughters make four of the cabal. . . . They wear away the indulgent happy hours according to their own taste . . . an easy walk to their bower of bliss. The day and hour of their *rendezvous* is appointed beforehand; they meet, they caress they swear inviolable secrecy and amity. . . . They momently exclude the men: fortify themselves in the precepts of virtue and chastity against all their [the men's] detestable undermining arts . . . give rules to such of the Cabal who are not married how to behave themselves to such who they think fit they should marry, no such weighty affair being to be accomplished without the mutual consent of the society, at the same time lamenting the custom of the world, that has made it convenient (nay, almost indispensable) for all ladies once to marry. To those that have husbands, they have other instructions, in which this is sure to be one: to reserve their heart, their tender amity for their fair friend, an article in this well-bred, wilfully undistinguishing age which the husband seems to be rarely solicitous of. (155–56)

Marriage is as corrupt here as the politics that Manley satirizes in other parts of the novel: it is necessary for economic and social survival, but since husbands are "rarely solicitous of" their wives' hearts, those hearts may as well be reserved for "their tender amity for their fair friend." This accords well with the relations between Katherine Philips and her friends, her relation with her husband defined in terms of duty and honor, her passion reserved for Rosania and Lucasia; but Philips's was certainly a rather more innocent historical moment. Manley writes for a more knowing, more cynical age that regards with irony the "mysterious innocence" of the past.[89] Female same-sex relations are now, at the turn of the century, openly acknowledged and described in ways that make clear a context of shared understanding, but they continue to be unnamed—that is, they are not identified by the discourse of tribadism or other slang—insofar as they describe persons who are socially well-placed.

Erotic Discourse(s), Libidinous Energies

The dissemination of knowledge about tribadism and other sexualities was hastened in the years between the late 1650s and about 1690, when a spate of French pornography was translated and imported into England: familiarity with transgressive behaviors then became more widespread and more available to women than it had been before the Restoration, when Latin texts and their English translations were the primary sources of such information.[90] In the years immediately following the Restoration, then, women in England had increased access to—and therefore more readily available knowledge of—erotic and pornographic materials imported from the Continent, as well as to more recently translated materials in the vernacular. The appearance, not too long after Philips's death, of writing by women such as Behn, Cavendish, and Manley, corroborates women's increasing familiarity with, and a willingness on the part of some to write about, a transgressive same-sex erotics. While this erotics continues to be not named, its existence has become part of a shared cultural knowledge that is communicated obliquely.

Although female same-sex sexual activities were being publicly articulated by women by the late 1660s, they stand in an at best ambiguous relation to actual intimate behaviors between ordinary women—that is, women of the middling sort, not of the gentry or aristocracy. Direct sources that might document the connections between erotic discourse and erotic physicality between women in sixteenth- and seventeenth-century England are absent in part because tribadism was not named as a reason for prosecuting women and explicitly descriptive private documents are exceedingly rare to nonexistent.[91] In English cultural mythology, tribades as a class of transgressors were classed with sodomites, and probably papists; but we do not at present have more reliable documentation of the activities of women engaged in same-sex relations who were not regarded, and did not regard themselves, as tribades, as we do about those of male homosexuals.

Alan Bray has described the change that took place in male homosexual life in England from 1650 to 1700. According to his research into court records and other documents, it was at this time that "molly houses" came into being as a symptom of the increasing isolation of practicing homosexuals from traditional institutions. This was the beginning of what we might now call a male homosexual subculture that evidently did not include women, though the appearance of explicitly female same-sex literary subject matter (especially Manley's Cabal) certainly suggests the existence of contemporary female networks. Of course, as Bray suggests, at the point of emergence of a subculture, the dominant culture officially recognizes that such individuals do indeed exist. Bray hypothesizes, on substantial grounds, that before about 1650, and before the official acknowledgment of the existence of homosexual behavior, "the conflict between individual desire and the values of society as a whole" was resolved by a "cleavage . . . between an individual's behaviour and his awareness of its significance."[92] Pursuing the work of Michel Rey, Bray extends this view in an essay about "the body of the friend at the onset of the modern world and its loss" in which he examines the public contexts of male friendship and its expression in the embrace, the table, the bed, and the chamber pot, as emblems of "the social cohesion that could be signified by the symbolic gift of the friend's body" and "the place of comforting security such relationships afforded in an insecure world."[93] Before about 1650, then, we might say that there was a happy collusion between the individual and his culture to avoid making the connections between this behavior and the perversion of sodomy. Male homosexuality was in this way an unacknowledged, but hardly unusual, activity in such respectable institutions as public schools, the apprentice-master and master-servant systems. But this situation was in flux during the late seventeenth century as the erotics of friendship became more dangerous: these erotics gradually became more clearly associated with the transgressive perversities of sodomy and the life of a subculture began to take shape to accommodate this evolution in sexual understanding.

The general situation of ordinary women during the early modern period in England has recently been explored by Margaret R. Hunt in a review of historical evidence, such as parish registers and living arrangements, to determine the kinds of opportunities that the circumstances of daily life might have made available for female same-sex erotic activities. Even into the eighteenth century, she notes "the everyday character of close relations between women" and "the ease of access of women to other women" in a society in which it was common for individuals to share beds well into adulthood, in which there was a high percentage of single women living in households headed by women (15 percent in London; 20 percent in rural areas),[94] and in which female servants often assumed a companionate relation with their mistresses. Hunt's conclusion, based primarily on this reconstruction of living arrangements and the texture of everyday life, is not unlike Bray's description of male-male intimate relations, and supports my own hypothesis that female homoeroticism was a "seamless part of everyday life."[95]

It is not surprising, therefore, that influential late-twentieth-century lesbian-feminist debates about an appropriate definition of lesbianism do not offer an even remotely satisfactory approach to describing the erotic experience or self-understanding of women before the mid–eighteenth century, at a time when open acknowledgment of female sexual subjectivity was often inhibited and when individuals had a great deal at stake in *not* recognizing their own complicity in same-sex erotic relations and in *not* defining their friendships in terms of the discourse of tribadism. Bonnie Zimmerman summarizes the attempts during the 1970s and early 1980s by Adrienne Rich, Catharine Stimpson, and Lillian Faderman to establish a useful working definition of lesbianism for historical scholarship; she cautions us to avoid the "simplistic universalism" that results when we use the overly inclusive "lesbian continuum" described by Rich as well as the exclusive genital sexuality of Stimpson's definition, which may have political utility now but inhibits attempts to reconstruct female eroticism in earlier historical periods.[96] Faderman's use of the convention of "romantic friendship"—a descriptor of women's erotic relations for the period from the mid–eighteenth century to the self-identification of lesbians in the early twentieth century—as a *via media*, a middle way, between the opposing definitions proposed by Rich and Stimpson leaves much to be desired: it evades the nature of the erotic content of much of the earlier literature she discusses and defuses its implications.[97] Zimmerman's cautions continue to be relevant: scholars are no closer to defining "lesbian" for the new millennium than they were for the end of the twentieth century. As mainstream thinking increasingly valorizes genital definitions of the sort advocated by Stimpson,[98] feminist scholars expend less energy problematizing "lesbian" and focus instead on expanding the vocabulary of performative identities, an enterprise whose historical utility has yet to be proved. Marilyn Farwell, however, provides a perspective that is useful for our efforts to recover the historical experience of same-sex erotics: she discusses the possibility of lesbian identity "defined as a discursive position" or as "a discursive construction."[99] Recognizing that female same-sex erotic relations are defined as discursive positions or constructions can free us to comprehend their historical particularities and to explore the various discursive constructions of same-sex erotic relations that may be in play at any specific historical moment.

Because "the historical relationship between genital sexuality and lesbianism remains unclear," we must recognize that certain earlier *texts* describe female same-sex erotics to the extent that they convey an experience of passion that expresses "libidinous energy," whether or not it includes verifiable experience of genital activity.[100] The *writers* of these texts may have been lovers of other women insofar as they evidently understood and were able to convey "libidinous energy" between women, even though it may never be possible to verify the precise nature or extent of their physical activities.[101] Such attention to a textual erotics avoids the Procrustean distortion of writers' experiences and is consistent with what we now know about early modern pre-binary understandings of sexuality. Thus, it is critical that we avoid the dichotomizing perspective of "heterosexuality" and "homosexuality" as mutually exclusive identity categories in order to recognize the ways in which eroticism between early modern Englishwomen is manifested.

Katherine Philips produced poetic texts that focus on eroticism between women. That these texts not only are now amenable to lesbian reading, but also spoke to contemporary female readers of their own feelings and attachments, is evidenced by the response of Philo-Philippa and by the popularity and influence of Philips's texts among the seventeenth-century women writers who followed her.[102] She created a discursive construction and shaped a discursive strategy that nicely served the purposes of women writers who sought to express their erotic passions toward one another but did not recognize any connection between those passions and proscribed transgressions; though as the seventeenth century wore on, this disconnect became ever more difficult to maintain.

We can argue, then, that erotic behavior among respectable women was, until the coalescence of distinct hetero- and homosexual identities during the eighteenth century, carried on in ways similar to male homo-eroticism before about the 1650s. There was a "cleavage" between consciousness and behavior that allowed the individual and her society to evade recognizing possibly transgressive behaviors, unless like Behn, Cavendish, or Manley, she was willing to ignore the pressures to maintain a publicly chaste demeanor and to admit her sexual knowledge; later, in the eighteenth century, unnamed erotic and possibly transgressive behaviors were to be institutionalized and made acceptable in the convention of "female romantic friendship." Thus, the work and life of Katherine Philips furnished an example that made possible the expression as well as the acceptance of eroticized friendships between women as a respectable alternative to the specter of unnatural vice.

Fig. 5

Title page, Richard Brathwait, *The English Gentlewoman* (London, 1631). The title page from Brathwait's *The English Gentlewoman* illustrates the volume's topical divisions; *clockwise from top right,* they are Honour, Gentility, Fancy, Estimation, Decency, Complement, Behaviour, and Apparell. Friendship between women is notably absent.

CHAPTER IV

DOUBLING DISCOURSES
IN AN EROTICS OF
FEMALE FRIENDSHIP

e′clipsis. *Gram.*
[ad. Gr. ἔκλειψις, noun of action f. ἐκλειπειν to leave out; . . . perh.
Confused with *ellipsis*. . . .]
. . . An omission of words needful fully to express the sense. *Obs.*
1538 COVERDALE *Prol. N. T.*, The cause . . . is partly the figure called eclipsis.
1589 PUTTENHAM *Eng. Poesie* III. xii. (Arb.) 175 Eclipsis or the Figure of default.

—OED—

IN THIS CHAPTER, I demonstrate that as sexual acts between women
began to be identified as transgressive by public discourse in the vernacular, "respectable" women[1]—whose connections with one another might
today be read as "lesbian"—developed a second, more sexually evasive yet
erotically charged language of female friendship to describe female same-
sex intimacy. I characterize this language of female friendship and intimacy as a "double discourse" because its emergence parallels the publicly
disseminated discourse of overt transgression. It was the growing acknowledgment of female same-sex sexual behaviors in the public sphere
and the corresponding opprobrium directed at them that made this
double discourse possible, and necessary. Those women who were sheltered, privileged, and "respectable," and who were loath to see themselves
or to express their desires in ways considered transgressive, developed
more acceptable discursive strategies to contain or to deflect desires that
might otherwise have threatened to overwhelm them. This double discourse constitutes a poetic tradition that begins in the impulse to create
idealized female communities in the work of Katherine Philips and Aemilia Lanyer and culminates in the mid–eighteenth century with the impassioned poems of Mary Leapor.

In order to understand these different discourses, overt and covert, it is useful to place them in the context of the indeterminability of sexual definition recognized by much current thought and writing about same-sex female erotics. Annamarie Jagose in *Lesbian Utopics*, for example, describes "the fundamental uncertainty of the category 'lesbian'" and its "definitional intractability."[2] Martha Vicinus has commented that "definitional uncertainty is at the core of lesbian studies"; she describes as "lesbian-like" the murky passions of the Miss Pirie and Miss Scott of Lillian Faderman's *Scotch Verdict* and Lillian Hellman's *The Children's Hour*.[3] Terry Castle, in *The Apparitional Lesbian* (and also in her work on the historical legacy of Marie Antoinette), describes the "ghosting" of lesbian desire, that is, the representation of the lesbian and her desire through coded gesture and oblique reference.[4] These are only a few of the recent struggles to come to terms with the by now traditional critical oppositions between Adrienne Rich's assimilation of as many women as possible into a cultural feminist paradigm of "women-loving women" in a "lesbian continuum" and Catharine Stimpson's objection that lesbianism concerns sexual desire and that to diminish the power of sexuality between women reinforces the negation of female subjectivity.[5]

The obstacle of these definitional impasses has exacerbated the reluctance of critics and historians to confront the problems of female same-sex sexuality and eroticism in the period before 1800 in England, long before Freud, the sexological revolution, and the creation of modern sexual identities. This is seen in the persistence of a refusal even to acknowledge the possibilities for a historically early understanding of female same-sex erotic activity. However, the work of Valerie Traub, Katharine Park, Patricia Simons, myself, and others demonstrates that the isolation and description of certain behaviors (following classical precedent for their nomenclature) were used during the sixteenth and seventeenth centuries to identify and to stigmatize a distinct category of transgressive woman, albeit one often beyond the experience or knowledge of "respectable" women.[6]

By the mid–seventeenth century, public discourse about identifiably sexually transgressive women is presented with increasing ambiguity and self-consciousness and is increasingly relegated to two distinct categories of printed text. On the one hand, it appears in medical treatises, travel narratives, erotica, and other texts that could provoke and satisfy pruriently misogynist interests; on the other hand, it becomes evident in allusions by male writers and in literary works by women willing or able to be unconventional, as in the examples of Aphra Behn, Margaret Cavendish, and Delarivier Manley.[7] While descriptions and allusions by male literary figures provide a discourse that explicitly describes the nature of sexual activities of women with one another, the emergence of clear descriptions of same-sex erotic activity in writing by women is also striking at this historical moment. Yet this willingness to be transgressive apparently encouraged a more self-protective discourse in other female contemporaries, as well as in subsequent women writers, who wished to dissociate themselves from transgression.

In this fashion, women not willing to flout social mores developed an erotically charged yet shadowed language of female same-sex friendship, while other women not unwilling to be seen as flamboyantly overstepping the bounds of convention wrote in a more explicit language of sexuality. These more apparently conventional women sought the rewards of "respectable" social status—that is, marriage, family, economic security—at the same time that they gestured against conventional confinement. It was Katherine Philips who established the model of an eroticized female friendship that set a precedent and was emulated by the female poets and playwrights who followed her in the later seventeenth century. Philips's work established a tradition and a discourse for the expression of passions not otherwise given voice in nontransgressive ways. Yet although Philips's work was demonstrably produced by her own emotional and erotic impulses, it was grounded in a particular set of circumstances and a particular kind of discourse—a rhetoric that echoes the fervent emotionalism of male-male platonic friendship and the literary conventions of metaphysical (male-female) love poetry—that were conventional and acceptable in the homosocial culture of the mid–seventeenth century. The women writers who followed her were mindful that a path had been cleared for the expression of a passionate emotional attachment between women. The splitting off of an erotically charged yet shadowed language from an explicitly transgressive discourse created a space that pointed the way for the later development, in the mid–eighteenth century, of a socially acceptable language of female romantic friendship as the dominant discourse defining "virtuous" and "chaste" female friends.[8]

In short, then, a change in discourse about female same-sex eroticism in England in the mid–seventeenth century took place in rough coincidence with and following the Restoration. The language of literature and respectable society becomes more evasive as the existence of female same-sex transgressive behaviors is increasingly acknowledged by other dimensions of public discourse. With the approach of the eighteenth century, the definition of female same-sex relations and its expression in public discourse had become more narrowly focused on a specific set of forbidden sexual behaviors. This transgressive sexuality and its discursive articulation were increasingly circumscribed and split off from representations and understandings of the relations between "respectable" women. Those who were defined as transgressing were over time ever more conclusively ostracized, and in all likelihood relegated to a liminal existence in a subculture analogous to, though probably much less public than, that of London's male "mollies." But the acceptability of the discourses and behaviors of "respectable" women not so relegated is likely to have been unquestioned, and surely regarded as beyond reproach.

"Respectable" Intimacies and Erotic Ellipsis

Others have noted recently in connection with the definitional impasses encountered in reading lesbian texts that the very powerful role played by the unspoken or by the elliptical in literature by women cannot be underestimated in nineteenth- and twentieth-century lesbian studies. Karla Jay has remarked that "lesbian eroticism must often be read in the silent spaces in an otherwise heterosexual text. Often, it is the ellipses or breaks in the text that mark the feelings between women that cannot be spoken."[9] Jane Garrity points out that "the sign of lesbian presence is frequently . . . lodged in textual places that expressly demand that we become adept at multilayered readings."[10] Similarly, we need to be attentive to the possibilities of *erotic ellipsis* in order to understand the nuances of meaning that inhere in a powerfully charged poetry of friendship by "respectable" women writers of the mid– to late seventeenth century. The poets discussed here chose to write after the model of eroticized discourse established by Philips rather than make any connections between themselves and the synchronous and much more explicitly sexual references to female same-sex activities by Behn, Newcastle, or Manley. It is probable that they did not recognize any connections between their own emotional attachments and those identified by more explicit discourses of transgression; if they did recognize any connection, they would almost certainly have chosen to suppress such a recognition in the interests of social comfort and safety from ostracism.

"Erotic" in this early modern context, and as I use it here, describes that spectrum of sometimes diffuse but clearly sensuous feelings and intense emotions found in discourses of passionate engagement between women. While these feelings and emotions probably included a physical dimension, they would not necessarily have been genitally focused. By extension, in those instances in which they were genitally focused, they were not likely to have been defined or recognized as sexual, or as transgressive, because they would not have been modeled on valorized male penetrative action.[11] An *erotic ellipsis,* then, may be said to occur when these feelings and emotions are discursively expressed, but not explicitly acknowledged in connection with sexuality or with sexual transgression. An examination of the poetry of Ephelia, Lady Mary Chudleigh, Anne Finch, countess of Winchelsea, and Jane Barker, among others—writers who ignored the possibilities offered by the more explicitly sexual discourse of some of their contemporaries—illustrates the strong presence of passionate poems by women to one another in which such erotic ellipsis is apparent.

Women produced a body of writings to one another in a society that limited the range of literary subjects available to women who sought positive recognition from male peers and the maintenance of their reputations. The kinds of poems written by women to one another fall into several clearly definable categories that were approved by tradition: poems to a social superior, acknowledging or soliciting patronage; elegiac poems either to a woman friend or to a child who has died, the former admiring a life of strength, courage, and honor, the latter regretting a life too early taken; poems of friendship, either encomia to a beloved friend or invectives on disappointed affections; poems on woman's prescribed social role: virginity, marriage, female vanity, relations with men; poems on women writing or reading; and dedicatory poems written for other women's plays or poetry. Examples of these abound.[12] Respectable writing women also wrote many kinds of poems that did not entail address to one another or to another woman; however, because they could not utilize the perspectives of political scurrility and explicit sexuality,[13] they usually confined themselves to the genres of meditation, contemplative philosophy, pastoral dialogue, and courtly compliment. Of the kinds of poems written by women to one another, poems of friendship, which often also combined themes from the other categories, offered forms of expression through which an erotically charged poetry of intimacy could and did emerge.

The *consolidation* of possibilities for the production of a poetry of impassioned intimacy between women coincides with the broad social, demographic, and economic changes taking place throughout England, and especially in London, during this period. Following the civil war, the deposition, and the subsequent Restoration, the well-known permissiveness with respect to sexual matters of the post-1660 period becomes apparent; but in addition, a different understanding of sexuality and the body emerges with the confluence of a number of critical social changes in the fabric of English life. Among these were the professionalization of women's writing; the greater dissemination of texts in the vernacular, including medical, travel, and midwifery texts; and the increasing urgency of education and literacy for women. These changes in the production of knowledge existed alongside, and were intimately related to, the pressures of an increasingly populous London, the shifting of class structures to accommodate the development of a bourgeoisie and the rise of a middle class, and the development of ideologies associated with domesticity, including what has been called the "emergent ideology of married love."[14]

The growing professionalization of literature and the system of patronage for writers of the middling sort in the early seventeenth century were factors particularly relevant for women writers.[15] The new professionalization is perhaps first clearly recognizable in the unusual, and striking, number of dedicatory poems to women patrons written by Aemilia Lanyer for the prefatory matter of the 1611 edition of *Salve Deus Rex Judæorum:* she addresses ten women individually, including such eminent personages as the queen and the countesses dowager of Kent, Pembroke, and Cumberland, and concludes with a dedication "To the Vertuous Reader," who is clearly female: "I have written this small volume, or little booke, for the generall use of all vertuous Ladies and Gentlewomen of this kingdome."[16] Her stated intent is to hold up women for praise and to bring forth their virtues. As her editor Susanne Woods has noted, Lanyer, in reworking her biblical materials, also introduces "digressions focussing on women" that "interweave the story."[17] Lanyer's poetry flourishes in and for a community of women, composed both of patrons and peers, that nourishes and sustains her creative efforts.

It is this same impulse to community that was developed and extended by Katherine Philips's "Society of Friendship."[18] Because the discourse of female same-sex eroticism Philips created was outside the boundaries of contemporaneous sexual understandings, it was also safe from interpretations that would constrain her and those who pursued her model. From the often highly self-conscious tributes to Orinda by numerous women writers, we see a poetry of female intimacy taking shape—even becoming increasingly conventional—in the later seventeenth and early eighteenth centuries in a broad range of poems expressing a variety of intensely intimate emotions by, among others, Ephelia,[19] Lady Mary Chudleigh, Anne Finch, countess of Winchelsea, and Jane Barker. In what follows, I take up in a roughly chronological order the work of these writers as they develop a tradition of female affective intimacy, beginning with the anonymous Ephelia and moving through the women writers at the court of Mary of Modena.

Ephelia and Negotiations of Homage

The work of Ephelia is particularly illuminating with respect to the development of a tradition in which strategies of erotic ellipsis take shape: her anonymity and the absence of biographical information force us to avoid speculatively biographical readings, and she is likely to have been the youngest of the writers after Katherine Philips to have assimilated her poetic forms. In "To the Honoured *Eugenia*, commanding me to Write to Her," probably written to her patroness, Ephelia explicitly and with deliberation pays tribute to the discourse of intimate friendship and encomiastic gesture associated with Katherine Philips. She also acknowledges and intensifies the elements of Philips's discourse by calling attention to moments of silence, or the intrusions of erotic ellipsis.

Like Philips, Ephelia uses the device of pseudopastoral names both for herself and for her friends; her choice of identity as Ephelia is a clearly recognizable echo of Philips's assumption of the literary identity of Orinda: "Fair Excellence! such strange Commands you lay, / I neither dare Dispute, nor can Obey: / Had I the sweet *Orinda's* happy Strain, / Yet every Line would Sacriledge contain" (1–4).[20] The social disparity between the speaker and Eugenia is underlined at the outset to create the opportunity for an erotics that would narrow that breach: Eugenia is a "Fair Excellence!" who lays "strange Commands" to write to her that the speaker struggles to meet, acknowledging the thrill of embarrassment that accompanies her ambivalent need to submit ("Obey"), with its *frisson* of sadomasochism.[21] The following two lines suggest that, had she the poetic skills of Orinda, "every Line" would overflow the bounds of convention, "would Sacriledge contain." Further, the speaker's punning use of "contain" points to the operations of a shadowed eroticism, an erotic ellipsis, by suggesting the arrest or inhibition of the threatened "Sacriledge" at the same time as it is conveyed through speech; thus is "Sacriledge," quasi-religious transgression, rejected so that it can be invoked. The erotic charge carried by shadowed discourse here reveals itself explicitly as a threatened pressure against boundaries. Ephelia continues:

> Like to some awful Deity you sit,
> At once the Terrour and Delight of Wit:

> Your Soul appears in such a charming Dress
> As I admire, but never can express:
>
> .   .   .   .
>
> Pardon, dear Madam, these untuned Lays,
> That have Prophan'd what I design'd to Praise.
> Nor is't possible, but I so must do,
> All I can think falls so much short of you . . .
>
> (ll. 5–8, 27–30)

As does Philips in so many of the poems that established her reputation, Ephelia writes with the intense devotion and self-deprecation of one awed by and infatuated with the object of her poetic attentions. While this compliment to Eugenia is in some ways rather conventional, it is like so much of Philips's writing inflected with a more personal emotional cast.[22] The articulation of the inexpressibility of feeling suggests an intensity that of necessity remains latent and yet evokes the passionate submission not only of suppliant (male) lover toward (female) beloved, but also of subject toward ruler or religious suppliant toward deity ("Like to some awful Deity you sit"). These subject positions are all invoked and at play in these lines.

Ephelia also pays homage to Aphra Behn in an encomium "To Madam *Bhen* [*sic*]" in which she establishes her subject position as one of an agency that falls short of transgression. In this poem, she notes the power of emotion, especially of the admiration of one woman for another, to silence discursive expression: "Madam! permit a Muse, that has been long / Silent with wonder, now to find a Tongue: . . . / As in your Self, so in your Verses meet, / A rare connexion of Strong and Sweet: . . ." (ll. 1–2, 15–16). As in the poem to Eugenia, she has been tongue-tied with awe, though not with the intense submission she expresses there. Here, voicing her admiration for Behn, Ephelia describes her predecessor's poetic and erotic reputation as "A rare connexion of Strong and Sweet" and thereby characterizes Behn's transgressiveness as both complexly configured and attractive. Yet this moment of fascination with Behn's transgression is neatly coterminous with Ephelia's unwillingness to incorporate any similarly overt transgressiveness into her own work and her preference for the virtues of silence and ellipsis.

In "To a Proud Beauty," whose emotional trajectory echoes that in Philips's similar "On Rosania's Apostacy, and Lucasia's Friendship" and "*Injuria amici*,"[23] Ephelia's rage at another woman's scorn is not a simple jealousy in the competition for male attention; instead, the lines are choked by the speaker's conflicted and only semi-articulated passions. She passionately desires the approval of a woman who appears to reject her; she directs condemnation, contempt, and rage at the unresponsive object of her need; and she imagines herself successfully retaliating through the power of language. The underlying erotic charge here is indicated by the lack of proportion between the size of the emotions and the stated offense:

> Imperious Fool! think not because you're Fair,
> That you so much above my Converse are,
> What though the Gallants sing your Praises loud,
> And with false Plaudits make you vainly Proud?
> . . . .
> Know too, you stately piece of Vanity,
> That you are not Alone ador'd, for I
> Fantastickly might mince, and smile, as well
> As you, if Airy Praise my mind cou'd swell:
> . . . .
> Since then my Fame's as great as yours is, why
> Should you behold me with a loathing eye?
> If you at me cast a disdainful Eye,
> In biting Satyr I will Rage so high,
> Thunder shall pleasant be to what I'le write,
> And you shall Tremble at my very Sight. . . .
> (ll. 1–4, 13–16, 23–28)

The speaker's intense anguish and passionate longing vibrate in the interstices between the rage and invective that are her ineffectual gestures of lament for unrequited affection. Following closely in the emotional footsteps of Orinda, Ephelia enlarges on the strategy of erotic ellipsis by calling attention to the silences opened up, by what is in other words unspoken.

Women Writers and Female Community at Court

The court of Mary of Modena, second wife to the duke of York, later James II, was known for its cultivation of literature and the other arts, particularly for bringing Italian art and music to England in the 1670s and for elaborate court games, rituals, and performances, including performances of *Pompey* and *Horace*, Katherine Philips's translations from Corneille.

Mary's waiting women were surely familiar with Philips's poems as well, and with the writing of their French and Italian contemporaries. Adopting the language of Carroll Smith-Rosenberg's account of nineteenth-century American female homosocial culture, Carol Barash describes Mary of Modena's court as "a female world of love and ritual": "As Duchess of York [Mary of Modena] created a place where women's education and women's imagination were taken seriously, a world in many ways anticipating the Protestant academy Mary Astell later described in *A Serious Proposal To the Ladies* (1694)."[24] Among Mary of Modena's attendants there developed a marked intimacy focused on a shared commitment to their education and artistic development, as well as the shared pleasures of their creative projects.

These attendants included several writers whose work exemplifies the discourses of passionate engagement and affectivity between women that I have been examining here. Notable are Anne Killigrew (1660–1685), whose untimely death at the age of twenty-five must have been a potent reminder of Katherine Philips, and Anne Kingsmill, later Anne Finch, countess of Winchelsea (1661–1721).[25] Jane Barker (1652–1732) is likely to have been known at court; though she was not, like Killigrew and Finch, a maid of honor, the court played an important symbolic role in her creative imagination, as it had in Katherine Philips's immediately following the Restoration.[26] These writers were also committed royalists faithful to a Stuart succession and, for that reason, the varieties of a literary pastoralism of exile and retreat appealed to them in ways that evoke the escapism of Katherine Philips's idealized rural landscapes during the Interregnum.

We might also keep in mind that the court of Charles II, during the time that James and Mary of Modena occupied it as duke and duchess of York, was known for its libertinism. The court wits—of whom the best known was John Wilmot, earl of Rochester, renowned for his flagrantly open sexual escapades with both boys and women—had taken the literary place of the more lyrically inclined cavalier poets who had populated the literary milieu of the court before the Restoration. Mary of Modena's attendants and other educated women who were, like Barker, less immediately occupied at court were almost certainly privy to an atmosphere in which transgressively erotic liaisons and sexual infidelities were part of the fabric of daily life. In other words, it was impossible at court, or near court, during this time to remain naive or ignorant of the range of erotic and sexual behaviors known and discussed among one's peers. Women at court, then, including circles of female friendship and of women writers, were exposed to knowledge of a broad range of sexual behaviors that included tribadism and the vernacular vocabulary for tribades.

Women Writers at the Court of Mary of Modena: Anne Killigrew

Most interesting and perhaps most idiosyncratic among these writers is Anne Killigrew, whose slim volume of poems was published in 1686 not long after her death, edited by a male relative[27] and with a dedicatory poem by John Dryden, "To the Pious Memory of the Accomplisht Young LADY Mrs Anne Killigrew, Excellent in the two Sister-Arts of Poësie, and Painting. An ODE." In his encomium, Dryden compares Killigrew with Sappho:

> But if thy Præexisting Soul
> Was form'd, at first, with Myriads more,
> It did through all the Mighty Poets roul,
> Who *Greek* or *Latine* Laurels wore.
> And was that *Sappho* last, which once it was before.
> If so, then cease thy flight, O Heav'n-born Mind!
> Thou hast no Dross to purge from thy Rich Ore:
> Nor can thy Soul a fairer Mansion find,
> Than was the Beauteous Frame she left behind:
> Return, to fill or mend the Quire, of thy Celestial kind.
>
> (sig. a2–a2ᵛ)[28]

Dryden places Killigrew in a long tradition of classical poets, suggesting that her soul once animated Sappho. Though Dryden draws only on the poetic aspect of the Sapphic tradition,[29] it should be apparent that, by the late seventeenth century, a glance at the nature of Sappho's love for her companions was unavoidable in any invocation of her name, and Dryden is likely to have been including at least a gesture toward erotic friendship in his allusion. He goes on to compare Killigrew even more strongly with Orinda, whose fate she shared; he laments the "Murder" inflicted by "cruel Destiny":

> O double Sacriledge on things Divine,
> To rob the Relique, and deface the Shrine!
> But thus *Orinda* dy'd:
> Heav'n, by the same Disease, did both translate,
> As equal were their Souls, so equal was their Fate.
>
> (sig. bᵛ)

The additional comparison to Orinda using an image traditional in the language of friendship ("equal were their Souls") underlines the connections between Killigrew and the traditions of the friendship poetry of a female homosocial milieu from the classics to the very recent poetic past. This encomiastic move of comparison with both Sappho and Orinda was very soon to become a conventional trope in commending female poets.

Killigrew also seems to have seen herself as Orinda's spiritual and poetic legatee. She compares herself explicitly to Philips in "Upon the saying that my Verses were made by another":

> *Orinda,* (*Albions* and her Sexes Grace)
> Ow'd not her Glory to a Beauteous Face,
> It was her Radiant Soul that shon With-in,
> Which struck a Lustre through her Outward Skin;
> . . . .
> Nor did her Sex at all obstruct her Fame,
> But higher 'mong the Stars it fixt her Name;
> What she did write, not only all allow'd,
> But ev'ry Laurel, to her Laurel, bow'd!
>
> (sig. G3ᵛ)

In the context of this poem's assertion of Killigrew's passionate ambition for recognition, Orinda is an icon of female poetic achievement in a culture that emphasizes female physical desirability. Killigrew here constructs herself as a tragic figure denied her achievement by "Th' Envious Age"; she is the poet as *vates*, "Divinely Inspired and possest" by Phœbus, and a prophet willing to "accept Cassandras Fate, / To speak the Truth, although believ'd too late" (sig. G3ᵛ).[30] Barash points out that Killigrew's "battle with a personified Fame is an attempt to mediate between the opposing demands of heroic and prophetic discourses" in the more than half of her poems that develop her ambivalent desires for poetic glory.[31] In "A Pastoral Dialogue between Dorinda and Alexis," Killigrew again pays homage to Orinda: "Immortal Laurels and as lasting Praise, / Crown the Divine Dorinda's matchless Laies" (sig. C2). As we shall see, Killigrew's reference to Philips was not only iconic; she also adopted Orinda's ideals of friendship and the themes associated with ideal pastoral communities of women, though she often echoed them only to play against Philips's characteristic form and tone.

Among the thirty poems in the 1686 volume attributed to Killigrew is a range of occasional poems (e.g., "To the Queen," "On a young Lady whose Lord was Travelling") as well as several experimental poems on classical or mythological themes (e.g., "Penelope to Ulysses"). Apart from these, a large proportion of the poems address pastoral topics, many of them from a unique and unusually dark perspective. Two elements in particular are striking harbingers of Killigrew's more explicit entanglements with transgression in the three odes that conclude the volume: the thematic tensions between reason—that Augustan ideal standard of feeling—and passion that are a consistently central concern in many of her poems and her transvestite ventriloquizing of a male poetic voice through which to express these tensions.

A relatively uncomplicated example of Killigrew's ventriloquized male voice is "The Second Epigram. On Billinda," in which the speaker describes a love quarrel:

> Wanton Bellinda [*sic*] loudly does complain,
> I've chang'd my Love of late into disdain:
> Calls me unconstant, cause I now adore
> The chast Marcella, that lov'd her before.
> Sin or Dishonour, me as well may blame,
> That I repent, or do avoid a shame.
>
> (sig. C4–C4ᵛ)

This seems an exercise in the manner of Roman poetry, the male speaker condemning female unchastity and assuming an androcentric posture that classifies women according to the binaries "Wanton" or "chast"; having taken his pleasure, the speaker concedes "Sin or Dishonour," cynically admitting "That I repent, or do avoid a shame." "A Farewel To Worldly Joys," however, turns on a comparison between the situation of the unnamed male speaker and Ulysses' struggle with the Sirens. In this brief poem, the speaker abjures the follies of "Unsubstantial Joyes," the "Gilded Nothings, Gaudy Toyes" that too long "have my Soul misled":

> For when I hear such Sirens sing,
> Like Ithacas's fore-warned King,
> With prudent Resolution I
> Will so my Will and Fancy tye,
> That stronger to the Mast not he,
> Than I to Reason bound will be:
> And though your Witchcrafts strike my Ear,
> Unhurt, like him, your Charms I'll hear.
>
> (sig. D1ᵛ)

The tension between passion and reason that we see in so many of

Killigrew's poems is very clearly set forth here: Ulysses' struggle with the Sirens is the ideal vehicle for its expression. The speaker steels himself to counterpoise "Will and Fancy," the temptations of the Sirens, with "Reason" and "Resolution." One can only wonder at the identity of the Siren whose "Witchcrafts" and "Charms" the speaker wishes, unscathed, to hear. What could the young Killigrew have known of the self-discipline that enjoys yet avoids the pleasures and pains of seduction?

In "THE Complaint of a Lover," Killigrew again inhabits a male speaker grieving an unrequited love for his Rosalinda. At least we assume that the speaker is male because of the traditional posture of the lover and the conventional theme and pastoral setting of the poem. Yet this pastoral landscape is not a bucolic one, but is dark, dank, and depressing, characterized by the *absence* of shepherds, peasants, flocks, and birds; this landscape is an inverted reflection of the pastoral world with which we are familiar in classical poetry and in conventional laments for unrequited love by male Renaissance poets: "'Tis Barren as the Hopeless Flame, / That scortches my tormented Breast" (sig. D2). The speaker elaborates this barrenness in an underworld that functions as a perfectly Eliotesque objective correlative for grief:

> Deep underneath a Cave does lie,
>   Th'entrance hid with dismal Yew,
> Where Phebus never shew'd his Eye,
>   Or cheerful Day yet pierced through.
> In that dark Melancholy Cell,
>   (Retreate and Sollace to my Woe)
> Love, sad Dispair, and I, do dwell,
>   The Springs from whence my Griefs do flow.
>   (sig. D2–D2ᵛ)

The speaker sinks deeply into his lamentation in the Stygian gloom of this underground grotto, appropriately guarded by the yew, a graveyard symbol, and here a marker of the speaker's recognition of the death of a "Treacherous Love" that was like serpents beneath flowers, whose appearance betrayed reality:

> So Innocent those Charms then seem'd,
>   When Rosalinda first I spy'd
>
> · · · · · · · · · ·
>
> Beneath those sweets conceal'd lay,
>   To Love the cruel Foe, Disdain
>   (sig. D2ᵛ)

In the final stanzas of the poem, the speaker uses a fanciful metaphor of
self-comfort when he calls on the nymph Echo to help alleviate his
"Mighty Woe" by flattery or chiding; finally, he asks Echo, "My Passion
either sooth, or School" (sig. D3ᵛ). As in "A Farewel To Worldly Joys," the
speaker's primary concern, here evident in the strong finality of the concluding "or School" as the poem's last words, is with control of his passions, with the modulation of an extreme emotion that overwhelms rationality. The persistence with which Killigrew adopts a male persona in
one respect demonstrates her interest in the exploration of a literary device; but in another respect it demonstrates her desire to assume metaphorically toward women a male subject position whose nuances seem to
fascinate her.

"The Miseries of Man" is a long, ambitious poem in the contemplative
mode in which Killigrew surveys the grimness of human existence and the
travails humanity brings on itself. The subject here is not erotic passion,
and so the choice of speaker is female: Cloris—typically a shepherdess's
name—speaks to a nymph who "murmur[s] for her Woes" on a dark and
gloomy hill that frowns over Arcadia. Cloris's lamentations begin with an
address to death and a protracted description of the miseries of poverty,
sickness, and war. Cloris's speech makes a rhetorical turn when she
identifies man as the cause of his own miseries:

> But, Shame to Reason, thou art seen to be
> Unto thy self the fatall'st Enemy,
> Within thy Breast the Greatest Plagues to bear,
> First them to breed, and then to cherish there
> (sig. F4, ll. 152–55)

Human misery is thus wrought by the failure of reason in "Man": "Un-
manag'd Passions which the Reins have broke / Of Reason, and refuse to
bear its Yoke" (F4ᵛ, ll. 156–57). The poem concludes with Cloris urging
humanity to "rouse thy self as from a Sleep, / The long neglected Reins
let Reason keep," and, in a reformulation of the classic Aristotelian metaphor, she likens the relation of man and his passions to the horses and
driver of a chariot in which the passions/horses are controlled by rea-
son/the driver so that well-governed horses pull the chariot in a lawful
way. The last stanza is a passionate plea for self-discipline:

> The Charret mount, and use both Lash and Bit,
> Nobly resolve, and thou wilt firmly fit:
> Fierce Anger, boggling Fear, Pride prauncing still,
> Bounds-hating Hope, Desire which nought can fill,

Are stubborn all, but thou may'st give them Law;
Th' are hard-Mouth'd Horses, but they well can draw.
Lash on, and the well govern'd Charret drive,
Till thou a Victor at the Goal arrive,
Where the free Soul does all her burden leave,
And Joys commensurate to her self receive.

(G2ᵛ; ll. 218–27)

This poem resonates intimately with Killigrew's other poems that speak of the failure to govern passions and of the need for an almost violent governance ("use both Lash and Bit").

Killigrew's near-obsession with the control of unruly passions and with self-discipline is repeatedly reworked throughout her poems in a variety of pastoral and classically mythological settings, often with a grim urgency that suggests a personal investment rather than uncomplicated adherence to Augustan convention. "Penelope to Ulysses," for example, concludes with Penelope's elaboration of the conventional trope of fire for passion, so that Troy and Ulysses' sexual passions are mutually inflamed:

... [T]hou art captiv'd by some captive Dame,
Who, when thou fired'st Troy, did thee inflame
And now with her thou lead'st thy am'rous Life,
Forgetful, and despising of thy Wife.

(sig. L4–L4ᵛ)

Ulysses embodies the destructiveness of ungoverned passions both here and in "A Farewel To Worldly Joys." Whether Killigrew might not identify with him is an unavoidable, and unanswerable, question raised by these poems. Is Penelope in this poem her higher self urging discipline on her passionate, desiring (male) self?

In the second of two lengthy pastoral dialogues, both titled "A Pastoral Dialogue," an old shepherd Melibæus, a "Most Reverend Swaine," plays out Killigrew's repeated theme of reason and the control of passion as he sings of love to a group of young shepherds and shepherdesses. As Melibæus finishes the tale of Rodanthe and Alcander the "Fond Rover," whose moral is "Remember when you Love, from that same hour / Your Peace you put into your Lovers Power" (sig. K3, ll. 134–35), Alcimedon, one of the young shepherds, attacks and accuses him of being old and passionless and of discouraging women from loving men; but Melibæus responds that his precepts in support of rationality apply as well to men as to women, that is, in favor of a kind of equal opportunity gender restraint in love: "Young man, if my advice thou well hadst weigh'd, / Thou would'st have found, for either Sex 'twas made" (sig. K4, ll. 188–89). This last is an interesting and curious version of customary pastoral injunctions: Killigrew might be described as writing anti-pastorals both with respect to their often Stygian landscapes and their refusal of the comfortable platitudes of heterosexual love. Instead, her poems almost universally reject the possibilities of idyllic romance, offering in their place a bleak view of the destructive and overwhelming powers of passion, more often than not articulated through a ventriloquized male speaker.

As heir to Philips's poetic legacy, Killigrew reframes the pastoralism in which Philips had situated her female friends; she uses pastoral names and settings but emphasizes the inverted conventions of her own gloomily barren landscapes, the failures of human reason confronted with sexual passion, and the futility of erotic relations between men and women. Killigrew gestures toward the ideals of friendship on a number of occasions, but her stance in relation to these ideals is complex and ambivalent. "On a young Lady Whose Lord was Travelling" is a rather conventional statement that pays tribute to a woman's virtue—Celinda, almost certainly a pseudonym for a friend at court, is "At once a Noble Virgin, and a Wife"—and enjoins her husband to return to "Heaven at Home." The poet describes an idyll between mother and daughter during the husband's absence through the language of friendship: "They Smile, they Joy, together they do Pray, / You'd think two Bodies did One Soul obey" (sig. L2ᵛ). And again in "The Miseries of Man," when Cloris addresses Death, she uses the conventionally idealized language of friends:

> The Two, whom Friendship in dear Bands has ty'd,
> Thou dost with a remorseless hand devide;
> Friendship, the Cement, that does faster twine
> Two Souls, than that which Soul and Body joyn:
> Thousands have been, who their own Blood did spill,
> But never any yet his Friend did kill.
>
> (sig. F1ᵛ)

This allusion to the ideals of friendship to describe the intrusion of Death is a mark of Killigrew's unusual sensibility. While she incorporates Orinda's themes of friendship and pastoralism, she "tells it slant," to borrow a phrase from Emily Dickinson. But for Celinda's relation with her mother in "On a young Lady . . . ," Killigrew's relation to the ideals of friendship seems to be as negative and disillusioned as her view of love generally. In "The Discontent," as in "The Miseries of Man," Killigrew writes a lengthy contemplative poem in which she inveighs against Fame, "black Dispaire," Avarice, War, and other treacheries of life.[32] Stanza 5, immediately following a brief mention of David's soothing of Saul with his lyre, is devoted to a description of friendship as seduction, as full of false promise:

> But Friendship fain would yet it self defend,
>   And Mighty Things it does pretend,
> To be of this Sad Journey, Life, the Baite,
> The sweet Refection of our toylsome State.
>   But though True Friendship a Rich Cordial be,
>   Alas, by most 'tis so alay'd,
>   Its Good so mixt with Ill we see,
>   That Dross for Gold is often paid.
> And for one Grain of Friendship that is found,
> Falshood and Interest do the Mass compound,
> Or coldness, worse than Steel, the Loyal heart doth wound.
>   Love in no Two was ever yet the same,
>   No Happy Two ere felt an Equal Flame.
>
>   (sig. H4)

This jaundiced, one might say almost cynical, view of friendship is of a piece with her invective against the corruptions of humanity throughout this poem and in a large number of others. The last two lines of the stanza, by arguing for the inequality of love in friendship, deliberately invert the ideal of mutuality that was so cherished by Katherine Philips and male writers of the sixteenth and seventeenth centuries. We might conclude that this poem and others like it among her works are examples of youthful poetic experimentation in which Killigrew is assuming the posture and voice of worldly disillusion and disappointment, that she is choosing the role of gadfly or malcontent, which is of course possible. However, her stance is not one of fashionable ennui but of active distress; it militates in favor of her having chosen this posture, among others poetically available to her, because it suited her temperament and experience, and perhaps it suited as well her ambitions to compete with the satirical writing of some of her male contemporaries. The inappropriately "crude virility"[33] attributed to her surely was the result of more than one impulse. She was young, but not so young as not to have had sufficient experience of disappointment to rail at human frailties.

The three odes that conclude this small volume, and its most distinctive poems, confirm this point, gesturing as they do toward an experience that may have been transgressive and that perhaps overstepped the bounds of what was more acceptably idealized in the doubled discourses of so many other female poets. These odes are preceded by the anonymous editor's disclaimer that "Theſe Three following ODES being found among Mrs Killigrews Papers, I was willing to Print though none of hers."[34] Because there are numerous points of continuity and connection between these poems and the others in the collection, critics have tended either to accept them as Killigrew's on the basis of internal evidence—despite the editorial disclaimer and the absence of archival evidence that would confirm the attribution—or, in the case of Barash, to evade the issue of attribution altogether by focusing on the cultural production of the poems at the court of Mary of Modena.[35] My own view is to accept the poems as Killigrew's because of their thematic and discursive continuities with her other poems, because of their discovery among her papers, and because of the circumstances of their publication. It seems more likely that the editor's disclaimer is the result of the perhaps controversial subject matter of these poems than it is of their spurious authorship. A possibility not yet considered is that the editor, confronted with three Killigrew poems that he found embarrassing or discomfiting, resolved his dilemma by printing but disclaiming them, thereby ensuring their place among her written works while also protecting her reputation.

In these concluding poems, Killigrew develops further her use of an inverted pastoralism in which the traditional elements of the classical pastoral in its use after the Restoration in England are eroticized and turned topsy-turvy to suggest their opposites. As we have seen, Killigrew's pastoral landscapes and their trappings (e.g., the pseudoclassical names of shepherds and shepherdesses) do not conventionally offer escape and solace from the world of the court or from the larger world of human folly and viciousness; rather, her inverted pastoral world is a grim landscape from which to rail against human corruption. The pastoralism of these odes may be thought of as an armature that shapes her friendship themes and that reveals the underside of eroticism within a familiar but at times distorted and surreal landscape; this inverted pastoralism, in other words, acts as a vehicle for the shadowed language of erotic ellipsis.

The first of the three odes, "Cloris Charmes Dissolved by EUDORA" (sigs. M2–N), is a narrative addressed to Cloris as a "Clue" in which the speaker describes a journey through a presumably allegorical Dantesque, Stygian landscape that represents the hellish wanderings of betrayed lovers; the journey of despair is concluded only with the approach of Eudora to dispel the darkness of the grief presumably caused by Cloris's

"Wandring Fire." Killigrew makes no attempt to identify the sex of the speaker as she so clearly does when taking up a male posture; this suggests that the speaker is female and that Killigrew, having dissolved the distinction between herself and her poetic persona, is in all likelihood speaking autobiographically, as Ann Messenger has astutely suggested.[36] The speaker opens by declaring her conviction that Cloris is gone from her:

> Not that thy Fair Hand
> Should lead me from my deep Dispaire,
> Or thy Love, Cloris, End my Care,
> And back my Steps command
>
> (sig. M2)

The speaker wanders along "the Rocky Northern Shore," "Where on the Strand lye spread, / The Sculls of many Dead" (sig. M2ᵛ), and then moves on past a dark "Grove of Fatal Ewe" through which runs a brook whose flood "Poyson[s] the Creatures of the Wood." The landscape becomes increasingly macabre as the speaker passes "a Murderers Walk" and a place where "Witches . . . Nightly Dance." The speaker sees "a Shadow of a Man," perhaps an alter ego who expresses her grieving a beloved, "She is not; and she ne're will be," and calls for "Despair and Death [to] come swallow me" (sig. M4). The speaker finds solace only in "a Cave, / Dreadful as Hell, still as the Grave" that echoes the tumultuous passions she endures:

> This is the place I chose,
> Changeable like my Woes,
> Now calmly Sad,
> Then Raging Mad,
> As move my Bitter Throwes.
>
> (M4ᵛ)

At the nadir of her misery, when all seems joyless, Eudora appears as "A Form Divine and bright" and disperses the monsters and the "Terrors of the Cursed Wood"; she enjoins the speaker to send Cloris this "Clue" of the dissolution of the spell that has held her bound to grief and perhaps also to wish this "Phantastick Hell" on her. Like a (male) courtly lover, the speaker has been bewitched by the "Charmes" of Cloris and is released by the "Gentle Power" of another woman's love: "Dissolv'd is Cloris spell, / from whence thy Evils fell." Whether Eudora is actually a new beloved or merely a very powerful adviser and friend, the speaker describes her presence and intervention as evoking love and admiration. If the speaker is indeed a woman, as there seems no reason to doubt, the relation with Cloris is explicitly passionate and erotic in the tumultuous emotions it has unleashed, particularly in its parallels with the postures of courtly love. The emotional conflicts manifested in these poems describe the intensities of a complex erotic connection with another woman in which the tension between a more tender eroticism and the titillation of punishment drives the transgressiveness of Killigrew's emotional trajectory.[37] This tension is also the ground from which the erotic ellipses emerge: the presence of transgression is apparent but never named.

For Killigrew, transgression also inheres in the failure itself to contain passion. In this ode, she anatomizes the miserable consequences of having unleashed the erotic passions that she represents as successfully fended off by reason in her other poems. The connection between this and her other poems is one of obverse relations: here, the failure to contain passion by reason results in a transgression *within* the subject that severely disturbs her balance. Further, the passions expressed in this first ode echo the triangulated emotional expressions of Katherine Philips in poems like *"Injuria amici,"* in which her relations with Rosania have soured and are shortly to be replaced by Lucasia, and of Ephelia in the poems in which she evokes Orinda.

The second ode, "Upon a Little Lady Under the Discipline of an Excellent Person" (sig. N1ᵛ–N4ᵛ), opens with the narrative of a mock-epic tumult and turmoil among despairing Cupids in heaven that causes distress in the natural world and unease and darkness in the cosmos. The speaker asks, "what can that Sorrow be, / Disorders Heaven, and wounds a Deitie" (sig. N2), only to be answered by an angry Cupid whose spitefully loosed arrow returns to slay him. The tone is one of mockery and humor, deflating the high seriousness of epic confrontations in heaven. The "Scene from whence Loves grief arose, / And Heaven and Nature both did discompose" (sig. N2ᵛ) is one in which a young woman is dominated and disciplined by Eudora, an older and more powerful personage; stanza 3 concludes:

> A little Nymph whose Limbs divinely bright,
> Lay like a Body of Collected Light,
> But not to Love and Courtship so disclos'd,
> But to the Rigour of a Dame oppos'd,
> Who instant on the Faire with Words and Blows,
> Now chastens Error, and now Virtue shews.
>
> (sig. N3)

What ensues is a frequently ambiguous account of the speaker's coming to terms with Eudora's apparent cruelty as a disciplinarian and/or a reversion in Eudora's demeanor and carriage to her earlier kindness and generosity. An erotic "discipline" by an "other" now replaces the reason that controls passion in her other poems, and this "discipline" excites through suggestions of bodily containment and release. Ambiguity—the shadowed language of erotic ellipsis that serves to disguise and to complicate the communication of transgression—arises from a slippage in the reader's attempts to reconstruct the identity of the speaking voice at various points in the poem. In stanza 4, for example, the poet counterpoises Apollo, emblem of rationality, and Diana, virgin huntress, both gods associated with music and harmony, to the destructiveness of Eudora:

> . . .—But see!
> By Apollos Sacred Tree,
> By his ever Tuneful Lyre,
> And his bright Image the Eternal Fire,
> Eudoras she has done this Deed
> And made the World thus in its Darling bleed!
> I know the Cruel Dame
> Too well instructed by my Flame!
> In her Temple such is Diana's Grace!
> Behold her Lute upon the Pavement lies,
> When Beautie's wrong'd, no wonder Musick dies!
> (sig. N3–N3ᵛ)

If the speaker here, the "I," is presumed to be one of the Cupids that populates the opening of the poem, then the allegory of the ricochet of the Cupid's dart is clarified: "Too well instructed by my Flame," Eudora carries passion to the extremes of pain, cruelty, and blood, destroying the harmonies of love; the lute and lyre (traditional emblems of female sexuality as well as of harmony)[38] are set aside to be recalled at the poem's conclusion. Finally, Eudora's cruelty is attributed to her pride and arrogance, her self-deification. As the poem moves into its concluding stanza 6, in which there is a turn toward reconciliation and harmony, the poet seems to return as speaking persona: "While thus I did exclaime, / And wildly rage and blame . . . / The little Loves burn'd with [a] nobler fier / Each chang'd his wanton Bow, and took a Lyre" (sig. N4). As the heavenly Cupids seem to confer approval, the speaker reconsiders:

> I turn'd the little Nymph to view,
> She singing and did smiling shew;
> Eudora led a heav'nly strain,
> Her Angels voice did eccho it again!
> I then decreed no Sacriledge was wrought,
> But neerer Heav'n this Piece of Heaven was brought.
>
> (sig. N4–N4ᵛ)

The cause of this movement from darkness to light, and from the speaker's rage to understanding, is opaque, unexplained, yet it is clear that the speaker has not only come to terms with what appeared to be a transgressively erotic behavior but now finds it desirable. The last lines of the poem are unmistakable in their erotic suggestiveness:

> Eudora also shew'd as heretofore,
> When her soft Graces I did first adore.
> I saw, what one did Nobly Will,
> The other sweetly did fulfil;
> Their Actions all harmoniously did sute,
> And she had only tun'd the Lady like her Lute.
>
> (N4ᵛ)

A well-worn symbol for female sexuality in Elizabethan sonnets and courtly love poetry, the lute appears here in the familiar metaphor of tuning "the Lady like her Lute": Killigrew leaves no doubt about the nature of the actions taking place between Eudora and the Lady, who might be herself, or perhaps an alter ego through whom she recognizes her own desires. The poem tempts us to read it as an account of the poet/speaker's reconciliation with her own resistance to an erotics that seemed to her to be transgressive and painful. Instead, this erotics reveals itself as not only "no Sacriledge" but "sweetly" fulfilling. An apparently excessive passion is finally a sweetly satisfying affection. The pseudomythological, mock-epic, and sonneteering rhetorical devices used to structure the poem come together playfully in a shadowed language of erotic ellipsis to disguise the more serious nature of the poetic statement here. The poet has chosen a discourse full of ambiguity, one that invites multiple readings through its silences, to veil the transgressiveness of her narrative.

The third and final ode, "On the Soft and Gentle Motions of Eudora"—a mere twenty lines long as compared to the 130-odd lines of each of the previous odes—opens with the image of the lute that concludes the

last poem and elaborates a metaphor comparing the gentleness of Eudora's motions to music; the poet pays tribute to Eudora's exquisite movement: "How downie, how smooth, / Eudora doth Move, / How Silken
her Actions appear" (sig. O). The couplet that concludes the poem pays
Eudora the final compliment of describing her motions as surpassing music because they are "so soft, so Noyseless a Thing": "O This to express
from thy Hand must fall, / Then Musicks self, something more Musical"
(sig. O1ᵛ). Has the poet now taken the place of the little Lady of the second ode? One can only speculate. This poem, however, is a tribute to
the pleasure given by Eudora's motions, and we seem led to conclude,
given the context of this poem in following the two previous odes, that
the speaker now enjoys those erotic pleasures herself. Further, looking
back through the perspective of these last odes at other poems in which
Killigrew ventriloquizes a male speaker, we can begin to reread them with
more certainty as doubled discourses that cross-dress her desires.

Women Writers at the Court of Mary of Modena:
Anne Kingsmill Finch, Countess of Winchelsea

Both Anne Kingsmill Finch and Jane Barker, unlike Killigrew, lived sub-
stantially long adult lives marked by the complex changes at court and in
English culture through the end of the seventeenth century. Finch produced by far the most substantial body of poetic work, writing in almost
every form and style that was part of the contemporary repertoire. Anne
Kingsmill met and married Heneage Finch at court in 1684 and left the
service of Mary of Modena, but her husband remained as captain of the
halberdiers of the duke of York and gentleman of the bedchamber. Following the revolution of 1688 [39] and James II's exile, they underwent many
serious political and financial difficulties after Heneage Finch's rout from
court; they retired to their estates in Kent for many years, but returned to
London and the court of Queen Anne by 1708, after the restoration of the
Stuarts to the monarchy. Anne Finch was encouraged in her writing by
her husband and by the most prominent writers of her time, including
Jonathan Swift, Alexander Pope (who was many years her junior and with
whom she had an especially lively literary friendship), and Matthew
Prior. No doubt Finch's title, inherited in 1712, and family connections
among the nobility helped ease the progress of her literary achievements
and reputation. Unlike Jane Barker, whose background was less privileged, Finch was not seriously hampered and subsequently embittered by

the pressures that militated against female writing. She was, however, highly conscious of the public persona a female writer was constrained to present if she was to be successful, a lesson clearly conveyed by the opposed examples of Katherine Philips, exemplar of female chastity, and Aphra Behn, transgressing commoner.

While references to Philips occur frequently throughout Finch's poems, and there is an occasional reference to Sappho (including "Melinda on an Insipid Beauty: In imitation of a fragment of Sapho's"),[40] it is in "The Circuit of Appollo" that Finch articulates most fully and with considerable clarity and wit her relation to Behn and Philips. The poem uses mythological trappings as well as the pastoral pseudonyms popularized by Philips. She follows praise of Behn—who was no longer alive—with a negative gesture, making apparent her consciousness of Behn's transgressions. The poem opens with Apollo, Paris-like, seeking to encourage female poets by crowning the best, and then undercuts Behn's poetic superiority by alluding to her subject matter:

> He lamented for Behn o're that place of her birth,
> And said amongst Femens [*sic*] was not on the earth
> Her superior in fancy, in language, or witt,
> Yett own'd that a little too loosly she writt. . . .
> (92; ll. 11–14)

Finch's additional note on Behn's background and place of birth underlines the low origins associated with the "looseness" that mars her literary superiority, leaving little doubt that she intends to distance herself from Behn: "M ʳˢ Behn was Daughter to a Barber who liv'd formerly in Wye, a little market Town (now much decay'd) in Kent: though the account of her life before her Works pretends otherwise; some persons now alive Do testify upon their knowledge that to be her Original."[41] These remarks can be read as displaying a class snobbery that is in conflict with the expressed admiration of Behn's poetic gifts. The effect is one of balance . . . or perhaps of ambivalence. As Apollo continues his search for the best female poet, he encounters four candidates for his prize: Laura (Mary of Modena), Orinda (Katherine Philips), Valeria, and Ardelia (Finch herself), but having learned his lesson about the jealousies of women from Paris and the fall of Troy, he alters his plan:

> Since in Witt, or in Beauty, itt never was heard,
> One female cou'd yield t' have another preferr'd,
> He changed his dessign, and devided his praise,

And said that they all had a right to the Bay's,
And that t'were injustice, one brow to adorn,
With a wreath, which so fittly by each might be worn.

(94, ll. 60–65)

The poem thus concludes with the god's gracious and witty self-satisfaction at having found so nice a solution to his dilemma: the matter will be referred to the Muses on Parnassus for decision since no man in heaven or on earth would dare "loose three parts in four from amongst woman kind."[42] While Finch in this poem establishes a community and a tradition of female writers, presided over by Mary of Modena and with herself as heir to Behn and Philips, she also distances herself from Behn and further ruptures possibilities for erotic passion among the poets by assuming the masculine persona of an Apollo who wittily mediates their jealousies. Paradoxically, Finch here removes herself from the blemished reputation of those writers who would write "too loosly" at the same time that she metaphorically embraces a powerful, and male, subject position.

Finch's introduction to the 1713 edition of her poems picks up her concern with Behn's too "loose" writing and makes very clear the nature of her agenda with respect to a female erotics and her calculated intention to emulate the apparent reserve of Philips in sexual matters. While she finds it puzzling that writing of love should be scandalous, she acknowledges the need to use a more socially expedient, circumspect discourse. She says of her poems:

> For the subjects, I hope they are att least innofensive; tho' sometimes of Love; for keeping within those limmitts which I have observ'd, I know not why itt shou'd be more faulty, to treat of that passion, then of any other violent excursion, or transport of the mind. Tho' I must confesse, the great reservednesse of Mrs. Philips in this particular, and the prayses I have heard given her upon that account, together with my desire not to give scandal to the most severe, has often discourag'd me from making use of itt, and given me some regrett for what I had writt of that kind. . . .[43]

While distancing herself from those who might overstep the borders of propriety in their writing, and even noting "regrett for what I had writt of that kind," she expresses her doubts about the wisdom of censoring "Love": "I know not why itt shou'd be more faulty, to treat of that passion, then of any other violent excursion, or transport of the mind." Finch affirms a generous recognition of the role of the passions in human life, so that love is only one of many "transport(s) of the mind." The "Love" in question here is a male-female one since Orinda's same-sex erotics were considered "chaste," but Behn's were not because they crossed a boundary into recognizably transgressive same-sex sexual behaviors (e.g., "To the Fair Clarinda") that Finch was certainly aware of. Desiring praise, she follows Orinda's example of elliptical erotic expression rather than Behn's more outspoken descriptions. Like Orinda, she also makes frequent use of the conventions of pastoral and pseudopastoral names, though she does not employ these with the consistency observable in Philips's poems.

Finch wrote a number of poems in which her regard for her husband is passionately expressed and suggests a certain sexual contentment. Among these "A Letter to Dafnis April: 2D 1685" is most notable for the often-quoted statement that "They err, who say that husbands can't be lovers."[44] Among her other poems are also a number that describe her intense commitments to and enjoyment of intimacies with female friends and community. For example, in the dialogue "Friendship between *Ephelia* and *Ardelia*," Ephelia[45] presses Ardelia for a clear definition of friendship beyond her stated "'tis to love, as I love you" (l. 20). Finch gives us at once a witty comment on the limits of what can be spoken and an intense expression of passion between women for which the form of the pastoral dialogue is a convenient and deceptively conventional vehicle:

EPH[ELIA]. This indeed, though carried high;
This, though more than e're was done
Underneath the rolling sun,
This has all been said before.
Can Ardelia say no more?
ARD[ELIA]. Words indeed no more can show:
But 'tis to love, as I love you. (46, ll. 14–20)

Ephelia here scorns Ardelia's earlier description of the generosities of true friendship as a mere echo of traditional expressions of ideal friendship by male writers. The exchange in these closing lines of the poem goes on to delineate the inadequacies of language—"Words indeed no more can show"—and the inexpressibility of erotic emotion between women, which can be spoken only as a self-explanatory "*But 'tis to love, as I love you.*" Ardelia's love, which no language can articulate, which is greater than any words can compass, is itself the definition of love: it can only be silent in its inexpressible, unspeakable fullness. Ardelia's closing line, then, "*But 'tis to love, as I love you,*" states clearly the nature of erotic ellipsis and the unspeakability of certain affective attachments.

Finch's poems repeatedly convey a passion for her female intimates that would appear to have been not incompatible with sexual love for her husband. A poem in the Wellesley manuscript addressed to Ann Tufton, daughter of Lady Thanet and a much younger friend to Finch, illustrates Finch's playful projection of richly sensual feeling through the persona of a white mouse and provides a striking example of the shadowed language of female erotics. In "The white mouses petition to Lamira the Right Hon: ᵇˡᵉ the Lady Ann Tufton now Countess of Salisbury," Finch as the white mouse describes a fanciful seduction:

> I sue to wear Lamira's fetters
> And live the envy of my betters
> When I receive her soft caresses
> And creeping near her lovely tresses
> Their glossy brown from my reflection
> Shall gain more lustre and perfection
> And to her bosom if admitted
> My colour there will be so fitted
> That no distinction cou'd discover
> My station to a jealous Lover
>
> . . . .
>
> And if by a genteel behaviour
> 'Tis but my lot to gain her favour
> To her my life shall be devoted
>
> . . . .
>
> Where loss of freedom shall be owing
> To her whose chain my value raises
> And makes me merit all your praises.
>
> (Wellesley ms. 92–93) [46]

The description of "soft caresses" and "lovely tresses" invites an erotic appreciation of female beauty and moves toward a more intimately tactile connection when the white mouse declares its safety from a "jealous Lover" should he be admitted to her bosom. Read allegorically, this passage suggests that the speaker's (i.e., Finch's) "colour" (i.e., the whiteness of the white mouse against the white breast or even—taking this further into what might be a real-world situation in which a woman poet writes in the person of a mouse—her femaleness) would make her invisible as a competitor for erotic favors. The mouse speaks from the subject position of a courtly lover who longs for the pleasure of the "fetters" and the "loss of freedom" entailed by submission "To her whose chain my value raises."

But such a reading perhaps makes tortuous a simpler, more direct, imaginative leap on Finch's part: the poet projects her erotic appreciation for her friend and her desire for a "chaste" or "innocent" (again, the mouse is white) physical connection with her through the eyes of a charmingly smitten mouse of indeterminate sex. And so the poet is able to communicate her erotic attraction to Lamira and they can both safely enjoy their passions through this imaginative ploy. Ann Tufton appears again in "On the Death of the Queen," an elegy on the death of Mary of Modena. She is again Lamira and her relation to Finch is again intimate: she comforts the poet in a loss "that is at once both private and public, both personal and political."[47]

In yet another poem, "An Epistle: From Ardelia To Mrs. Randolph in answer to her Poem upon Her Verses," addressed to an obscure poet who has named Finch heir to Orinda's legacy in one of her poems, Finch returns to Sappho to assert that women "To Poetry renew our Ancient Claime." She thanks Randolph graciously for having "enhanc'd / My humble worth, and so, my fame advanc'd . . . / It stands inferiour only to your own." Finch, as Ardelia, then compares her relation to Randolph with Orinda's friendships, emphasizing both the literary and the personal aspects of their connection:

> And whilst Orinda's part you far transcend,
> I proudly bear that of her glorious Friend,
> Who though not equaling her lofty Witt,
> Th' occasion was, of what so well she writt.
> Might I the paralell yett more improve,
> And gain as high a Station in your Love,
> Then shou'd my Pen (directed by my heart)
> Make gratefull Nature, speak the words of Art,
> Since Friendship, like Devotion clears the mind,
> Where every thought, is heighten'd and refin'd.
>
> (96, ll. 31–40)

Finch gives Randolph the part of superior poet, surpassing even Orinda, while she herself is proud to take that of "her glorious Friend," the subject of her poems. But Finch seeks more from this connection, desiring to "gain as high a Station in your Love" as that held by Orinda's beloved friends. Here, Finch sees herself as the object of literary attention and a friendship "like Devotion," sacred as it was to Orinda. Poetry, then, makes "gratefull Nature" into art, formalizing feeling, as friendship, like devotion, transmutes, sacralizes, heightens, and refines it. Ardelia goes on to use a famous male friendship as a metaphor for the power of friendship to create art:

> Had Saul alone, upon Mount Gilboa fell,
> David had sung, but had not sung so well;
> Describ'd th' abandon'd Sheild, and broaken Bow,
> But, to the love of Jonathan we owe
> The Love, which that of Women did surpasse,
> Of that sweet Elegy, the mournfull grace;
> The Brother Jonathan, peirc'd deeper far
> Then all the Spears of that destructive war.
>
> (96, ll. 41–48)

Comparison with Philips's poetic strategies is instructive here. Whereas Philips had asked Jeremy Taylor a genteel question concerning female capacity for friendship and never presumed explicitly to compare any of her friendships with those of any traditionally idealized male couples, in the next generation Finch now boldly compares her own situation vis-à-vis a desired friendship with Randolph to the famous male friendship between David and Jonathan, a passion "which that of Women did surpasse." If we recall Abraham Cowley's *Davideis* at this point, Ardelia's comparison to the passionately erotic—if presumably disembodied—ideal of male friendship gathers considerable force as part of Philips's legacy. Cowley describes as follows the union of David and Jonathan in contrast to male-female relations:

> Never did *Marriage* such true *Union* find,
> Or mens desires with so glad violence bind;
> For there is still some tincture left of *Sin*,
> And still the *Sex* will needs be stealing in.
> Those joys are full of dross, and thicker farre,
> These, without matter, clear and liquid are.
> Such sacred *Love* does he'avens bright *Spirits* fill,
> Where *Love* is but to *Understand* and *Will*,
>
> . . . .
>
> There [in Heaven] now ye sit, and with mixt souls embrace,
> Gazing upon great *Loves* mysterious Face[48]

Thus Ardelia evokes not only Orinda's passionate friendships, but also the erotic power of Cowley's well-known unfinished epic poem and Orinda's implicit indebtedness to it and to the ideals it adumbrates.

Another of Finch's pastoral poems ironically reworks the friendship theme. In "A Pastoral Dialogue: Between Two Shepherdesses," Silvia attempts to persuade Dorinda to beguile the time with her in the woods, away from the shepherds who would woo her, but Dorinda will have none of this seduction to solitude by a woman and persists in looking after a variety of swains. Finally, the dialogue between the two shepherdesses is reduced to a competition in which Dorinda has the last word: "That Woman-kind's peculiar Joys / From past, or present Beauties rise" (147, ll. 79–80). Not only is ideal friendship not extolled, but female social vanity reigns supreme as Finch satirizes the hetero-erotic stresses placed on female intimacies. Immediately following these shepherdesses' dialogue, Finch assumes a male persona in "The Cautious Lovers." Here, as in a carpe diem, the suitor begs his beloved Silvia to follow him to a retired life away from the infidelities that surround them; but she responds with the tale of false Theseus and Ariadne, saying that she will be more cautious than to be "A flying Nymph." The assumption of a male poetic persona was a bold gesture for a woman writer conscious of overstepping the bounds of propriety, but, as we saw in the case of Killigrew, it evidently had become a permissible gesture in the generation following Katherine Philips. In both these poems, Finch toys with cynicism and plays with idealizing traditions, illustrating her wit and her sophistication about matters of the heart.

Finch's poetry is not only a tribute to the elliptical strategies she integrated into her work from the study of Katherine Philips. It also develops and refines those strategies into new areas, especially by assuming a greater variety of speaking positions and heightening the erotic intensity of the shadowed and elliptical language of female affective relations.

Women Writers at the Court of Mary of Modena: Jane Barker

Jane Barker (1652–1732) published a volume of fifty-three poems in 1688 as part 1 of *Poetical Recreations;* the second part is a series of poems "By several Gentlemen of the UNIVERSITIES, and others."[49] Part 1, the poems by Barker, is also introduced by a long series of commendatory poems by these same gentlemen so that the double volume often reads like a dialogue between Barker and her male admirers and in a fashion recalls the posthumous praise accorded Katherine Philips in the elaborate prefatory materials that introduced the 1667 edition of her poems. The comparison is no accident since Barker's male admirers indulge in profuse comparisons between Barker and Philips. The pseudonymous Philaster of St. John's College sets the tone in the first encomium:

> Soon as ſome envious *Angel*'s willing hand
> Snatch'd Great *Orinda* from our happy Land;
> The Great *Orinda*, whoſe *Seraphick* Pen
> Triumph'd o'er *Women*, and out-brav'd ev'n *Men:*
> Then our Male-*Poets* modeſtly thought fit,
> To claim the honour'd *Primacy* in *Wit;*
> But, lo, the *Heireſs* of that Ladies *Muſe,*
> Rivals their Merits, and their Sence out-do's;
> With ſwifter flights of fancy wings her *Verſe,*
> And nobler Greatneſs valiant Acts reherſe.
>
> . . . .
>
> A genuine ſweetneſs through her Verſes flow,
> And harmleſs Raptures, ſuch as Shepherds know;
>
> . . . .
>
> *Spencer*'s aſpiring fancy fills your Soul,
> Whilſt lawfull Raptures through your *Poems* rowl,
> Which always by your guidance do ſubmit,
> To th'curb of Judgment, and the bounds of Wit.
>
> (sig. A5–A5ᵛ)

This poem and the ones that follow do not merely compare Barker and Philips, but they specifically take up and repeatedly emphasize the chasteness that had been attributed to Orinda. Philaster underlines the comparison by repeating "harmless Raptures" and "lawfull Raptures," "Which always by your guidance do ſubmit, / To th' curb of Judgment, and the bounds of Wit." So it is not the comparison to Philips per se that is significant, but the likening of Barker's virtue to Orinda's. Again, E. C. Esq. writes:

> She cloaths her *Sence* in ſuch a modeſt *Style,*
> That her *chaſt Lines* no Reader can defile.
>
> . . . .
>
> Pure unmix't rays (juſt ſo *Ethereal* fire
> Will ſhine above the *Atmoſphere* of groſs deſire,)
> Brisk Ayrs, chaſt Sence, and moſt delighting Lays;
>
> (sig. a1ᵛ)

E. C. Esq. sees Barker's modesty and chastity defying the imagination of even the most lustfully inclined reader. Hers is an *"Ethereal* fire / . . . above the *Atmoſphere* of groſs deſire" and full of "chaſt Sence." Another pseudonymous friend, Fidelius, addresses the sixth and last commendatory poem "To the Incomparable Galæcia, On the Publication of her Poems" (sig. a2), clearly echoing the epithet so often used to describe Philips, "The Matchless Orinda." Several of the men writing these encomia also assume pastoral names in an apparent effort to re-create and to include themselves in a circle of friendship like that associated with Philips. In these commendatory poems, as in those to Orinda, it is the female writer's chastity and virtue that are emphasized and her ability to curb her passion into acceptable and often pastoral channels. As becomes evident throughout this volume, the pastoral form becomes for Barker a double discourse, a vehicle for the containment, even the sublimation, of erotic feeling.

These themes introduced in the commendatory section of volume 1 of the 1688 *Poetical Recreations* are picked up again in the second volume of poems by Barker's male Cambridge friends. Volume 2 is bound with the first volume: "MISCELLANEA: or the Second Part of Poetical Recreations. / Compos'd by ſeveral Authors." The conjunction of the usual comparisons with Behn and Philips and the mention of Barker's chastity are especially evident in "To Mrs. JANE BARKER, on her moſt Delightfull and Excellent *Romance* of SCIPINA, now in the Preſs. / *By* J. N. *Fellow of* St. John's Colledge *in* Cambridge": "Thy *Lines* may paſs ſevereſt *Virtue's Teſt,* / More than *Aſtræd's* ſoft, more than *Orinda's* chaſt" (sig. Cc8ᵛ). J. N. reveals himself as Philaster, in keeping with the pseudopastoral conventions of the Cambridge friends.

Compared with these elaborate emphases on Barker's chaste passion, encomia to Killigrew or Finch evoking Orinda and/or Sappho seem relatively perfunctory. We might ask why Barker should have elicited such commendations averring her chastity. Unlike Killigrew or Finch, she was not safely dead or comfortably married; as a "spinster," she was an anomalous social figure whose sexual virtue evidently needed to be repeatedly reconfirmed and extolled. We might speculate that her singleness at the advanced age of thirty-six when her poems were published occasioned some anxiety in a culture—both at court and more generally surrounding the court—marked by the not infrequently intemperate sexual behavior of its population. Barker addresses these issues directly in a number of her poems in which she asserts the virtues of singleness and in others in which she denigrates marriage and the infidelity of (presumably her) suitors.

The organization of the poems in her part of the volume is carefully established to lead the reader into a community and to address the gendered themes that most concern her. Because it is generally acknowledged that Barker's poetry is heavily autobiographical, I will assume that the first-person female speaker in all her poems is, for all intents and purposes, Barker herself.[50] The first poem is a response to the writers of the preceding encomia. "An Invitation to my Friends at Cambridge" describes a pastoral retreat from worldly pursuits that in many respects echoes Orinda's many poems on this theme. Like Philips, Barker solicits her friends' companionship in an idyllic rural landscape of "gentle Solitude and Innocence": "No avarice is here, but in the Bees, / Nor is Ambition found but in the Trees. / No Wantonness but in the frisking Lambs" (sig. B1ᵛ). The next three poems (i.e., "To Mr. HILL, on his Verses to the Dutchess of YORK, when she was at Cambridge," "To my Cousin Mr. E. F. on his Excellent PAINTING," and "To my Reverend Friend Mr. H——. on his Presenting me The Reasonableness of Christianity, and The History of King CHARLES the First, &c.") are gestures of appreciation and flattery to men whose attention she solicits. However, the next poem introduces the themes of single blessedness and her disdain for marriage that are to recur throughout the poems in this volume. "To Mr. G. P. my Adopted Brother; on the nigh approach of his Nuptials" begins by stating her consciousness of her own situation as a "Musty Maid" and then warns Mr. G. P. against marriage, which will ruin his capacities for good humor, wit, and friendship and make him "grave and dull, as standing Pond"(B6ᵛ): "let not Marriage thee in danger draw, / Unless thou'rt bit by Love's *Tarantula,* / A Frenzy which no Physick can reclaim" (sig. B6).

"A Virgin Life," which follows immediately after, creates in its affirmation of the joys of the single life a clearly demarcated space that legitimizes and rationalizes Barker's rejection of a sexual imperative enforced by the cumulative forces of social control. This poem addresses a problematics of marriage in which for perhaps the first time a woman writer voices her active resistance to hetero-erotic attachment. Barker confronts the issues attendant on her being a "Musty Maid" and offers a passionately felt defense of virginity. The poem opens with a comment on the pressures that cause women to internalize the language of disapprobation used by society to enforce strictures against female independence:

> Since, O ye Pow'rs, ye have bestow'd on me
> So great a kindness for Virginity,
> Suffer me not to fall into the Pow'rs

> Of Mens almost Omnipotent Amours;
> But in this happy Life let me remain,
> Fearless of Twenty five and all its train,
> Of slights or scorns, or being call'd Old Maid,
> Those Goblings which so many have betray'd . . .
>
> (sig. B6ᵛ)

This is a sophisticated analysis of the ways in which language ("being call'd Old Maid") serves as social control to propel women into marriage. She asks "O ye Pow'rs" for courage to ignore the arbitrary cultural constraints that betray women into unhappy unions under "the Pow'rs / Of Mens almost Omnipotent Amours." She concludes by connecting the virgin's contentment with the joys of religious commitment, intellectual pursuits, and friendship:

> Her Closet, where she do's much time bestow,
> Is both her Library and Chappel too,
> Where she enjoys society alone,
> I'th' Great Three-One—
> She drives her whole Lives business to these Ends,
> To serve her God, enjoy her Books and Friends.
>
> (sig. B7)

Her stated obligations "To serve her God" and an emphasis throughout the poem on the innocence, chastity, and piety of virgin life thus provide an impassioned rationale for female singleness.

The next poem, "*To My Friend* Exillus, *on his perſuading me to Marry Old* Damon," continues to address what I want to call the problematics of heterosexual attachment—marriage—and demonstrates Barker's unexpected imaginings of a heterosexual eroticism that she rejects. She struggles to subdue the erotic passions she believes would lead to an imprisonment in marriage. She pleads with her friend Exillus to desist from his confederacy with Old Damon because her heart is "without defence, / No Guard nor Art but its own innocence"; she moves from chastising her friend and her fears that her fortified innocence is not sufficient to protect her against collusion between friends and lovers, to an imagined acquiescence in a heterosexual erotics whose emotional and physical "Idolatry" or "homage" alarm her:

> Ah, why would'st thou assist my Enemy,
> Who was himself almost too strong for me?
> Thou with Idolatry mak'st me adore,

And homage do to the proud Conquerour.
Now round his Neck my willing Arms I'd twine,
And swear upon his Lips, My Dear, I'm thine,
But that his kindness then would grow, I fear,
Too weighty for my weak desert to bear.

(sig. B7^v)

The rest of the poem details the male jealousy and other miseries that would follow such acquiescence. Barker observes, "Not only He-friends innocent as thou [*Exillus*], / But he'll mistrust She-friends and Heav'n too." "She-friends" almost certainly refers to tribades or *fricatrices*,[51] and her phrasing suggests that any association between herself and this category of "She-friends" would be absurd. The poem concludes with descriptions of increasingly less-appetizing suitors and situations in which her revulsion at conjured images of male-female attachment is marked; she refers to prospective suitors as "some debauch'd pretender to lewd wit" or as some "covetous, conceited, unbred Citt [citizen]," and to herself as a "brave Horse . . . forc'd at last to tug a nasty Dray" (sig. B8). She is revolted at the notion of marriage, yet she articulates a desire she cannot accept in its socially approved form of marriage, or in its identifiably transgressive same-sex embodiment.

In contrast, the revulsion expressed in this poem is counterbalanced, or even perhaps augmented, by the emotions sketched in a number of other poems: disillusionments in love and failed attempts at heterosexual attachment, on the one hand, and rejections of a too youthful suitor, on the other. In these poems, the speaker expresses abiding sorrow, frustration, and anger at the loss of hetero-erotic possibility. For example, "*To Dr. R. S. my indifferent Lover, who complain'd of my Indifferency*" tells of a suitor whose primary interest is money: "Your Flames and Sighs only for Money were"; wiser in the ways of love, the speaker rejects the position of female beloved: "Yet there's a kindness in this false Amour, / It teaches me ne'er to be Mistress more" (sig. C). A number of other poems very strongly suggest an autobiographical connection by elaborating on a May–December infatuation,[52] by describing the speaker's distress in love, as in the jealous fears of betrayal expressed in "Parting with—" (sig. G5–G5^v), and by urging her lover to submit to duty and his father's disapproval of their attachment ("A SONG [Give o'er my Fidelius, my Fidelius give o'er]" (sig. G1^v). The tone in this last poem is one of an almost easy resignation in which pastoral elements operate to disguise and to distance any more intense emotions and at the same time to invoke the long tradition of patriarchal authority that presides over pastoral lovers.

The ambiguities of the subject positions assumed by the speakers Barker inhabits suggest an emotionally eroticized experience with several male friends and a familiarity with the passions of intimacy. Unlike her contemporaries Killigrew or Finch, in her published poems she does not hesitate explicitly to describe the sexual attachments with males that she rejects. Barker's stance is that of a realist confronted by the unpleasant facts of marriage and gendered social requirements, and she comments on these repeatedly.[53] Barker's courtship poems may well convey the personal unhappinesses—no doubt exacerbated by the difficulties of the monarchy and court—that caused her to follow Philips's example in turning to a pastoral escapism.[54] For Barker this escapism was more than figurative: eventually, she converted to Catholicism and was one of the forty thousand royalist supporters who followed the court into exile near Paris, at Saint-Germain-en-Laye, at the time of James II's flight to France during the revolution of 1688; she did not return to England until 1704.[55]

A sequence of three pastoral poems, along with the last poem in part 1, prepares for her removal to France and deploys conventional pastoral elements to disguise and to distance more painful emotions: *Poetical Recreations* was published shortly before she was to leave London in 1688. The pastoral sequence opens with "The Prospect of a LANDSKIP, Beginning with a GROVE" (C2ᵛ), characterized by its escapism and description of landscape very much in the tradition of Orinda with its allusions to political difficulties and a vehement contrast between court and country:[56]

> In some small Village, and adjacent Grove,
> At once your Friendship and your Wit improve;
> Free from those vile, opprobrious, foolish Names,
> Of Whig or Tory. . . .
>
> (sig. C4)

"Sitting by a Rivulet" and "A HILL" elaborate the idealized rural escapism in this poem while "Resolved never to Versifie more," the poem that concludes part 1—addressed to her friends the Cambridge men who wrote the introductory encomia and the poems in part 2—counterbalances the pastoral theme of solitude and contemplation already established by saying that she will write no more because "in this Town they [her verses] will not thrive." She comments cynically on the failure of urbanity in the city: "No more than Beauty, without Wealth, can move / . . . No more can Verse in London grow" (sig. H7ᵛ). There is a constant seesawing movement in these poems between a contemplative, innocent, and pastoral ideal that blunts grief and an angry, knowing rejection of court and city follies.

Barker's development of the traditions established by Philips focuses on the pastoral as a vehicle for escape from political distress. However, very much unlike Philips or her "virtuous" contemporaries in or near the court, she expresses familiarity with erotic desire yet denigrates marriage as an institution that is damaging to women. The strategy that makes this daring stance socially acceptable, and prevents her from joining the literary ranks of an Aphra Behn, is the refuge she takes in her virginal, and pious, singleness.

What, then, of Barker's use of the more obliquely veiled language of erotic ellipsis? Barker's expression differs from that of the other writers we have examined insofar as she makes much of her male friends and suitors in her volume of poems and does not scruple to write of her own attractions to men. But she also expresses deeply erotic feeling in unexpected contexts. A more shadowed erotic language can be located in the one poem she writes with passion for a female friend, in several poems to her brother, and in a section of her novel *A Patch-Work Screen for the Ladies*.

It is in "On the DEATH of my Dear Friend and Play-fellow, Mrs E. D. having Dream'd the night before I heard thereof, that I had lost a Pearl," that we read most clearly in Barker's poems an erotic ellipsis that concerns same-sex relations; for it is primarily in this poem and in her poems to and about her brother that Barker's voice breaks through the confines of poetic convention to speak in its most passionately intimate tone. Here, the speaker begins with a conventional statement of the traditional pieties about friendship (including the requisite uniting of two hearts in one) before moving on to a more impassioned account of sensuous pleasures between the two friends. In the lines that follow, Barker expresses a depth of sensuous pleasure that goes well beyond the more serene and contemplative pastoral descriptions in her other poems; the landscape is particular—"ye Wilsthorp-Fields"—rather than generally bucolic:

> We had no by-designs, nor hop'd to get
> Each by the other place amongst the great;
> Nor Riches hop'd, nor Poverty we fear'd,
> 'Twas Innocence in both, which both rever'd.

> Witness this truth ye Wilsthorp-Fields, where we
> So oft enjoyd a harmless Luxurie;
> Where we indulg'd our easie Appetites,
> With Pocket-Apples, Plumbs, and such delights.
> Then we contriv'd to spend the rest o'th' day,
> In making Chaplets, or at Check-stone play;
> When weary, we our selves supinely laid
> On Beds of Vi'lets under some cool shade,
> VVhere th' Sun in vain strove to dart through his Rays;
> Whilst Birds around us chanted forth their Lays;
> Ev'n those we had bereaved of their young,
> VVould greet us with a Querimonious Song.
>
> (sig. Cɪᵛ–C2)

The pastoral descriptions and encomia in other poems to her friends are pallid and generalized by comparison. Free of any ulterior motives—"We had no by-designs"—this friendship is innocent. Their enjoyment of "a harmless Luxurie" and indulgence in their "easie Appetites, / With Pocket-Apples, Plumbs, and such delights" suggests shared joy in the sensuousness of pure bodily pleasure, as does the statement that "When weary, we our selves supinely laid / On Beds of Vi'lets under some cool shade." The remaining third of the poem asks her muse to teach her to mourn and concludes, ". . . to my Muse and Me; / Fate shall give all that Fame can comprehend, / Ah poor repair for th' loss of such a Friend" (sig. C2).

Barker's intense emotionality toward her brother presents a different kind of erotic ellipsis but, like the lines on the death of Mrs. E. D., opens up a dimension of possibly transgressive feeling that can be expressed only through erotic ellipsis and the reworking of literary conventions to accommodate it.[57] "To my BROTHER, whilst he was in France" is something more than a conventional lament. She describes their walks and communion in a lush natural setting, but worries for his safety and deeply grieves his absence:

> Instead of this, and thy Philosophy,
> Nought but my own false Latin now I see;
> False Verse, or Lovers falsest of the three:
> Ev'n thoughts of formor [*sic*] happiness augment
> My Griefs, and are my present punishment;
>
> (sig. D7ᵛ–D8)

To describe his absence as her "present punishment" suggests a passion perhaps more than sisterly in the customary sense of that relation. "On the DEATH of my Brother," which follows immediately, confirms the impression of a passion that partakes of erotic undercurrents. She uses a language of sexuality in which sorrow is now her "faithfull'st Lover" to whom her thoughts of her brother are "only Pimps":

> Come Sorrow, come, embrace my yielding heart,
> For thou'rt alone, no Passion else a-part;
> Since of my Dear by Death I am bereft,
> Thou art the faithfull'st Lover I have left;
> And so much int'rest thou hast got in me,
> All thoughts of him prove only Pimps to thee:
> . . . .
> But hold, fond Grief, thou must forbear a while,
> Thy too too kind Caresses, which beguile
> Me of my Reason,—retire whilst I
> Repeat the Life, the Death, the Elogy,
> Of him my Soul ador'd with so much pride,
> As makes me slight all worldly things beside;
> Of him who did by his fraternal Love,
> More noble Passions in my Bosome move,
> Than e'er cou'd be infus'd by Cupid's Darts,
> Or any feign'd, adulterate, sordid Arts;
>
> (sig. D8–D8ᵛ)

Thoughts of her brother provoke erotic language and a comparison with other lovers who use "feign'd, adulterate, sordid Arts": "him who did by his fraternal Love, / More noble Passions in my Bosome move, / Than e'er cou'd be infus'd by Cupid's Darts." She continues to deify him, and to control her passions rather more sternly as the poem continues. But this opening invokes erotic metaphors only to refuse their taint, thereby suggesting her own struggle with passions she prefers to describe as "More noble" than those of her suitors. She pursues this theme in the long "On the same. A Pindarique ODE," whose opening stanza is arguably the most impassioned in all her poems. I quote this stanza in its entirety to illustrate the way Barker begins with a passionate outcry against the death of her love and then fits the intensity of her grief into the acceptably conventional parameters of friendship, in which comparisons with lustful male lovers nevertheless persist as an erotic undercurrent:

What have I now to hope or fear,
Since Death has taken all that's dear
In him, who was my joy, my love,
Who rais'd my Passion far above
What e're the blind God's shafts cou'd doe,
Or Nymph or Swain e'er knew:
For Friendship do's our Souls more gently move,
To a Love more lasting, noble, and more true,
Than dwells in all the Amorous Crew;
For Friendship's pure, holy, just,
Without canker, soil, or rust
Of Pride, Covetousness, or Lust;
It to Ambition makes no room,
Nor can it be by Int'rest overcome,
But always keeps its proper state,
I'th' midst of most injurious Fate;
Ev'n Death it self to 'ts Bonds can give no date.

(sig. E2)

In succeeding stanzas, Barker leaves behind the idea of purity to describe the relationship with her brother as one of lover-companions. The second and third stanzas serve to illustrate the intimacies she experiences:

But O Tyrant! [Death] thou
Canst at one blow
Destroy Fruition's happiness,
Wherein we Lovers place our bliss;
. . . .
Ah Death, thou wast severe,
Thus from me to tear,
The Hopes of all my future Happiness,
The Co-partner of my present Bliss,
The Alleviator of my Care,
The partaker of what ever Fate did share,
To me in my Life's progress;
If bad, he wou'd bear half at least,
Till the Storm was over-blown or ceas'd;
If good, he wou'd augment it to excess,
And no less joy for me than for himself express.

(sig. E2ᵛ–E3)

For Barker, then, this brother-sister intimacy, chaste though it may be, has the erotic affectivity of the greater intimacy of friends/lovers/companions whose lives are completely interwoven. His role is that of "*Co-partner* of [her] present *Bliss*" (my emphasis), a role arguably more than fraternal, yet one not explicitly named but shadowed by an allowable discourse of familial relations. Its erotics are silent, though present and communicated in the interstices between conventional discourse and the unconventional passions for which it serves as vehicle.

One is tempted to ask whether it is in fact the *permissibility* of love for one's female friend(s) and for one's brother that clears a space for the passionate expression of erotic feeling. Barker's erotic feeling for brother or female friend can remain situated within the boundaries of innocence and chastity because it is only within the confines of a heterosexual matrix that passion is recognized as sexual, that the presence of the male organ makes for "unchasteness."

A striking example of the way in which an unarticulated same-sex erotics ruptures the matrix of male-female relations and transgresses class boundaries occurs in the story of "The Unaccountable Wife," one of the inset-tales in Barker's 1723 novel *A Patch-Work Screen for the Ladies*.[58] This is the tale of a ménage à trois in which, at the husband's instigation, he and his wife for years share their bed with a female servant. When the husband tires of the arrangement and of supporting the illegitimate children that are its result, he banishes the servant and her children to her parish; at this, the wife follows the servant into the country, saying that she is her "only Friend," and spends her remaining days begging in the streets to support servant and children. As Kathryn King has pointed out, the narrator "apparently regards the wife's actions as proceeding from a species of desire so bizarre as to baffle understanding. She calls the wife an 'infatuated Creature' whose 'unaccountable' behavior inspires 'amazement.' The narrator returns again and again to her sense of bewildered amazement" and employs a "rhetoric of disapprobation."[59] The visible transgression here is that of class: a "respectable" woman of the middling sort who leaves the social and economic safety of her husband's home for the mean existence of a beggar is indeed "unaccountable" in indulging an infatuation that violates strenuously policed class norms. The invisible transgression here, though, is one that is barely below the surface of the text, constantly intruding and introducing unspoken questions. It is "there-not-there," as King observes. The wife is "unaccountable" also, and most importantly, because her "respectability" cannot be reconciled with the recognized categories of same-sex transgressive women, with tribades/*fricatrices*/rubsters/tommies. Barker's struggle not to acknowledge the correspondence between her portrait of the unaccountable wife and the behaviors of sexually transgressive women creates a subtext that repeatedly, yet invisibly, disrupts the main text. That Barker should have chosen to tell this story at all points to a need to disavow these desires. But the disavowal nevertheless brings to the surface the silently refused sexual transgression as a palpably unspoken presence.

In the context of Barker's poetry, the tale of "The Unaccountable Wife" underlines Barker's constant renegotiations of liminal desires through the use of discursive conventions that will serve to contain and render those desires acceptable, or at least "unaccountable"; that is, such desires are "there-not-there," not visibly transgressive in ways that would force either Barker or her readers to acknowledge them. Ellipsis then serves for Barker the powerful function of emphasizing the virtues of spiritual and familial bonds, in the case of brother or female friend, and the follies of class and economic recklessness, in the tale of the unaccountable wife—without ever acknowledging the ambiguity of passions that might drive them.

Toward Sapphic Intimacies in the Eighteenth Century

Lady Mary Chudleigh, in "To *Clorissa*" (1703), draws on the device of pseudopastoral names and echoes Philips's pastoral themes of a half-century earlier. The poem opens with an erotic statement both of the speaker's desire and of the seductiveness of her friend: Marissa seeks the comforts of Clorissa's "Bosom" as the site of a "sacred Friendship" invited by "ten thousand Charms." The joyfulness expressed by the lines that describe her "gentle Passion" and the "sacred Flames" that "dilate themselves" in every part of her being suggests a most welcome immersion in erotic feeling and the forging of an intense, quasi-religious ("sacred"), connection:

> To your lov'd Bosom pleas'd Marissa flies:
> That place where sacred Friendship gives a Right,
> And where ten thousand Charms invite.
>
> . . . .
>
> Next these Delights [60] Love claims the chiefest Part,
> That gentle Passion governs in my Heart:
> Its sacred Flames dilate themselves around,

And like pure Aether no Confinement know:
Where ever true Desert is found,
I pay my Love and Wonder too . . .
(ll. 1–3, 45–50)

In the concluding stanza, the speaker represents with exactness the terms of spiritual union and passionate attachment between women initially given voice by Katherine Philips. The speaker describes a kind of emotional fusion ("We'll live in one another's Breast") in which the lives of the "friends" are so commingled that they will find their perfect condition in an afterlife ("in each other there eternally delight"). Their union is characterized by sweetness, by tenderness, by a complete sharing and joining of interests ("be but one"):

O! let our Thoughts, our Interests be but one,
Our Griefs and Joys, be to each other known:
In all Concerns we'll have an equal share,
Enlarge each Pleasure, lessen ev'ry Care:
Thus, of a thousand Sweets possest,
We'll live in one another's Breast:
When present, talk the flying Hours away,
When absent, thus, our tender Thoughts convey:
And, when by the decrees of Fate
We're summon'd to a higher State,
We'll meet again in the blest Realms of Light,
And in each other there eternally delight.
(146–48, ll. 66–77)[61]

The terms used to describe this relation are neoplatonic and charged with an emotional intensity that suggests erotic as well as emotional attachment. The tone is erotic, if not sexual, the content sapphic.[62]

Conventional form was and continued to be of critical importance to expressions of same-sex passion, and women writers continued to seek models in their predecessors. Jane Brereton's "Epistle to Mrs Anne Griffiths. Written from London, in 1718" (but not published until 1744) explicitly articulates this deployment of conventional form. Having raged against the vanities of male critics and their censures of women writers, she reiterates the standard themes of women's writing, replicating (perhaps because she has internalized them) the judgments of those same misogynistic male critics. The burden of maintaining status as a "respectable" woman writer is apparent in the speaker's rejection of the sexually tainted female writers represented by Aphra Behn and Delarivier Manley. In evoking Orinda, the architect of respectability for later women poets, Brereton colludes with male authority in circumscribing acceptable possibilities for women's writing. The poem's disingenuous closing lines, however, demonstrate Brereton's mastery of a shadowed discourse. Disdaining the world's opinion and seeking only to "amuse" herself and "please" her "friend," the poet gestures toward an elliptically erotic subtext:

> Fair modesty was once our sex's pride,
> But some have thrown that bashful grace aside:
> The Behns, the Manleys, head this motley train,
> Politely lewd and wittily profane;
> Their wit, their fluent style (which all must own)
> Can never for their levity atone.
> But Heaven still, its goodness to denote,
> For every poison gives an antidote:
> First, our *Orinda*, spotless in her fame,
> As chaste in wit, rescued our sex from shame.
>
> . . . .
>
> For me, who never durst to more pretend
> Than to amuse myself, and please my friend;
> If she approves of my unskillful lays,
> I dread no critic, and desire no praise
>
> (ll. 18–27, 32–35)[63]

These poems represent only a sample of those written and a partial list of women writing them from the mid–seventeenth century through the first quarter of the eighteenth century. It should be evident from this survey that "respectable" women of the middling sort desiring to express their attachment, however eroticized, to other women gravitated to the shadowed discourse developed by Katherine Philips to articulate her intense passions for her friends.

This discourse of veiled eroticism, developed in response to a more public language of overt transgression, appears to culminate in the writing of the working-class poet Mary Leapor (1722–1746), where it points the way for the development of the discourse of female romantic friendship that was to follow shortly thereafter. In the last months of her life, Leapor was passionately attached to her "friend and mentor" Bridget Freemantle, who saw to it that her poems were published posthumously.[64] In the long "Essay on Friendship," addressed to Artemisia, Freemantle's pastoral pseudonym, Leapor echoes Philips and the writers who followed her example in elevating friendship to a "sacred" aspect of the soul: "'Tis not to *Cythera's* Reign nor *Cupid's* Fires, / But sacred Friendship that our Muse inspires" (I: sig. F5ᵛ). By juxtaposing the "Essay on Friendship" with "David's *Complaint,* ii Samuel, *chap.* 1," which precedes it, Leapor revisits the impulse that had compelled Katherine Philips to question Jeremy Taylor about friendship between women.[65] Leapor's "David's *Complaint . . . ,*" a passionate lament for Jonathan, takes up the traditional theme of male friendship in the impassioned soul-union of friends and the anguish of survival when one of the pair has died: "He was my Soul's best Pleasure while alive, / And is he blasted?—then do I survive?" (I: sig. F5).[66] But this then leads Leapor, as it had Philips, to the vexed question in the "Essay on Friendship" of whether women can have similar attachments: "The Wise will seldom credit all they hear, / Tho' saucy Wits shou'd tell them with a Sneer, / That Womens Friendships, like a certain Fly, / Are hatch'd i'th Morning and at Ev'ning die" (I: sig. F5ᵛ). In response to this denigration of women's higher capacities, the speaker's rhetorical strategy is to detail at length the virtues of moderation, so that "Celestial Friendship with its nicer Rules" becomes "the justly tempered Flame" that "Will glow incessant, and be still the same" (I: sig. F7). Yet, as in Lady Mary Chudleigh's "To *Clorissa,*" the connection between sacredness ("Celestial Friendship") and passion ("the . . . Flame") is the defining notion on which the poem turns. Finally, Leapor's answer to the scoffers at women's friendship is a description of perfect intimacy, now in its aspect of mutual comforting: "The Soul's Relief, with Grief or Cares opprest, / Is to disclose them to a faithful Breast" (I: sig. F8ᵛ).

In both "The Beauties of the Spring" (I: sigs. B8–C1ᵛ) and "*Colinetta*" (I: sig. C5ᵛ–C7ᵛ) Leapor creates female community. In the first of these poems, community emerges through escape to an idyllic sylvan setting with "a Friend" who evokes an erotic response from nature: "At Sight of thee the swelling Buds expand, / And op'ning Roses seem to court thy Hand. . . . / To thee, my Fair, the chearful Linnet sings" (I: sig. C1–C1ᵛ). The response attributed here to sylvan flora and fauna suggests that the speaker's own feelings toward her "friend" have been displaced, creating a palpably erotic ellipsis. In "*Colinetta,*" a dying old shepherdess lies in the lap of another shepherdess lamenting her passage from a beloved world. She creates a community of women by bequeathing her goods to the other shepherdesses and makes a point of never having envied the heterosexual conquests of other women: "When *Damon* wedded *Urs'la* of the Grange, / My Cheek with Envy ne'er was seen to change" (I: sig. C7). In both poems, female community is predicated on the absence of heterosexual concerns and on the sharing of an eroticized experience of nature.

"Silvia and the Bee" describes, in the language of the male lover to his female beloved, an erotic allegory in which the bee, "Soft humming round the fatal Bow'r" (I: sig. S8), provokes Silvia to destroy him. The last stanza is a fancifully erotic compliment to Silvia, who, having been described as the motive for her garden's burst of intensity, now is its most desirable ornament: "Believe me, not a Bud like thee / In this fair Garden blows; / Then blame no more the erring Bee, / Who took you for the Rose" (I: sig. T). This compliment is familiar as a heterosexual gesture. Ventriloquized by a female poet/speaker who is addressing another woman, it creates a wholly different erotic dynamic, fraught with all the covert sexual implications of bees and stinging. "Song to *Cloe*, playing on her Spinnet" (sig. I4ᵛ–I5ᵛ) is also highly eroticized, thick with "trembling Strings" and Cloe's orphic powers. In "Complaining *Daphne*. A Pastoral" (II: sig. F4ᵛ–F8), Leapor is even more explicit in conveying a sense of same-sex eroticism in contrast to a damaging heterosexual passion. The poem concludes with a sustained "feminine pastoral idyll":

> Her Care convey'd me to a Beechen Shade.
> There with her Hand she press'd my throbbing Head,
> And laid me panting on a flow'ry Bed;
> Then sat beside me in the friendly Bow'r;
> Long Tales she told, to kill the tedious Hour;
> Of lovely Maids to early Ruin led, . . .
> And still howe'er the mournful Tale began,
> She always ended—*Child, beware of Man.* . . .
> Ye Sylvan Sisters! come; ye gentle Dames,
> Whose tender Souls are spotless as your Names!
> Henceforth shall *Daphne* only live for you;
> Content—and bid the lordly Race Adieu;
> See the clear Streams in gentler Murmurs flow,
> And fresher Gales from od'rous Mountains blow.
>   (II: sig. F7–F8)

The unequivocal rejection of male-female relations here opens a space for the implicitly superior intimacies between women, as the narrated perils of heterosexual seduction titillate the present bucolic connection of "gentler Murmurs." In "The Disappointment," which immediately follows "Complaining *Daphne*" in the second volume (II: sigs. F8–G), Mira

(Leapor's poetic persona) recounts a rejection by a friend that in its bitterness emphasizes the intensity of Leapor's passion for women. Sophronia's seductively "consenting Smile" renders Mira nearly prostrate in a language usually reserved for male lovers: her eyes are "dazled"; her brains are "giddy"; her dreams are "golden." But having been disappointed by Sophronia's "imagin'd Favours," Mira lashes out to salve the wounds of her unrequited passion:

> When you, *Sophronia*, did my Sense beguile
> With your Half-promise, and consenting Smile;
> What Shadows swam before these dazled Eyes!
> Fans, Lace, and Ribbands, in bright Order rise:
> Methought these Limbs your silken Favours found,
>
> . . . .
>
> No longer *Mira*, but a shining Belle.
> Such Phantoms fill'd these giddy Brains of mine;
> Such golden Dreams on *Mira*'s Temples shine;
> Till stern Experience bid her Servant rise,
> And Disappointment rubb'd my drowsy Eyes.
> Do thou, *Sophronia*, now thy Arts give o'er,
> Thy little Arts; for *Mira*'s Thoughts no more
> Shall after your imagin'd Favours run,
> Your still-born Gifts, that ne'er behold the Sun.
>
> (II: sig. F8–F8ᵛ)

The suggestions of transgressive eroticism are palpable in Leapor's work, securely masked by the respectabilities of female friendship and the evasions of conventional literary form, often (as in the case of Katherine Philips) by the uses of pastoralism. Donna Landry has noted "the eroticism of Leapor's textuality"[67] in "An Hymn to the Morning" (I: sig. C4–C5) in which the female protagonist vies with the poetic and, presumably, with the erotic skills of Sappho. The shadowed language here is developed through the iconic use of the lyre, the instrument most closely associated with Sappho, and with Sappho's "song":

> Thus sung *Mira* to her Lyre,
> Till the idle Numbers tire:
> Ah! *Sappho* sweeter sings, I cry,
> And the spiteful Rocks reply,
> (Responsive to the jarring Strings)
> Sweeter—*Sappho* sweeter sings.
>
> (I: sig. C5)

Given the double tradition of Sappho's reputation in early modern England—as the world's preeminent female poet and as an example of prototypical female sexual transgression—it is difficult to avoid the conclusion that Mira, singing "to her Lyre," identifies herself directly with the ambiguities inherent in that tradition.

I have been describing the historical process through which an eroticized discourse of intimate relations evolved, most often in the guise of patronage or friendship poetry, among literate women; this discourse developed apart from the more explicitly sexualized discourses of male-authored and male-read anatomies, travel narratives, advice manuals, and so on, and from purposefully transgressive writing by women around the mid-seventeenth century and after. What we see—with Amelia Lanyer at the end of the sixteenth and opening of the seventeenth centuries and Mary Leapor in about the second quarter of the eighteenth century, historically flanking Katherine Philips on either side—is the shaping of a largely poetic discourse of female same-sex intimacy.[68] Distancing themselves, as they were bound to do, from increasingly explicit and more widely acknowledged discourses of transgression, in certain writers this intimacy became erotically charged and expressed an affectional intensity for which the women in question would have had no language of definition.

Fig. 6

Diana in costume for *Calisto,* in Eleanore Boswell, *The Restoration Court Stage (1660–1702)*
with a Particular Account of the Production of Calisto (1932). The elaborate costumes designed
especially for the production of John Crowne's *Calisto: or the Chaste Nimph* (1674/75) at the
court of Charles II are illustrated by this portrait of Diana as huntress.

~~~~~

CHAPTER V

CONFIGURATIONS OF DESIRE: THE TURN OF THE CENTURY AT COURT

TO SUMMARIZE my review of materials to this point: accounts of the behaviors of transgressive women in a variety of texts in the vernacular—travel narratives, anatomies, marital advice books, and other extraliterary texts—initially provided the language through which a female same-sex erotics entered verbal consciousness in early modern England. By the mid–seventeenth century, however, conscious understanding about female same-sex relations in England was sufficiently strong and widespread, and those behaviors were sufficiently denigrated, that discourse in English literature began to be inhibited. My survey of literature, especially poetry, by women as well as of extraliterary accounts of female sexuality confirms that such an inhibition took place among the middling or better sort of women and that a change in discourse, if not in behavior, concerning female sexuality occurred sometime in midcentury, around 1650. Women writers reshaped literary forms such as the pastoral poem and the utopian narrative to facilitate expressions of passion and to accommodate understandings of themselves that would not engage definitions of transgressive desire. The broad range of texts and writers I have surveyed illustrates that the languages of literature and of respectable society became increasingly evasive and even oblique as the existence of female same-sex sexuality was more openly acknowledged by other dimensions of public discourse in the vernacular. Respectable women of the middling sort, of the gentry, or of the aristocracy who did not identify themselves as transgressive developed a language and literary forms of indirection and of doubled discourses to describe desires that they would have been reluctant to acknowledge more explicitly and that might otherwise have situated them outside the margins of social acceptability. Further, any demarcations between friendship and female same-sex desire became increasingly vague, so that distinctions between intense or passionate friendship and erotic desire became indistinct and a friendship that might include erotic physicality would have been indistinguishable from one that did not.[1]

Previous chapters have demonstrated this historical trajectory of the discourses of female same-sex relations in sixteenth- and seventeenth-century England in representations of Sappho's tribadism in mostly male-authored texts, in the tradition of an eroticized poetry of female friendship initiated by the poems of Katherine Philips after the Restoration, and in the work of some few women—like Behn, Cavendish, and Manley—willing to write knowingly and transgressively without actually using the vocabulary of public denunciation. In this final chapter, I examine the implications for a female same-sex erotic discourse posed by early modern interpretations of the Ovidian myth about a cross-sex-disguised Jove who impregnates one of Diana's nymphs. I pursue the development of those implications in English and their culmination in *Calisto,* a masque by John Crowne presented at the court of Charles II, a production that was to be a harbinger of the complex erotic dynamics that later informed the court of Queen Anne and set an example for England at the turn of the eighteenth century. Insofar as *Calisto* presents us with a male-authored manipulation of female same-sex erotics in the last quarter of the seventeenth century, it represents a different development of the public discourse of tribadism and female same-sex sexual transgression that coexists alongside the evasively eroticized language of female friendship poetry by women that anticipated the language of "romantic friendship" in the later eighteenth century.

In 1674/75 John Crowne hastily wrote *Calisto: or the Chaste Nimph,* a version of the myth based on book 2 of Ovid's *Metamorphoses,* for a performance in which the then-adolescent princesses Mary and Anne took principal roles among an all-female cast of seven speaking roles and an additional five nymphs attending Diana.[2] This hastily written masquelike play became one of the most elaborately and frequently staged perform-ances of its time. A vehicle of considerable expense and even extraor-dinary display, it provided a rich resource for future theater historians. Eleanore Boswell, who has furnished extensive analysis and documenta-tion for the production, has called it "a magnificent extravagance" and re-marked on the hybridity of its form, which partakes of the pastorals that had been "dear to Henrietta Maria" as well as of the operatic scenarios that were later to become popular.[3] Yet Crowne himself denigrated the haste of his composition and regretted the sloppiness of his work. In his preface "To the Reader," Crowne has this to say about the composition of his *Calisto:*

> And as men who do things in haste, have commonly ill fortune, as well as ill conduct, I resolving to choose the first tolerable story I could meet with, unhappily encountered this, where, by my own rashness, and the malice of fortune, I involved myself, before I was aware, in a difficulty greater than the invention of the Philosopher's Stone, that only endeav-ours to extract gold out of the coursest metals, but I employed myself to draw one contrary out of another; to write a clean, decent, and inoffen-sive play on the story of a rape, so that I was engaged in this dilemma, ei-ther wholly to deviate from my story, and so my story would be no story, or by keeping to it, write what would be unfit for Princesses and Ladies to speak, and a Court to hear.[4]

Here Crowne draws attention to the connections between the haste of his composition and the inappropriateness of his choice of subject matter for performance by the young princesses: his chief anxiety, and it is not an un-founded one, is that this "first tolerable story" he meets with not prove an embarrassment to himself or to the sensibilities of the girls and women in the production.

It is an inappropriateness that was to continue to draw comment long after the time of Queen Anne. In their 1873 edition of Crowne's works, James Maidment and W. H. Logan remark on "the virtuous Evelyn['s]" description of the modesty and suitability of the play since "The fable is one not exactly adapted, it might be supposed, for a Royal Masque," though it might "nevertheless be quite adapted to the taste of most of the distinguished audience that witnessed its representation," made up, as it is bound to have been, of "the class of individuals who fluttered about Charles and his brother" and who were no doubt not "free from the taint of the period."[5] The obliqueness of this Victorian commentary—with the sexual innuendoes evoked by "individuals who *fluttered*"—points to the continued opprobrium associated not only with the court of Charles and the later rumors and speculations surrounding Queen Anne and her favorites, but also to the subject matter of the Calisto myth itself.

What was the nature of this "inappropriateness"? Was it merely this particular Jovian escapade in shape-shifting and rape that seemed so scandalous? In the original Ovidian tale, a cross-dressed Jupiter infiltrates the precincts of Diana's nymphs in pursuit of Calisto, the most recent addition to Diana's train. When he reveals himself to Calisto and she resists his advances, he rapes her. Later, Diana discovers Calisto's pregnancy during the bathing of the nymphs and angrily rejects her, forcing her into exile. In jealous revenge after the birth of her son Arcos, Juno transforms her into a Bear. Eventually, however, Jupiter transforms her again into the constellation Ursa Major and her son Arcos into Arcturus or Boötes. Crowne's alterations to the Ovidian myth are perhaps instructive: he adds a subplot with Mercury and a jealous nymph, Psecas, who colludes with Juno to get revenge on Calisto, and he provides Calisto with a companion, Nyphe, in place of her Ovidian son Arcos. Princess Mary played Calisto, while Princess Anne was Nyphe. Mercury was played by Sarah Jennings, maid of honor to the duchess of York, and eventually the powerful and clever duchess of Marlborough, possibly anticipated by her role here as a sly trickster god. In addition, Jupiter's rape of Calisto is obliterated from the action. These changes shift the balance and focus of the myth to accommodate heterosexual jealousies among Diana's nymphs, to place an increased emphasis on Juno's revenge and to create a less culpable Jupiter. Crowne's explanation of his choice of story seems disingenuous in light of these alterations:

> That which tempted me into so great a labyrinth, was the fair and beautiful image that stood at the portal, I mean the exact and perfect character of Chastity in the person of *Calisto,* which I thought a very proper character for the princess to represent; nor was I mistaken in my judgment, the difficulty lay in the other part of the story, to defend chastity was easy, the danger was in assaulting it; I was to storm it, but not to wound it. . . .[6]

A comparison between Crowne's theatrical version of the Calisto story and the contemporary sexual valences of female eroticism among Diana's nymphs in the Calisto myth makes clear, as we shall see, that the vaunted "inappropriateness" of the Ovidian narrative was located in the female same-sex ambiguities of its erotic dynamics. To rationalize his choice of story, Crowne reshapes Calisto by drawing on the part of the tradition that depicts her as an emblem of chastity. Crowne's version suppresses the rape but just barely suppresses the historical presence of same-sex erotic elements in the myth, while at the same time invoking them and encouraging their circulation in an audience that was well aware of the myth's complexly eroticized dynamics.

Calisto and Diana's Nymphs: Visual Representations

The female same-sex dynamics of the Calisto myth had a textual and visual currency in England from as early as the mid–sixteenth century in the availability of emblematic representations of Calisto with Diana's nymphs and in translations of and commentaries on Ovid's *Metamorphoses.* [7] The history of representations of this myth is instructive for our understanding of the ways in which Crowne manipulates its elements late in the seventeenth century. At least two early combined visual and textual representations of the myth clearly delineate tribadic activity and suggest a tradition of associations between female same-sex eroticism and Diana's nymphs and the myth of Calisto.

The first of the two illustrations considered here appears in Barthélemy Aneau's emblem book *Picta Poesis* (Lyons, 1564). Beneath the caption "Imitatio Captatrix" [Imitation, the Pursuer] is a woodcut depicting ten figures ranged in groups in a pastoral setting with trees, hills in the background, and a stream that runs from the middle- to the foreground (see figure 7). Toward the left of the frame and closest to the foreground is a partially clothed, disheveled-seeming couple engaged in erotic touching; both figures appear to be women and one has evidently hung her bow and quiver of arrows on the nearby tree while the other still keeps hers about her. The composition then causes the reader's eye to move farther into the center of the frame where a group of three women are standing in close proximity to one another so that the two outer, naked figures fondle the partially clothed body of the third who stands between them. To the right of this group, extending to the frame's border and on the same plane, another group of three women stand in the stream and gesture toward the central threesome. Further back along the tree line an additional two figures are barely discernible. Presumably the most prominent couple, the one on the left to whom our eye is drawn initially, is Calisto with Jupiter. But their frolics are not isolated; rather, they mirror the behavior of the nymphs in the center of the frame who appear to be erotically engaged with one another. Any sexual ambiguity in the engraving is to be found in this central trio of figures, who are arguably intended to represent the

Fig. 7

"Imitatio Captatrix," in Barthélemy Aneau, *Picta Poesis* (Lyons, 1564). This emblem illustrates
the rape of Calisto by Jove and its consequences. It depicts both the sexual ambiguity and the
transgressions that are integral to the myth transmitted by Ovid in the *Metamorphoses* and was
circulated in a book of emblems, apart from the Ovidian narrative.

two nymphs disrobing Calisto for Diana's better view of her pregnant
belly; but their gestures, instead of appearing to "manage" the central
figure, unambiguously depict an erotic touching among the nymphs. The
implication of the engraving, then, is that Diana's nymphs are erotically
intimate as part of their usual bathing activities (i.e., when they are at the
stream and disrobed). The poem below the engraving—the third part of
the tripartite emblem structure of caption, illustration, and poem—reads
as follows:

> SI QVIS foemineum tentat corrumpere sexum
>   Foemineos mores induat, ac habitus.
> Seposita grauitate viri, multitia sumat.
>   Imberbisque velut foemina, comptus eat.

Chromate tum fucus faciemque, manusque coloret,
  Pingat et adductam purpura rubra cutem.
Sic instructus, eam quam quaerit, vadat adortum
  Verbaque det mistis blandula delicijs.
Oscula mox iungat, nudos post oscula tactus.
  Caetera vis sine vi dißimulata dabit.
IVPPITER hac stuprum simulata Diana Calisto,
  CLAVDIVS vxori Caesaris, arte tulit.

(sig. B8)

[If someone is going to try to seduce the female sex,
  He should assume feminine character traits and habits.
First he needs to lay aside manly solemnity and put on soft, splendid
  [garments],
  And, beardless like a woman, go about all spruced up.
Then he should apply colored makeup to his face and hands
  And a ruddy purple garment to his wrinkled skin.
So informed, let him now go ahead and approach the woman he seeks,
  And offer charming words when joined with his darling.
Next he should join kisses, and after this caress her nakedness.
  Feigned force will deliver the rest without violence.
By this artifice, Jupiter pretended to be Diana and sexually violated Calisto;
  Claudius [did likewise] to the wife of Caesar.] [8]

This emblem, then, becomes advice to the male reader, offering him a strategy for gaining the sexual favors of a woman: pretend to be another woman and your advances will be accepted. The rape of Calisto is repressed, yet at the same time evoked, in order to emphasize the favor with which women, particularly Diana and her nymphs, regard erotic relations among themselves.

The second illustration, roughly contemporaneous with the first, appears in a 1565 Venetian edition of the *Metamorphoses* with commentaries by Raphael Volaterrani as well as other "most erudite men." It is significant that the Calisto myth is chosen for illustration in this elaborately annotated and important edition since only a very few of the myths are illustrated in this or any others of the early modern editions of the *Metamorphoses*. The choice to represent the myth of Jupiter and Calisto in the midst of Diana's nymphs suggests a marked interest in the visual representation of *this* myth and of *this* subject matter in preference to others. And so this choice almost certainly indicates a cultural interest in *depicting* and in *seeing* both the gendered ambiguities figured by a cross-dressed Jupiter with Calisto and the erotically charged touching among Diana's nymphs.

The elements that make up this second representation are quite similar to those in Aneau's emblem, though this woodcut is much more crudely executed (see figure 8). Again, our scene has a pastoral setting in the woods with a stream, but it is a more claustrophobic setting without an open background vista of hills and sky. Here, there is no attempt to create perspective either, so that the three groups of figures are all represented on the same plane, perhaps to suggest a temporal sequence of activity to be read from left to right. Jupiter-disguised and Calisto are shown embracing at the left of the frame; any doubt about their identities or any mistaking the figures for two embracing women—which is indeed what they appear to be—is erased by their identification in an inscription of both their names, Jupiter's beneath her/his figure, Calisto's on the skirt of her garment. To their right and in the center of the frame, two nymphs stand behind a third whom they touch, exposing her breast, as two more nude nymphs, immersed to the waist in a stream, gesture toward them from the right of the frame. A caption over the heads of the three central figures indicates to us that Calisto is the central figure and another caption beneath the figures in the stream tells us that one of them is Diana, an identification confirmed by the bow and arrow placed nearby on the shore. Reading the figures in this illustration from left to right as a temporal sequence presents a narrative in which Calisto is fondled by the two nymphs *after* her encounter with Jupiter. This narrative suggests at least two interpretive possibilities: the nymphs may be trying to hide Calisto's pregnant belly from Diana's view (one of the variant versions in translations of the myth), or, since the nymphs are standing behind Calisto and appear to be loosening her garments to explore her breasts, the nymphs may be attempting to expose Calisto's pregnant belly to Diana. In either case, the touching of the nymphs conveys an erotic charge that is in excess of any simply demonstrative gesture toward Calisto's belly for Diana's benefit.

In both these visual representations, Jupiter-disguised with Calisto in a sexual posture comprises one of two or more female groups shown engaged in erotic touching and apparent sexual pleasure. The ambiguities of the representations—that is, whether or not the central trio depicts the temporally later revelation of Calisto's heterosexual transgression to Diana—only serve to emphasize the association of the nymphs with female erotic intimacies. The multiplication of these visual statements would in-

Fig. 8

Calisto and the Nymphs of Diana, in Ovid, *Metamorphoseon Libri XV Raphaelis Regii . . .*
(Venice, 1565). This illustration of the rape of Calisto and the discovery and revelation of her
pregnancy appears in a well-known annotated edition of Ovid's *Metamorphoses* and sets forth
the sexual elements that continued to be associated with the myth. By permission of the
Folger Shakespeare Library.

dicate that there was a tradition of understanding female same-sex erotic
sports among Diana's nymphs, which no doubt accounts for Jupiter's un-
problematic ease in passing as a nymph and his success in gaining entry
into Diana's virgin inner circle. These representations confirm what later
literary versions also suggest: Diana's anger and subsequent punishment
of Calisto result not from the exposure of Calisto's erotic activity with
another seeming-woman but from the discovery that Calisto has had
heterosexual relations and is now suffering the pregnant consequence of
Jupiter's rape. In other words, the problem is not that there is erotic play
between two women but that the erotic play was between a male and a
female.

These combined literary and visual representations no doubt manifest
the same tradition of interpretation as the eroticized paintings and other
visual depictions of bathing women popular in Italy during this time.

Patricia Simons examines these representations as complex expressions of the erotic behaviors of *donna con donna*—woman with woman—through Italian art of the fifteenth and sixteenth centuries. Simons focuses especially on the complexity of myths of Diana and the folkloric traditions associated with her from pre-Christian times and into the early modern period. Diana's association with the moon and fecundity, with female community, and with the underworld was a classic tradition whose transmission complicates the iconography of the Christian cultures in which she appears as an emblem of chastity. Simons's exploration of representations of the myth of Diana and Acteon and clusters of bathing Dianic nymphs demonstrates the ways in which an "ostensibly . . . instructive tale about bridal purity and manly virtue . . . makes visible a counter-discourse about women's sensuality"[9] in which women appear to touch and fondle one another in an intimate fashion. Paintings and frescoes of Diana myths were produced by the best-known Italian Renaissance painters, including Paolo Veronese and Parmigianino, almost all of which include some display of nymphs in intimately physical contact. Of particular interest because it depicts the Calisto myth in an idiosyncratic way is Titian's well-known mid-sixteenth-century *Diana and Callisto* (1556–59), part of a Diana cycle that also portrays the Acteon story.[10] Here, a pregnant Calisto is brutally disrobed and held down by three nymphs for judgment and expulsion from the grove by an imperious Diana, nude and seated on a dais among admiring nymphs, two of whom appear to flirt with each other at the far right of the canvas. Titian's ungentle version of Calisto's dilemma underlines, as Simons points out, the double standard of the female need to be attractive to men and at the same time to retain chastity.[11] In this violent portrayal, an implicitly eroticized sadism obliquely suggests the female same-sex possibilities by now customarily embedded in the Calisto myth.

Calisto and Diana's Nymphs: Textual Representations

It is tempting to make connections between continental versions of the Calisto myth and English adaptations of these Ovidian materials, especially between English dramatic versions and the frequent Italian visual and operatic reinscriptions of the myth and of Diana and her bathing nymphs. While the English might not have had a direct knowledge of continental representations in the plastic or theatrical arts, they did have access to and were clearly familiar with moralized and reconfigured Ovidian myths in collections of fables and tales, with Ovidian texts and their Latin commentaries that were published in England, and with continental texts in Latin that would have been circulated in England. Among the many versions of the myth that would have been available in England is one that appears in the early- to mid-fifteenth-century manuscript by the Benedictine Thomas Walsingham, *De archana Deorum* [The Secrets of the Gods], which is in the tradition of the compendia of mythographers like Cartari or Ripa, and another in the considerably later Latin edition of *The Metamorphoses,* with commentaries by the Swiss Daniel Crispinus, published at Oxford in 1696.[12] The versions of the Calisto myth that appear in Walsingham's manuscript and in the Oxford Latin edition of *The Metamorphoses* would have been circulated alongside English versions of the tale that appear frequently in many editions during the course of two centuries; the Calisto story is first told in English in John Gower's popular *Confessio amantis* (ca. 1390 in manuscript, of which forty are extant; published by William Caxton in 1483) and appears as an insert-tale in William Caxton's translation of Raoul Lefèvre's *Recuyell of the Historyes of Troye* (ca. 1474), in William Warner's *Albion's England* (1586–89), and in W. N.'s *The Barley-Breake, or a Warning for Wantons* (1607); the "Englished" *Metamorphoses* by William Caxton (1480), Arthur Golding (1565), and George Sandys (1621–26), which are so much more familiar to modern readers, provide a fuller account of the myth and no doubt furnished the primary textual sources in English.[13] Thus, continental traditions associated with the Calisto myth, as well as with many others, would have made their way into England through the circulation of a variety of textual materials in Latin as well as in English. It is important to recognize as well, I believe, that the commentaries that circulated in the Latin Ovidian editions were not available to readers of the English editions and therefore furnish a significant dimension of the textual history of the myth that we overlook when we consider only the "Englished" editions.

For these reasons, the emblematic representations that we have examined in Aneau's and Volaterrani's texts help establish that an originary visual representation of same-sex erotics among Diana's nymphs (which had also appeared in the bathing nymphs of Italian paintings portraying Diana and Acteon as well as Diana and Calisto) was being disseminated textually on the Continent and became part of the tradition later circulated into England. It was this century-old habit of representation on the Continent, then, that was to emerge as one of the most spectacularly elaborate examples of late-seventeenth-century post-Restoration English court drama, in a cultural milieu in which familiarity with female same-sex eroticism was becoming increasingly common through other sources.

However, earlier in the seventeenth century, the dramatist Thomas Heywood's (1573/74–1641) several treatments of the Calisto story in poetry and for the stage demonstrate the currency of the Calisto myth as a representation of unambiguously erotic female same-sex relations in England before the Restoration. Heywood's first full-length recounting of the tale is in cantos 2 and 3 of his epic poem *Troia Britanica or, Great Britaines Troy* (1609).[14] In this vernacular treatment, the implications of a female same-sex eroticism associated with Diana's nymphs are rather explicitly developed. The distinguishing feature of Heywood's account is its (often misogynistic) humor, beginning with his elaborate description of Jupiter's donning of his nymph's disguise and his learning to walk and talk like a girl:

> . . . he makes speed to where the Virgins stay,
>   And by the way his womanish steps he tride,
>   And practis'd how to speake, to looke, to stride.
>
> To blush and to make honors (and if need)
> To pule and weepe at euery idle toy,
> As women vse. . . .
>   Of all effeminate trickes (if youle beleeue him,)
>   To practise teares and Sempstry did most greeue him.
>
> (45)

Diana's review of his qualifications for her train plays overtly on sexual ambiguity and particularly on female masculinity, which in this instance — unbeknownst to Diana — is masculine femininity:

> *Diana, Ihoue* in euery part surueyes,
> Who simpers by himselfe, and stands demurely,
> His youth, his face, his stature she doth praise,
> (A braue *virago* she suppos'd him surely)
> Were all my trayne of this large size (she saies)
> Within these Forrests we might dwell securely:
>   Mongst all, that stand or kneele vpon the grasse,
>   I spy not such another Manly Lasse.
>
> (47)

Diana privileges what she sees as female masculinity in the nymph we know is Jove. Though we know that it is Heywood who slyly privileges masculinity for his readers, these lines also play with Diana's admiring gaze at this "Manly Lasse" and evoke the tradition of eroticism among the nymphs. A few lines further on, Heywood lingers on the erotics of Jove's attempts to seduce Calisto, evoking the *frisson* of an apparent flirtation between women—one that includes the presence of a male organ, and so reinscribes the erotic tradition of Diana's nymphs:

> *Calisto* for his bed-fellow he chose:
> > With her all day he works, at night he lies,
> > Yet euery morne, the mayde, a Mayde doth rise.
>
> For if he glaunst but at a word or two
> Of Loue, or grew familiar (as Maydes vse)
> She frownes, or shakes the head (all will not doe)
> His amorous parley she doth quite refuse:
> Sometime by feeling touches he would woo;
> Sometime her necke and breast, and sometime chuse
> > Her lip to dally with: what hurt's in this?
> > Who would forbid a mayd, a Mayde to kisse?
>
> And then amidst this dalliance he would cheere her,
> And from her necke, decline vnto her shoulder,
> Next to her breast, and thence discending nearer
> Vnto the place, where he would haue bin boulder:
> He finds the froward Gyrle so chastly beare her,
> That the more hot he seem'd, she showed the colder,
> > And when he grew immodest, oft would say:
> > Now fie for shame, lay by this foolish play.
>
> > > (47–48)

Heywood glances at accepted physical contact between women, especially Diana's nymphs, by using parentheses: "Maydes vse" to be familiar but, unlike some others—"(all will not doe)"—Calisto "frownes, or shakes the head." The acceptability, or customary nature, of physical intimacy between women is again remarked in the question "Who would forbid a mayd, a Mayde to kisse?" Of course, there is no harm because no male organ is present between women. But Heywood uses this opportunity to describe a dalliance that goes just to the point of (presumably genital) transgression before Calisto's chaste rejection: "Next to her breast, and thence discending nearer / Vnto the place, where he would haue bin boulder." Thus, the descriptions of Jove's attempts to seduce Calisto as another woman are founded on the initial assumption that a *donna con donna* erotics among Diana's nymphs is acceptable. Jove's manipulations work on dual erotic levels: as the titillation of female same-sex flirtation with the additional irony of our sharing a sexual secret with Jupiter and Heywood at Diana and her nymphs' expense.

Somewhat later, perhaps around 1625, Heywood again reworked the Calisto myth in the first act of *The Escapes of Jupiter,* a play made up of scenes from his two earlier plays, *The Golden Age* and *The Silver Age* (1609–12).[15] In this version, Heywood dramatizes the action described in *Troia Britanica* so that Jupiter's cross-dressing enables a variety of explicitly sexual verbal ironies. Before Jupiter's entrance, Calisto's arrival among Diana's nymphs provides the opportunity for a colloquy that establishes the two-by-two pairings of the nymphs as bedfellows and companions:

> *Calisto,*
> All sensuall thouughts are Into vapour turnd
> To vanishe Into no thinnge, I am nowe
> Composed off finer temper late repur'd
> wth wch Loathd society off man
> Can Clame no more Alliance:
>
> *Diana,*
> Excellent virgin
> In this you' Indeere vs to you, and wee lyst you
> next to our selff in the ffyrst royall ffyle
> off princes and kinges doughters.:
> . . . .
>
> *Calisto,*
> these apprehensions drewe mee to yʳ servyce
> And I am nwe your hand-mayde.
>
> *Diana,*
> wheres atlanta,
>
> *A[t]llanta,*
> Heare madam:
>
> *Diana,*
> what princesse, that Can equall her in byrth
> Is sinngle and wthout a Cabin mate.
> To sleepe wth her

Atlanta,
none Lady that I knowe.
And all our Cupples are so sweetly matcht
and twin'd in love amongst vs theres scarce one
that Can bee [moved] woon to Chandg her bedffell<o

Diana,
Calisto then, as you are singular
you must bee single till another com
shee that is next admitted off our traine
must bee your bedd-companion, so tis' lotted—

(11–13)¹⁶

Calisto's move to join Diana's train is motivated by her rejection of male-female relations, of the "Loathd society off man": she has fled her father's court following the uncivil approach and abusive language of Jupiter sans disguise. The erotics among the nymphs is made obvious by Atlanta's commentary during the course of this discussion, in which it is made clear that the newly arrived Calisto must await a companion: "all our Cupples are so sweetly matcht / and twin'd in love amongst vs theres scarce one / that Can bee [moved] woon to Chandg her bedffell<o." Diana and her train are clearly imaged as "Cupples . . . sweetly matcht and twin'd in love," as erotically attached in delimited relationships in which they share their lives intimately each one with another and secondarily with the larger society of nymphs. Jupiter's arrival in disguise follows shortly after this, and his induction as a nymph includes this exchange with Diana:

Diana,
you shall vowe Chastity

Iupiter,
thats more then I dare promisse, (well proceede.)

Diana,
you never shall wth hated man attone,
but lye wth woman, or elce lodge alone.

. . . .

Diana,
All your societye shall bee with vestalls.
Enterd (as you) Into our sisterhoodd

Iupiter,
Itt shall:

Diana,
Consort wth them att boord and bedd
And sweare no man shall have your madenhead.

Iupiter,
By all the gods boath Earthy and devyne
Iff [I] eare I loo'st, a woman shall have mine.

Diana,
you nowe are ours; y'are welcom,

(14–15)

The last exchange here, in which Jupiter comments that a woman shall have his maidenhead, is not an aside. It is an explicit acknowledgment of female same-sex eroticism to which Diana responds positively. Her immediate response that "you nowe are ours; y'are welcom" leaves little doubt about which erotics define her company of nymphs at the same time that it prepares for the comic ironies of the heavy seduction scene between Jupiter and Calisto, and the rape that follows it. In that seduction scene, Heywood again exacerbates sexual tensions between the principals by elaborating the complications of cross-dressing, already familiar from their uses in pastoral narratives and in Elizabethan drama. The language of seduction used by the disguised Jupiter to entice Calisto creates a heavily eroticized dramatic discourse of same-sex sexuality that plays on the reader/audience's knowledge of the real male identity of the new nymph and on Calisto's innocent responses to the blandishments of another seeming-woman. As in the version of the myth in his epic poem, Heywood creates here a complex sexual dynamic to whose success a same-sex erotics is necessary, for it is the explicit acknowledgment of the possibilities for a same-sex erotics that alone makes possible and enables Jupiter's duplicities. Jupiter's scheme depends entirely on the acknowledgment of these possibilities and on the reader/audience's concurrence in their presence.

Heywood's treatments of the Calisto myth help us to affirm that a female same-sex erotics was an integral part of the Calisto story current in English before the Restoration and long before Crowne created his masque by sanitizing the less chaste representations of Diana and her nymphs for performance at court by the princesses. The more frank early representation of a female same-sex erotics by Heywood also reaffirms the larger pattern of inhibition in representations of female same-sex erotics after about midcentury, when knowledge of sexually transgressive women was becoming more widely disseminated through vernacular texts.

John Crowne's Calisto: *Sappho at Court*

Returning then to Crowne's treatment of the Calisto story, it becomes clear that his attempt to de-eroticize the relations between the nymphs by creating a heteronormative paradigm suited to performance by the young princesses hardly succeeds in erasing the historical presence of its same-sex erotic elements. Instead, it invokes them and encourages their circulation in the audience at court, most of whose members would so late in the century have been well aware of the complexly eroticized dynamics traditionally associated with the myth of Calisto. Crowne's play refers to contemporary female same-sex behaviors when *Calisto* makes a clear allusion to a recent episode at court in which Miss Hobart, who was "Mother of the Maids of Honour" to the duchess of York, left her post under a cloud of scandal when it was rumored that she had attempted to seduce one of the new maids of honor. The event is described retrospectively by Anthony Hamilton in 1713, in French, well before the death of Queen Anne; his 1714 English account reads:

> 'Twas not long before the Report, whether true or false, of this *Singularity*, spread through the whole Court, where *People* being yet so *unciviliz'd* as never to have heard of that *Refinement* in *Tenderness* of *ancient Greece*, some imagined, that the *illustrious H——t*, who was so fond of the *fair Sex*, was something more than she appear'd to be.[17]

Ros Ballaster observes that "the 'something more' that Miss Hobart commands is suspected to be a penis";[18] but given the contempt Hamilton expresses here for English ignorance in sexual matters, this ironic remark about "something more" is more likely to be a scathing reference to English credulousness, that is, the English know no better than to think that Miss Hobart is a man. The remark might even more profitably be read as a sly allusion to Miss Hobart's use of a dildo or other phallic supplement. This salacious, voyeuristic account, with its coy euphemisms and slighting comparison between the lack of sophistication at the English court and French understandings of erotic "*Refinement*," brings into perspective a culture that, when it is not ignorant of erotic "*Refinement*," now fears and rejects those suspected of "this *Singularity*," tribadism. Imputations of female same-sex relations are thus coming to be used as instruments of

Fig. 9

Miss Hobart discovered, in Anthony Hamilton, *Memoirs of the Count de Gramont: Containing the Amorous History of the English Court under the Reign of Charles II* (London, [1713,] 1889). This nineteenth-century engraving illustrates Hamilton's account of the disgrace at court of Miss Hobart, "Mother of the Maids of Honour" to the duchess of York, following the revelation of her presumably lustful proclivities for her own sex.

social control, to silence female same-sex expression and to enforce a sexual imperative that was gradually moving toward binary, heteronormative sexual identities.

The cross-dressed Jupiter in Crowne's masque is easily recognized as a stand-in for Miss Hobart. The scene in which Jupiter-as-Diana (performed by Lady Henrietta Wentworth) makes an attempt on Calisto's chastity, a scene that apparently *and actually* takes place between two women, "cannot but have had an ambiguous power to remind many of the absent and disgraced Hobart, and to poke fun in the crudest way at the outdated pretensions of 'Platonicks'"; the way Jupiter's lines in the following exchange "skirt around the nameless passion creates precisely that effect of titillation which one would have supposed Crowne anxious to avoid":[19]

> [Jupiter/Lady Wentworth]:
> Oh! Princess! it is I that pity need,
> Shall I the secret tell? your merits breed
> In my lost heart a strange uncommon flame:
> A kindness I both fear and blush to name;
> Nay, one for which no name I ever knew,
> The passion is to me so strange, so new.
>
> [Calisto/ Princess Mary]:
> My wond'ring thoughts you into mazes guide!
> And your dark meaning close in riddles hide.
>
> (act 2)[20]

Indeed, whether deliberately or not, Crowne draws attention to the "dark meaning" of "a strange uncommon [and nameless] flame," the love that, two centuries later, still "dare not speak its name." Despite Crowne's efforts to emphasize Calisto's chastity, to reframe the tale as a *failed* attempt on it, and to highlight other heterosexual motifs, *Calisto* by no means succeeds in evading allusions to the very transgressions it presumes to repress. The ambiguities and ambivalences of those allusions are distinctly different from the playful use made of cross-dressing and of female same-sex relations by Heywood before midcentury. We might speculate that the excessively extravagant production of *Calisto*—with its elaborately costumed masquers, richly varied musicians, dancers, and professional performers, and elegantly refurbished theater—served to draw attention away from the problematic and inappropriate issues raised by the audience's knowledge of recent scandals at court and of the erotic traditions associated with Diana and her nymphs.

The ambivalently acknowledged subtext of Crowne's play was to be a harbinger of the reign of Queen Anne and the relations with women that shadowed it. Already during the period in which Crowne's play was being performed, Anne was manifesting in her attachment to Frances Apsley the emotional (and presumably erotic) preferences for female companionship that were to remain constant throughout her life, and that existed in conjunction with what were to all appearances happy and satisfying relations with her husband, George of Denmark. Her performance, when she was only eleven years old, in Crowne's masque—with its barely contained erotic subtext—eerily anticipates the trajectory of her future reign and the not very well-concealed scandal of her passionate attachments to particular women favorites in her court.

The Case of Queen Anne's Court

From the time of her youthful participation in Crowne's *Calisto,* then, the future Queen Anne lived at court in the presence of a great variety of erotic expression. Not only had she participated in the most flamboyant post-Restoration theatrical production, but she grew up among the women who surrounded her father's wife, the duchess of York, the Catholic Mary of Modena, second wife to the future James II. It was a cultural milieu that also included the writings of women, like Behn and Cavendish, who transgressed conventional boundaries in depicting women's erotic relations and female sexual subjectivity.

Anne's first confidante was Lady Frances Apsley, somewhat older and originally friend to Princess Mary. Edward Gregg, in his biography of Queen Anne, remarks: "The passionate correspondence between Lady Mary (even after she became Princess of Orange) and Frances Apsley reflected the excesses of the romantic French novel then so popular among educated ladies."[21] Indeed, these rhetorical "excesses" must in many instances have exemplified the fashion of the French novel at court. However, a closer examination of the reverberations of these "excesses" points to their use as acceptable vehicles for more tangible erotic passions. The younger Lady Anne's correspondence with Frances Apsley, once their intimacy had superseded that of Lady Mary and Frances, was one in which Anne assumed the role of Ziphares, a man who longs for a glimpse of his "faire Semandra." Years later, Queen Anne was to correspond in a similarly passionate way, as Mrs Morley and Mrs Freeman, with the woman who was to be her lifelong confidante and companion, Sarah Jennings, the future Sarah Jennings Churchill, duchess of Marlborough (1660–1744).

Gregg's comments on these impassioned correspondences are worth reading in detail:

> Too much can be—and perhaps has been—read into the adolescent ro-
> manticism and subconscious sexuality revealed by these letters, particu-
> larly in the light of Lady Anne's later close association with the future
> Duchess of Marlborough. To some extent, the later "Mrs Morley" and
> "Mrs Freeman" correspondence between the queen and the duchess was
> a repetition of the teen-aged Lady Anne's correspondence with Frances
> Apsley, a search for a fantasy world in which Lady Anne could shed her
> exalted rank and correspond with "faire Semandra" as an equal. More im-
> portantly, Lady Anne's choice of the male role in the friendship . . . sug-
> gests that Lady Anne intended to be the dominant partner in the friend-
> ship. Indeed, as we shall see, this intention became an automatic
> assumption in every close relationship which Lady Anne was to develop
> in later life.[22]

Gregg concedes here, even if dismissively, the nature of Anne's relationships both with Apsley and with Sarah Jennings Churchill. The "adoles-
cent romanticism and subconscious sexuality" were certainly not out-
grown by Anne, who maintained her passionate regard for the duchess of
Marlborough until the end of her life, though she eventually banished
Churchill from her presence for primarily political reasons. Was the sexuality "subconscious"? It could not have been in an era in which a "subconscious" had not yet been thought of, any more than were modern notions of sexuality. But we can say that the possibilities for an active
eroticism were surely motivating desires in these relationships. It is perhaps too easy to dismiss Anne's passionate writing as "a search for a fantasy world in which [she] could shed her exalted rank" since other rhetorical devices might have served that purpose as well. The isolation of
successors to the throne, the hothouse atmosphere of politics and intrigue
at court, the fear of relations with others, the conniving for position, in
combination with her temperament—her "bashfulness" and "personal reserve" and her "taciturn" demeanor in conversations[23]—would have made
the young Princess Anne particularly vulnerable to intense and passionate attachments that were more than airy fantasies. The availability of the
examples of Katherine Philips and her successors was no doubt enhanced
by the increased daring of the female literary assumption of masculinity
that we have noted in Cavendish and Behn, so that Princess, later Queen,
Anne had a channel for the articulation of her charged emotions, whatever embodiment they might have sought.

Princess Anne's marriage in 1683 to George of Denmark, a second cousin once removed, was accompanied by reassurances to Frances Apsley that even though "your Ziphares [Anne] . . . changes his condition yet nothing shall ever alter him from being ye same to his deare Semandra [Frances] that he ever was."[24] It is difficult not to see in these reassurances, in Lady Anne's acknowledgment of the rivalrous connection between "friendship" and marriage, an admission of the intensely erotic nature of her attachment to Apsley. This acknowledgment also recalls the passionate disappointment at the rivalry between marriage and friendship expressed by Katherine Philips to Sir Charles Cotterell after Anne Owen's marriage: "I find too there are few Friendships in the World Marriage-proof. . . . We may generally conclude the Marriage of a Friend to be the Funeral of a Friendship" (Letter 13).[25] But some twenty years after Philips wrote to Sir Charles of her bitter disappointment, Princess Anne configures her relations with Frances Apsley in terms of gender roles, herself assuming the posture of (male) lover, a possibility not available to earlier female friends. Protected by the status accorded her by her place in the succession, Anne did not scruple to express her passion for Apsley through a female masculinity.

It was at this time just before her marriage that Princess Anne was trying to ensure that Sarah Jennings Churchill would join her household. Princess Anne was five and Sarah Jennings ten when they first met in 1670 or 1671. Sarah Jennings began to live at court in 1673 as a maid of honor to the duchess of York (Mary of Modena) and appeared with the princesses in the production of *Calisto;* but the friendship "which would influence the destiny of Europe"[26] did not flourish until about 1683, when she took up service with Princess Anne, having married John Churchill in 1677 or 1678. The age difference between the two women was likely to have been fertile soil for an infatuation by the younger girl, an intense admiration perhaps, that if she were of the right temperament—as indeed she proved to be—Sarah Jennings would have known how to cultivate to her own advantage.

The difficulties of the years preceding Anne's accession to the throne in 1702 were the result, first, of Anne and Mary's Protestant opposition to the Catholic reign of their father James II,[27] who took the throne for the four brief years between 1685 and 1689. Second, they were the result of the constant maneuvering for position between the two royal sisters in the fragile alliance in which they conspired against their father to invade England, until James II fled the country and thereby appeared to abdicate the throne. Anne played an extraordinarily duplicitous game in which she betrayed her father and then, when it became clear that her cause to gain the throne was hopeless, in an unprecedented gesture abdicated her hereditary rights in favor of her brother-in-law William of Orange and her sister Mary. As her principal advisers, the Churchills were an integral part of Anne's maneuverings; they continued as her intimates and as both architects and executors of her plans during this period, through her falling-out with the Oranges, and well into her own reign. James II, before his departure from the throne, described clearly his younger daughter's attachment to Sarah Jennings Churchill, duchess of Marlborough, as *"une passion démésurée"* [28]—an immoderate or excessive passion. These words leave little doubt that he recognized their relationship as having overstepped the bounds of acceptable intimacy in friendship; he rightly feared the political consequences of the duchess's influence. James II's characterization of the relationship between Anne and the duchess as a *passion démésurée* underscores the political dimensions of the erotic dynamics between the two women and the layered complexities of their interactions. These were to continue for many years and, by 1692, they had caused relations between Princess Anne and now-Queen Mary to deteriorate into total hostility when Anne refused to acquiesce to her sister's, the queen's, demand that she dismiss the duchess of Marlborough.

By 1709, however, Queen Anne's affections had shifted to Abigail Masham, a woman of the bedchamber not nobly born,[29] and Sarah Churchill became increasingly troublesome in her rivalrous jealousy, making unpleasant accusations and in effect finally forcing the queen to terminate their relations and to request that her letters (which the duchess had threatened to publish) be returned. The duchess of Marlborough, driven by fears of losing her position and the benefices promised her heirs, recklessly pursued a course of importuning the queen. Over and over, she wrote reviling Abigail Masham, targeting especially her inappropriate social status: "[F]or I can't but think the Nation wou'd be of opinion that I have deserv'd better than to be made a sacrifice to the unreasonable passion of a bedchamber woman."[30] Ironically, the duchess's language about Masham—"the unreasonable passion"—echoes James II's phrasing about Anne's more youthful attachment to herself. Whining, she had earlier written:

> I appeal to your Majesty if I have not often asked you what my fault was, for I was sure I could mend, & if you have not as often answered not, till one day upon such pressing you said it was that I believed you had such an intimacy with Masham.[31]

The ambiguities in this passage open a space for interesting speculation.

The duchess's tone can be read as that of a lover scorned, complaining of the beloved's silence, begging for explanation and another chance. Is the queen's revelation that she is angry because the duchess has accused her of having "such an intimacy with Masham" to be read as "such an intimacy with Masham [as we have had]"? In other words, is the queen offended because the duchess has guessed the true nature of her relations with Masham? Or because the accusation is untrue? Would the duchess have kept repeating the gossip about the queen's relations with Masham did she not intend to goad her? The duchess seems to have been especially fond of expressing a disingenuous concern for the queen's reputation in which she was given to snide insinuations; of the pamphlets attacking the queen, the duchess wrote: "[B]ut that which I hated was the disrespect to the Queen & the disagreeable expressions of the dark deeds in the night."[32] The duchess's persistent gnawing at this issue of "the dark deeds in the night" made her rejection by the queen inevitable.[33]

The political machinations of Queen Anne's enemies took the form of pamphlets and narratives, like Manley's portrait of "the new Cabal," in which Queen Anne and her intimates were satirized. The duchess of Marlborough describes, with what I read as an almost lubricious enjoyment, a Whig pamphlet entitled "The Rival Duchess: or Court Incendiary. In a Dialogue between Madam Maintenon, and Madam Masham," published the previous year (1708):

> I had almost forgot to tell you of a new book that is come out: . . . the subject is ridiculous, and the book not well written, but that looks so much the worse, for it shews that the notion is extensively spread among all sorts of people. It is a dialogue between Madame Maintenon and Madam Masham, . . . and there is stuff, not fit to be mentioned, of passions between women. . . .[34]

The "I had almost forgot to tell you" is a *faux naïf* version of "I was afraid I might forget to tell you . . . as if I could." Mentioning that "there is stuff, not fit to be mentioned," rather nicely calls the reader's (i.e., the queen's) attention to these "passions between women" and excoriates their embodiment as well. The following lines are from a dialogue in the pamphlet that the duchess describes:

> MADAM MASHAM. Especially at *Court* I was taken for a more modish Lady, was rather addicted to another sort of Passion, of having too great a Regard for my own Sex, inasmuch that few People thought I wou'd ever have Married; but to free my self from that Aspersion some of our Sex labour under, for being too fond of one another, I was resolv'd to Marry as soon as I cou'd fix to my Advantage or Inclination.

MAINTENON. And does that Female Vice, which is the most detestable in Nature, Reign among you, as it does with us in *France* . . . ?

MADAM MASHAM. O, Madam, we are arriv'd to as great Perfection in sinning that Way as you can pretend to. . . .[35]

This passage echoes comments we have noted in earlier literature but expresses them in a way more characteristic of the historical moment just after the turn of the century. Anthony Hamilton's comment on the ignorance of *"Refinements"* at the court of Charles II is here answered in Madam Masham's acknowledgment of English proficiency in "that Female Vice." The language used to describe female same-sex transgression also evokes that in Hamilton's account of Miss Hobart's dismissal; Madam Masham is "addicted to another sort of Passion, of having too great a Regard for my own Sex."

This is a discourse that names without naming, that avoids the available discourses of tribadism, on the one hand, or of the erotic ellipses associated with ideal "friendship," on the other hand. The circumlocution of "that Female Vice" clears a path between those traditionally familiar extremes, as does Manley's sly description of "the new Cabal." The appearance of this discourse that names obliquely assumes a certain knowledge of the "Female Vice" and suggests that that knowledge is now widely circulated. Further, Madam Masham's remark that "few People thought I wou'd ever have Married; but to free my self from that Aspersion some of our Sex labour under, for being too fond of one another, I was resolv'd to Marry as soon as I cou'd fix to my Advantage or Inclination" delineates a clear opposition between same-sex behaviors and heterosexual marriage, an opposition that has become explicit and exclusive in ways that it had not been. The articulation of this opposition—the very fact that it is spoken—reveals that the notion of heteronormativity is being circulated and has become available as political cover. In this example, the Masham persona in the pamphlet does not suggest that she will discontinue her same-sex activities; she suggests only that marriage will clear her reputation because marriage is *thought* to be incompatible with same-sex behavior. Thus, the notion of the exclusivity of sexual orientations, and the heteronormative ideology that accompanies it, has come into being and is to evolve, albeit haltingly and uncertainly, into modern binary identities.

How, then, can we understand the constructions of a female same-sex erotics during this turn from the seventeenth into the eighteenth century? The texts we have been examining indicate that a salacious interest in tribadism and in other same-sex sexual behaviors was by this historical moment being incorporated into, and even facilitated by, literary discourse by women not unwilling to present themselves as transgressive. Particular literary genres, such as the roman à clef (e.g., Manley's *The New Atalantis*) and other satirical forms of the late seventeenth century no doubt enabled this explicitly sexual female same-sex discourse by women. Thus, by the late seventeenth century, we can confirm the currency of a vernacular and literary sexual discourse that circulated knowledge of female same-sex sexuality among both men and women; this vernacular discourse exists in contrast to the Latin texts and discourses that had earlier been the unique vehicles for the dissemination of such knowledge, and in contrast as well to the veiled erotic discourse of contemporary female pastoral friendship poetry deployed in the writing of "respectable" women. The currency of this overt discourse of female same-sex sexuality in the vernacular (in particular, the libidinously charged language of female sexual transgression of Behn and others) makes female same-sex emotional, and more generally erotic, relations vulnerable to description in its explicitly transgressive terms and also, as we have seen, in terms that are explicit but do not name. In short, as overt discourses of female sexuality gain currency, whether as discourses of tribadism or the more knowing and oblique "Female Vice," the ability to name and the availability of names—as after the Restoration the possibilities for naming female transgression become increasingly available to women—places a new burden on behaviors that might, or might not, be "innocent." In the case of Queen Anne, her feeling for the duchess of Marlborough and other female companions—her *"passion démésurée,"* as her father, James II, described it—was read as sexual whether or not her emotionally intense relations with other women ever sought physical expression. Crowne's attempted erasure of the sexually transgressive subtext of the Calisto myth only made that subtext more available for circulation and so ensured the return of what was being repressed. In this way, Crowne's *Calisto* might be said to mediate obliquely between contemporary discourses of overt and covert transgressiveness.

Notes

CHAPTER I

1. Though class status is invoked here to focus on women of a particular social position, I have purposely avoided problematizing ideas of class in themselves. Instead, I have chosen to reinscribe the language and understanding of social position likely to have been operative for the subjects of my study. The intent of this rhetorical strategy is to sustain my focus on early modern understandings of status and behavior. In using "the language of 'sorts' of people," I follow the work of Keith Wrightson, "'Sorts of People' in Tudor and Stuart England," in questioning the classical hierarchy of social order customarily accepted by students of the early modern period: "[I]n the later sixteenth century the English elaborated an alternative vocabulary of social description which reveals a world of social meanings untapped by the formal social classifications of literary convention, and . . . this language of 'sorts' of people was ubiquitous in late Elizabethan and early Stuart England" (36). Rosemary Kegl, *The Rhetoric of Concealment: Figuring Gender and Class in Renaissance Literature,* provides a differently nuanced perspective on our understanding of early modern constructions of class; she distinguishes between a sociological definition of class "on the basis of differences in rank, status or authority" and a more Marxist materialist definition "on the basis of their structural role in the production and extraction of surplus value" that yet retains the assumption "that rank, status, and authority were categories through which members of late-sixteenth-century society often experienced their relationship to economic exploitation and through which they often articulated their political demands for social change" (4–5).

2. Catherine Belsey, *The Subject of Tragedy: Identity and Difference in Renaissance Drama,* 33–34. See also John O. Lyons, *The Invention of the Self: The Hinge of Consciousness in the Eighteenth Century,* on the possible connections between the popularity of Venetian mirrors and the great number of self-portraits during the sixteenth century; though there is not "a comparable growth of self-portraiture in prose literature" (69), there is, as Belsey demonstrates, a perhaps commensurate display of interiority in the dramatic soliloquies of Shakespeare and his contemporaries.

3. Charles Taylor, *Sources of the Self: The Making of the Modern Identity,* 36; see also 528n. 12; and Regenia Gagnier, *Subjectivities: A History of Self-Representation in Britain, 1832–1920,* 11.

4. Katharine Park, "The Rediscovery of the Clitoris: French Medicine and the Tribade, 1570–1620," provides a detailed analysis of the interdependency of ideas about hermaphrodites and tribadism in early modern France. Patricia Simons, "Lesbian (In)visibility in Italian Renaissance Culture: Diana and Other Cases of

donna con donna," furnishes evidence of the presence of *donna con donna* in the paintings of Renaissance Italy. Valerie Traub, "The Perversion of 'Lesbian' Desire," pursues the dissemination of the Ovidian myth of Calisto as a transgeographical phenomenon in Europe, but does not focus on problems of historicity in the case of England. For a synopsis of this scholarship about female same-sex relations in early modern Europe, see also chapter 4.

5. Marie-Jo Bonnet, "Sappho, or the Importance of Culture in the Language of Love: *Tribade, Lesbienne, Homosexuelle,"* 149, locates the first appearance of "tribade" in French in Henri Estienne's *Apologie pour Hérodote* (1567), but see my chapter 2 for earlier Latin uses. Terry Castle, *The Apparitional Lesbian: Female Homosexuality and Modern Culture,* lists "a whole slangy mob" of words that have "always" been available "for pointing to (or taking aim at) the lover of women" (9). Rictor Norton, *Mother Clap's Molly House: The Gay Subculture in England 1700–1830,* esp. 232–47; and Randolph Trumbach, "London's Sapphists: From Three Sexes to Four Genders in the Making of Modern Culture," give accounts of the various names used to describe same-sex female transgressors in eighteenth-century England; Theo van der Meer, "Tribades on Trial: Female Same-Sex Offenders in Late Eighteenth-Century Amsterdam," 203, provides this information for the Netherlands.

6. The tenacity of this trope of the enlarged clitoris in the imaginations of male writers is evident in Richard von Krafft-Ebing's 1886 description of a female invert in *Psychopathia sexualis: a medico-forensic study,* perhaps the most influential work of nineteenth-century sexology: "Vagina, uterus, ovaries, normal; clitoris rather large" (350).

Valerie Traub, in "The Rewards of Lesbian History," takes as a given "the tribade's allegedly discrete bodily morphology—her clitoral hypertrophy" (374); however, my own research does not confirm the inevitability of such a connection between tribades and aberrant bodily morphology. That is, the tribade is not, as Traub suggests, *defined* by clitoral hypertrophy, though she is persistently associated with it. In a more recent essay, "Recent Studies in Homoeroticism," Traub provides an informative topical review of research in the field and a useful bibliographical survey.

7. Park, "Rediscovery of the Clitoris," 172–73. Valerie Traub, "The Psychomorphology of the Clitoris," makes a similar point about exoticism and travel narratives (85–89).

8. Nicolas de Nicolay, *Nauigations into Turkie* [London, 1585], 60; see chapter 2 for the Ovidian sources of de Nicolay's reference to Sappho's hundred women and unrequited love for Phaon, the young ferryman who made a bargain with Venus for his beauty.

I have in general attempted to convey the unique qualities of early modern texts by retaining in quotations their original spellings and other accidentals of typography, such as the use of *u* for *v* and the long *ſ*; however, in some instances, I have modernized and normalized excerpted materials for easier reading.

9. Quoted in Kate Aughterson, ed. *Renaissance Woman: A Sourcebook,* 129.

10. De Busbecq's Latin name, Augerius Gislenius Busbequius (1522−1592), was often used on title pages. The four epistles reporting on his embassies to Constantinople were written beginning in the fall of 1554. The third epistle, which I cite here, is dated as written at Constantinople on June 1, 1560. See Ogier Ghislain de Busbecq, *Works* (Batavorvm: Ex Officina Elzeveriana, 1633), and A[ugerius] G[islenius] Busbequius, *The Four Epistles of A. G. Busbequius Concerning His Embassy into Turkey*, 1st English ed. (London: J. Taylor and J. Wyat, 1694).

11. I take "against Nature" here to refer to anal penetration. Reading between the lines, it seems likely that acts husbands might perform with their concubines were not permissible with wives, in fact were so extremely offensive as to be grounds for divorce; nor were they namable, for when a wife approached a judge and "he asks the Cauſe, they ſay nothing, but pull off their Shoo from their Feet, and turn it up and down, which is a Sign among them of the unlawful uſe of Copulation" (sig. I7). Citations are to the 1694 English edition of Busbequius. I indicate signature location following quotes in the text. The translation and publication of this popular text certainly indicate that the English enjoyed reading the details of Turkish sexual customs and bodily functions.

12. The Latin of earlier editions is for the most part quite literally translated into English, but I have inserted two Latin phrases from the 1633 Dutch edition of Busbequius, sig. M5, for comparison. The English is both less and more condemnatory than the Latin: "burn in Love" versus "love among themselves," "refined Loves" versus "abominable loves."

13. Peter Anthony Motteux, ed., *Gentleman's Journal; Or, the Monthly Miscellany. By Way of Letter to a Gentleman in the Country. Consisting of News, History, Philosophy, Poetry, Musick, Translations, &c.*, vols. 1−3 (London, 1692−94), June 1694 issue, exactly contemporary with the English translation of Busbequius. In this story of a "Female Husband," Motteux writes of a hoax by a woman who crossdresses to regain her former lover by recovering his money from the "loose" woman who has robbed him. Finally, the female husband's chastity overwhelms the lasciviousness of the betrayer and all ends as it should, both the narrator and his readers, including women, having enjoyed the titillation of the female husband's inability to perform a husband's sexual role (149−52; sig. X2−X3ᵛ).

14. *The Gentleman's Journal*, December 1692 issue. This is a titillating account of a French provincial hermaphrodite "lately come to *Paris*," once a woman now legally forced to live as a man once "her" sexual ambiguity was discovered. "Margaret" becomes "Arnold" as Motteux describes a female body, hinting at a prosthesis or enlarged clitoris (19).

15. *The Gentleman's Journal*, April 1692 issue. The remainder of Motteux's description is as follows: "Courage is so natural to the English, that even the tender sex, give a frequent Mark of theirs: We have had but two years ago a young Lady on board the Fleet in Man's Apparel, who show'd all the Signs of the most undaunted Valour. . . . The last Letters from *Genoa* give us an account of an *English Heroin* who, they tell us, is of quality. She had serv'd two years in the *French* Army in *Piedmont* as a *Volunteer,* and was entertain'd for her Merit by the Governor of

Pignerol in the quality of his Gentleman of the Horse; at last playing with another of her Sex, she was discover'd; and the Governor having thought fit to inform the King his Master of this, he hath sent him word that he would be glad to see the Lady; which hath occasion'd her coming to *Genoa,* in order to Imbark for *France:* Nature has bestow'd no less Beauty on her than Courage; and her Age is not above 26. The *French* Envoy hath Orders to cause her to be waited on to Marseille, and to furnish her with all Necessarie" (22–23).

16. Mary Wortley Montagu, *The Complete Letters of Lady Mary Wortley Montagu,* edited by Robert Halsband. Vol. 1: 1708–1720 (Oxford: Clarendon Press, 1967), 313–14.

17. Anonymous, *Satan's Harvest Home [London, 1749] and Hell upon Earth: or the Town in an Uproar [London, 1729]* (New York: Garland Publishing, 1985), 18 [sig. D1ʳ]. Norton, *Mother Clap's,* also cites this passage. See chapter 2 for descriptions of Sappho in early modern editions of her poetry and in medical, anatomical, and other contemporary texts that mention her.

18. Norton, *Mother Clap's,* reviews the evidence for these locutions in chapter 15: "Tommies and the Game of Flats" (232–47). That this vocabulary was common has yet to be confirmed by textual examples in addition to the unique instances now known. It is of course also possible, and indeed probable, that these vernacular usages rarely made their way into surviving texts and that the absence of additional instances does not negate their existence as common discursive currency, at least within certain social circles probably not of the better sort.

19. Alan Bray, *Homosexuality in Renaissance England* and "Homosexuality and the Signs of Male Friendship in Elizabethan England," and Randolph Trumbach, "Sex, Gender, and Sexual Identity in Modern Culture: Male Sodomy and Female Prostitution in Enlightenment London" and "London's Sapphists," have provided the now-standard analyses of an emergent male subculture. See also the recent theoretical perspectives described by David M. Halperin, "Forgetting Foucault: Acts, Identities, and the History of Sexuality" and "How to Do the History of Male Homosexuality," as modifications of what he reads as critical misapplications of Foucault; Halperin's concern is exclusively with the historical continuities and discontinuities of male (homo)sexual relations and "prehomosexual models of male sexual and gender deviance" ("How to Do," 91).

20. See Bernadette Brooten, *Love between Women: Early Christian Responses to Female Homoeroticism,* esp. 1–28 and "Part 1: Female Homoeroticism in the Roman World: The Cultural Context of Early Christianity" (29–188). Brooten's analysis is a powerful and careful corrective to the work of the late John Boswell, *Christianity, Social Tolerance, and Homosexuality: Gay People in Western Europe from the Beginning of the Christian Era to the Fourteenth Century,* which virtually ignored women in its emphasis on male homosexuality, and to Judith C. Brown's work *Immodest Acts: The Life of a Lesbian Nun in Renaissance Italy,* whose undertheorized assumptions about the nature of "lesbian" behaviors was for a long time the only available study of female homoeroticism in this period. Now, however, Brooten's corrective is itself proving controversial, as is demonstrated by the commentaries devoted to her work by David M. Halperin, Ann Pellegrini, and others,

in "The GLQ Forum: Lesbian Historiography Before the Name? on *Love between Women.*"

21. I illustrate this process in chapter 2 of this study by analyzing representations of the contemporary reputation of Sappho.

22. For a sustained and rigorously elaborated essentialist perspective, see Castle, *Apparitional Lesbian*, 1–20.

23. Helena Whitbread, ed., *"I Know My Own Heart": The Diaries of Anne Lister, 1791–1840*, and Jill Liddington, "Anne Lister of Shibden Hall, Halifax (1791–1840): Her Diaries and the Historians."

24. Anna Clark, "Anne Lister's Construction of Lesbian Identity," 27.

25. Bray, *Homosexuality in Renaissance England*, comments that "when one looks at the circumstantial details of how [male] homosexuality was conceived of and how it was expressed in concrete social forms [e.g., institutionalized in public school rituals or as part of master-servant relations], it becomes obvious how very easy it was in Renaissance England—far more so than today—for a cleavage of this kind to exist, between an individual's behaviour and his awareness of its significance" (68). In the later "Homosexuality and the Signs of Male Friendship," Bray refines his views. In the case of female same-sex relations, there is the added complexity of defining behaviors as sexual in the absence of a phallus.

26. Carolyn Woodward, "'My Heart So Wrapt': Lesbian Disruptions in Eighteenth-Century Fiction," 845.

27. Martha Vicinus, "Distance and Desire: English Boarding-School Friendships," describes the "raves" of Victorian schoolgirls. These appear to have been a way of defining and isolating female same-sex relations to adolescence and to boarding schools.

28. I include in "visible subcultures" groups tacitly acknowledged by a dominant culture as part of its purpose in containing and marginalizing non-normative relations. So, for instance, molly houses served to locate and to contain "sodomites."

29. Michael McKeon, "Historicizing Patriarchy: The Emergence of Gender Difference in England, 1660–1760," 300.

30. McKeon, "Historicizing Patriarchy," 296, 300. He provides in this essay a useful survey of the recent literature on the molly subculture and its distinction from "precedent sodomitical activity" (307); see especially his review of the work of Bray and Trumbach (307–12, 319nn. 47–50, 320n. 55).

31. Randolph Trumbach, "Sodomitical Subcultures, Sodomitical Roles, and the Gender Revolution of the Eighteenth Century: The Recent Historiography," and Michael Roche, *Forbidden Friendships: Homosexuality and Male Culture in Renaissance Florence*, take up the problematic distinction between the use of "networks" of shared activities and "subcultures." First, Trumbach pointedly asks "whether the persons in a network have, as a consequence of the network, a sense of separate identity. In the case of eighteenth-century London it can probably be shown that the network gave such an identity to only a few." And he goes on to comment that "[i]t is necessary to make a distinction of scale between the networks of small towns and the subcultures of large cities" (116). In developing this distinction for

his analysis of male same-sex relations in Renaissance Florence, Roche emphasizes the notion of a separate identity based on *sexual* difference presupposed by
our general understanding of "subculture" (149–50); thus he describes "the collec-
tive aspects of homosexual activity" in Renaissance Florence "as a profusion of
networks" (151). Like Bray, *Homosexuality in Renaissance England,* Roche concludes that "[t]here was only a single male sexual culture with a prominent homoerotic character. . . . Sodomy was an integral facet of male homosocial culture"
(191). It is strikingly apparent that any female networks or larger subcultures need
to be described quite differently than those in which men circulated. We need to
keep in mind the much more public nature of men's relations, associations, and
meeting places. For women, any networks or subcultures that might take shape
would have to have been circumscribed by the geographical spaces that limited
women's lives. It is only when we come to describe transgressive activities at court
that women's same-sex relations achieve public visibility. These distinctions un-
dergird the discussions that follow.

32. Theodora A. Jankowski, "'Where there can be no cause of affection': Redefining Virgins, Their Desires, and Their Pleasures in John Lyly's *Gallathea,*"
describing the unstable gender representations in Lyly's *Gallathea,* comments that
"[e]ven though this play allows a space for woman-woman desire, the type of desire that occurs is represented as curiously 'chaste'" (264).

33. Rachel P. Maines, *The Technology of Orgasm: "Hysteria," the Vibrator, and
Women's Sexual Satisfaction,* 1–47.

34. Thomas Raynalde, *The Birth of mankynde, otherwyse named the womans booke*
([London, 1552?]), sig. K8ᵛ. Raynalde's lengthy prologue makes clear that the presentation of this material in English was controversial. He justifies Englishing
Eucharius Roeslin's Latin by noting that since this book is available throughout
Europe, English women and their midwives should also have access to its information, which can do much good; he further points out that evil people will make
evil of whatever they read and knowing women's "secrets" will not make good
men hate women (sigs. B1–C4).

35. Kathryn M. Kendall, "Women in Lesotho and the (Western) Construction of Homophobia," for instance, has found that this is the case in modern
Lesotho.

36. Perhaps the best illustration of the persistence of this masculine sexual paradigm is the by now famous example, from the Starr Report, of President Clinton's
use of this distinction in defense of his relations with Monica Lewinski. It is
abundantly clear from Clinton's legalistic parsing of the definition of sexual relations and from Lewinski's confirmation of his perspective (i.e., that oral sex is not
"real" sex and that they were just "fooling around") that an androcentric definition
of sexuality continues—albeit anachronistically and greeted by public derision—
to shape individual self-accounts well into the twentieth century.

37. I examine the erotically charged language of women's poetry in chapter 4 of
this study. See Kathryn R. King, "The Unaccountable Wife and Other Tales of
Female Desire in Jane Barker's *A Patch-Work Screen for the Ladies,*" and George E.

Haggerty, "'Romantic Friendship' and Patriarchal Narrative in Sarah Scott's *Millenium Hall*," on Barker and Scott, respectively.

38. Elizabeth Mavor, *The Ladies of Llangollen: A Study in Romantic Friendship*, continues to be the standard account of their life together.

39. The work of Thomas Laqueur in "'Amor Veneris, vel Dulcedo Appeletur'" and *Making Sex: Body and Gender from the Greeks to Freud*, though contested, has brought considerable attention to the fact that early modern constructions of the body and of sexuality do not conform to the binary system of male/female whose prevalence has coincided with the rise of modern science in the West. For corrective commentary on Laqueur, see Katharine Park and Robert A. Nye, "Destiny Is Anatomy: Review of *Making Sex* by Thomas Laqueur."

40. Sally O'Driscoll, "Outlaw Readings: Beyond Queer Theory," 37, 43. O'Driscoll provides a neat summary of the theoretical stances on both sides of the identity categories debate and outlines the far-reaching implications of using modern categories to read earlier lives and literatures.

41. Martha Vicinus, "Lesbian History: All Theory and No Facts or All Facts and No Theory?" For the origination of this term, see Judith M. Bennett, "'Lesbian-Like' and the Social History of Lesbianisms."

42. Deborah T. Meem, "Eliza Lynn Linton and the Rise of Lesbian Consciousness." At the same time that Meem says "I use the term 'protolesbians' to refer to women of the late nineteenth century who would today be called lesbians" (537n. 4), she remarks that the novelist Eliza Lynn Linton "cannot name—no one could in 1880" (551) the identity of a female character whose erotic desire clearly is directed toward other women, despite the availability of the phrase "l'amour sapphique" in England as early as the 1870s (547). "Cannot name" might more productively be understood as "will not name," a mark of middle-class reluctance to name what is proscribed and hidden rather than an indication of the lack of names for female same-sex erotics before 1900.

43. Anna Clark, "Anne Lister's Construction," 50. Despite her familiarity with current literature about language available to describe female same-sex relations during Lister's lifetime, Clark does not problematize "lesbian."

44. Elaine Hobby, "Katherine Philips: Seventeenth-Century Lesbian Poet," 202. Emma Donoghue, *Passions between Women: British Lesbian Culture 1668–1801*, makes available a broad range of early modern literary materials that suggest the nature of same-sex erotics, yet she does not provide an adequately theorized context in which to place those materials or a problematized language through which to discuss them. See also the review by Jonathan Brody Kramnick, "LGSN Review: The Lesbian Century."

45. The work of the late-nineteenth-century German sexologists Heinrich Ulrichs and Krafft-Ebing in systematizing a "scientific" understanding of a "third sex" is now well known, along with the four-part classification of the female "invert" by Krafft-Ebing that influenced Havelock Ellis. See Esther Newton's classic study of Radclyffe Hall's *The Well of Loneliness* for a description of the genesis of what was to become modern lesbian identity ("The Mythic Mannish Lesbian: Radclyffe Hall and the New Woman").

46. Jennifer Terry, "Theorizing Deviant Historiography," 277.

47. Castle, *Apparitional Lesbian,* 10, 11, 15.

48. See Adrienne Rich, "Compulsory Heterosexuality and Lesbian Existence."

49. I use quotes to draw attention to the fact that I wish to problematize the intellectual constructs described by "queer theory."

50. O'Driscoll, "Outlaw Readings," esp. 30–37, furnishes a useful analysis of queer theory.

51. See Lillian Faderman, *Surpassing the Love of Men: Romantic Friendship and Love between Women from the Renaissance to the Present,* 65–73. I summarize the debates about defining lesbian identity in chapter 3.

52. Germaine Greer, Susan Hastings, Jeslyn Medoff, and Melinda Sansone, eds., *Kissing the Rod: An Anthology of Seventeenth-Century Women's Verse,* 188. See also Merry E. Wiesner's cautions against reading lesbianism in *Women and Gender in Early Modern Europe.*

53. For example, see Theo van der Meer, "Sodomy and the Pursuit of a Third Sex in the Early Modern Period," particularly his accounts of sodomy, including female same-sex relations, in the Netherlands during the early modern period. Van der Meer, "Tribades on Trial," also takes up the question of the prosecution of female same-sex offenders in late-eighteenth-century Amsterdam. Katharine Park and Lorraine Daston, "The Hermaphrodite and the Orders of Nature: Sexual Ambiguity in Early Modern France," provide an astute analysis of the complexities in sexual definition raised by the early modern French preoccupation with hermaphrodites. Anna Clark, "Anne Lister's Construction," esp. 26n. 14, laments the lack of evidence for the existence of "lesbian networks or subcultures" in England, even as late as the late eighteenth and early nineteenth centuries; the situations in Paris or Amsterdam were of course quite different, and subcultures were identifiable among otherwise marginalized women, that is, those who were not respectably attached to a male-dominated household, for example, actresses, dancers, prostitutes.

54. Recent studies of transvestism during the early modern period can be found in Rudolf M. Dekker and Lotte C. van de Pol, *The Tradition of Female Transvestism in Early Modern Europe,* and in essays collected in Julia Epstein and Kristina Straub, eds., *Body Guards: The Cultural Politics of Gender Ambiguity.*

55. The anatomy texts of Ambroise Paré, *The Works of Ambroise Paré* (London: Richard Cotes and William Dugard, 1649), and Thomas Vicary, *Profitable Treatise of the Anatomie of Mans Body* [1577], among others, were widely translated and disseminated throughout Europe. See Laqueur, "'Amor Veneris,'" Park, "Rediscovery of the Clitoris," and my chapter 2, for detailed analyses of the dissemination of Latinate sexual terminology and early modern understandings of female sexual pleasure.

CHAPTER II

1. Joan DeJean, *Fictions of Sappho, 1546–1937,* 6.

2. See Sidney Abbott and Barbara Love, *Sappho Was a Right-on Woman: A Liber-*

ated View of Lesbianism, an important popular work that helped galvanize lesbians early in the second wave of the women's movement. Today, lesbians from around the world flock to Lesbos in the summer to pay homage to Sappho as foremother of lesbian desire. Jane McIntosh Snyder, *Lesbian Desire in the Lyrics of Sappho,* is the first book-length scholarly examination of Sappho's poetry from the perspective of lesbian desire and with an emphasis on the active female gaze in the texts and narrative voice. For Snyder, as for so many twentieth-century readers and writers, the Sapphic corpus represents Sappho as an icon for lesbian visibility. From another perspective, however, Sappho's iconic status in modern discourse is often almost entirely divorced from her poetry or her role as foremother; invoking her can be a rhetorically witty way of saying "lesbian": for example, during the summer of 2000, a three-week retrospective of lesbian cult films being shown in New York City was entitled "Sapph-o-Rama."

3. DeJean, *Fictions of Sappho,* 5, 121.

4. Donoghue, *Passions between Women,* 243, has also remarked on DeJean's lack of familiarity with the rich variety of texts available to English readers before the Enlightenment.

5. In Katherine Philips, *Poems* (London, 1667), sig. C1.

6. See Gregory Nagy, "Phaethon, Sappho's Phaon, and the White Rock of Leukas."

7. See Howard Jacobson, *Ovid's "Heroides,"* 277–99; Florence Verducci, *Ovid's Toyshop of the Heart: Epistulae Herodium,* 123–79; and DeJean, *Fictions of Sappho,* 60–78.

8. See Nagy, "Phaethon."

9. Unless otherwise indicated, translations are mine. Steve Oberhelman's assistance has saved me from numerous infelicities.

10. Traub, "Psychomorphology of the Clitoris," explores the theoretical implications of this orientalizing. The connection between tribadism and exotic locales seems to have been current during a considerable period of time. We find it, for example, in 1671, in Jane Sharp, *The Midwives Book* [London, 1671]: "[the clitoris] hangs forth at the ſlit like a Yard, and will ſwell and ſtand ſtiff if it be provoked, and ſome lewd women have endeavoured to uſe it as men do theirs. In the *Indies,* and *Egypt* they are frequent, but I never heard but of one in this Country, if there be any they will do what they can for ſhame to keep it cloſe" (45); and again in 1749, in the anonymous *Satan's Harvest Home:* "[tribadism] is practis'd frequently in Turkey, as well as at Twickenham at this Day" (18).

11. The full title of the later edition is both descriptive and explanatory: Thomas Heywood, *The generall History of VVomen, Containing the Lives of the most Holy and Prophane, the most Famous and Infamous in all ages, exactly described not only from Poeticall Fictions, but from the most Ancient, Modern, and Admired Historians, to our Times* (London, 1657).

12. Thomas Heywood, *GYNAIKEION: or Nine Bookes of Various History Concerninge Women; Inscribed by ye names of ye Nine Muses* (London, 1624), provides this version of Sappho's biography: "ELianus affirmes her to be the daughter of

Scamandronius; Plato, of Ariston; Suidas and other Greeke writers deliuer to vs that there were two of that name, the one called Erixia, a much celebrated Poetesse (who flourished in the time of the Poet Alcæus, of Pittachus, and Tarquinius Priscus) who first deuised the vse of the Lyre or Harpe with a quill; some giue her the honor to bee the inuentor of the Lyricke verse: the other was called Sapho Mitelæna long after her who was a singer and a strumpet, shee published many rare and famous Poems amongst the Greekes, and therefore had the honour to be called the tenth Muse . . . " (sig. Ll 2ᵛ; 388).

13. Janel Mueller, "Troping Utopia: Donne's Brief for Lesbianism in 'Sapho to Philaenis,'" 187.

14. Janel Mueller, "A Letter from Lesbos: Utopian Homoerotics in Donne's 'Sapho to Philaenis,'" 18–19, 48n. 41. But see also the richly textured reading of this play provided by Philippa Berry, *Of Chastity and Power: Elizabethan Literature and the Unmarried Queen*, 120–24: "[E]mphasis on the queen's withdrawal into an exclusive feminine world as another Diana is invested with a certain innuendo by its conjunction with the name of Sappho" (123).

15. For a very different perspective, see Michael Pincombe, "Lyly and Lesbianism: Mysteries of the Closet in *Sappho and Phao*" and "*Sappho and Phao:* A Toy Made for Ladies." Pincombe reviews some of the materials that confirm a knowledge of tribadism for Lyly's audience and goes on to read that tribadism throughout the play. While a female same-sex erotics might furnish a subtext for the play's all-female scenes, I find unconvincing further speculations about performances before Elizabeth I.

16. The mandrake was well known as an aphrodisiac.

17. Arist. *Rhet.* 1398b; qtd. in Willis Barnstone, trans., *Sappho: Lyrics in the Original Greek with Translations,* 167.

18. See DeJean, *Fictions of Sappho,* 313ff., for a listing of sixteenth- and seventeenth-century French editions of Sappho; and Janel Mueller, "Lesbian Erotics: The Utopian Trope of Donne's 'Sapho to Philaenis,'" 109, 127nn. 15, 16, for other editions. Mueller, "Troping Utopia," 184 ff., also furnishes a good account of the Sappho doxography and citation in humanist scholarship, especially by Politian and Giraldi. Marie-Jo Bonnet, *Un choix sans équivoque: Recherches historiques sur les relations amoureuses entre les femmes XVIe–XXe siècle,* provides an account of continental commentary.

19. *Phainetai moi,* also known as fragment 31v, was preserved by the first-century c.e. literary critic Longinus in his treatise *On the Sublime.* See Snyder, *Lesbian Desire,* 27–38, for a fresh analysis of the text of this ode. Snyder discusses the triangulation of desire in which Sappho eloquently voices her passionate response on seeing a woman she loves sitting near a man who gazes upon her. Snyder also explores the influence of Catullus's adaptation and interpretation of the fragment.

20. In Katherine Philips, *Poems* (London, 1667), sig. c1–c1ᵛ. See chapter 3 for a fuller account of comparisons between Philips and Sappho.

21. Delarivier Manley, *The Royal Mischief* (London, 1696), sig. A3ᵛ. See as well Catharine Trotter's *Agnes de Castro* (London, 1696) and *Fatal Friendship* (London, 1698).

22. See *OED*. I have been unable to find *"albathara"* in either English or Latin dictionaries.

23. See Ian Maclean, *The Renaissance Notion of Woman: A Study in the Fortunes of Scholasticism and Medical Science in European Intellectual Life,* esp. 28–46; and Thomas Laqueur, "Orgasm, Generation, and the Politics of Reproductive Biology."

24. I have not been able to find another printed occurrence of "Rubsters"; but its failure to appear frequently in printed texts should not be surprising since this term is likely to have been used as street slang and to have been available collo-quially. The other terms we have noted were for the most part more clinically de-tached and therefore regarded as more appropriate for use in medical and other printed texts.

25. Park, "Rediscovery of the Clitoris," provides an important analysis of this material.

26. These materials are very usefully surveyed by Peter Wagner, "The Discourse on Sex — or Sex as Discourse: Eighteenth-Century Medical and Paramedical Erotica."

27. Martial, *Epigrams,* translated by Walter C. A. Ker, 2 vols., I:468–71. My translation. Donne and other early modern readers were also familiar with Philae-nis's appearance in *The Greek Anthology* (Mueller, "Lesbian Erotics," 110). Philae-nis is in addition mentioned a number of times by Athenaeus in the *Deipnosophists,* whose 1556 Venetian edition by Natalis Comes would have been widely known; Athenaeus writes to exonerate Philaenis: "To her is ascribed the authorship of the scandalous treatise on love which Aeschrion of Samos, the iambic poet, says the Sophist Polycrates forged to defame the woman, though she was most chaste" (viii.335), in Athenaeus, the *Deipnosophists,* translated by Charles Burton Gulick, 7 vols., 4:23.

28. Heywood, *GYNAIKEION,* sig. Ll 6; 395.

29. Lilius Gregorius Gyraldus, *Opera Omnia, duobus Tomis Distincta.* 2 vols. (Lei-den, 1696), sig. Ll 3ᵛ; col. 171–72. Even Gyraldus is at pains to distance the same-sex eroticism of Philaenis from her heterosexual wantonness by using the device that early modern readers had found in the two Sapphos of the *Suda:* he refers to "Alteram Philænem Tribadem" [another Philaenis Tribade].

30. Heywood, *GYNAIKEION,* sig. Ll 6; 395.

31. Martial's epigrams would have been easily available to readers of Latin. I have consulted the 1655 Paris edition: Martial, *Epigrammes,* translated by Michel de Marolles (Paris, 1655).

32. Robert Burton, *The Anatomy of Melancholy,* translated by Floyd Dell and edited by Paul Jordan-Smith, pt. 3, sec. 2, mem. 1, subs. 2, 652–53.

33. Quoted in Mueller, "Lesbian Erotics," 11.

34. Quoted in George Klawitter, "Verse Letters to T.W. from John Donne: 'By You My Love Is Sent,'" 91. See Klawitter for a detailed reading of this poem, as well as for an analysis of Donne's verse letters to Woodward and their clearly ho-moerotic implications. My own reading here is indebted to his work.

35. See Mueller, "Lesbian Erotics" and "Troping Utopia." Herbert J. C. Grierson, ed., *The Poems of John Donne*, 2 vols., dates the poem around 1597–98 (2:91). It is also possible that Donne recalls here Woodward's earlier poem, elaborating and reshaping its female erotics. "Sapho to Philaenis" has recently received a good deal of detailed attention: James Holstun, "'Will you rent our ancient love asunder?' Lesbian Elegy in Donne, Marvell, and Milton"; Elizabeth D. Harvey, "Ventriloquizing Sappho: Ovid, Donne, and the Erotics of the Feminine Voice"; and Paula Blank, "Comparing Sappho to Philaenis: John Donne's 'Homopoetics,'" offer differing critical perspectives. I find Mueller's the most congenial reading and incorporate several of her insights here.

36. My citations of the poem are from Sir Herbert Grierson, ed., *The Poems of John Donne*, 110–12.

37. See Stephen Coote, ed., *The Penguin Book of Homosexual Verse*, 56–74, for selections from *The Greek Anthology*, especially the epigrams of Catullus.

38. Edward Howard, *Poems, and Essays: With a Paraphrase on Cicero's Lælius, or Of Friendship. Written in Heroick Verse.* (London, 1673). A second edition of this volume appeared the following year, 1674, which suggests that it was actively circulated. Edward Howard (fl. 1669) wrote a number of plays and poems centered on contemporary political themes. According to the *DNB*, Howard was a figure of some controversy. Evidently, his work was ridiculed by Rochester, among others, while Orrery, Sir John Denham, Aphra Behn, and Thomas Hobbes prefixed commendatory verses and prose epistles to his work; in his turn, Howard wrote commendatory verses for Behn's 1685 *Poems* and John Dryden's 1697 *Virgil*. Pepys remarked of the *Change of Crowns*, "acted before a crowded house at the Theatre Royal on 12 April 1667 . . . as 'the best that I ever saw at that house being a great play and serious.' Some passages in the play gave offense . . . " (*DNB*). Though Howard's work has not been recognized after his own time, he was certainly a well-known, if not always well-regarded, member of London's literary and theatrical milieu during his creative years.

39. Howard, *Poems*, 10 (sig. B5ᵛ). I am much indebted to Jackson Boswell for calling this poem to my attention and for transcribing it when it was unavailable to me.

40. See Eric Partridge, *Shakespeare's Bawdy*.

41. See Norton, *Mother Clap's*, esp. 232 ff. Norton cites the "history of lesbianism" provided by the anonymous author of *Satan's Harvest Home*; it is striking that, in 1749, as a new vocabulary is becoming current, Sappho continues to be the chief exponent of female same-sex transgressiveness: "*Sappho*, as she was one of the wittiest Women that ever the World bred, so she thought with Reason, it would be expected she should make some Additions to a *Science* in which Womankind had been so successful: What does she do then? Not content with our Sex, begins *Amours* with her own, and teaches the Female World a new Sort of Sin, call'd the *Flats*" (*Satan's Harvest Home*, 18). Norton glosses "the Game of Flatts" as "a reference to games with playing cards, called 'flats,' and an allusion to the rubbing together of two 'flat' female pudenda" (233).

42. Mary McIntosh, "The Homosexual Role," 184.

43. Bray, *Homosexuality in Renaissance England,* 74.

44. Bray, *Homosexuality in Renaissance England,* 80, 85. Trumbach, "Sodomitical Subcultures," takes issue with McIntosh and Bray, though he finally comes to agree with McIntosh, but with reservations. See also Jeffrey Weeks, *Sex, Politics, and Society: The Regulation of Sexuality Since 1800,* 96 ff.; Eve Kosofsky Sedgwick, *Epistemology of the Closet,* 182 ff.; and Bray, "Homosexuality and the Signs of Male Friendship," for a fuller discussion of the issues at stake in this scholarship. Whatever the outcome of the contested historicizing of a homosexual role and subculture, it is important to keep in mind that the construction of sexuality in London was certainly different from that in other northern European capitals, as it was also from that in the rest of England, during this historical moment.

45. Bray, "Homosexuality and the Signs of Male Friendship," 54, 51.

46. The phrase "lesbian continuum" was first introduced into feminist discourse in 1980. See Vicinus, "Lesbian History," and Annamarie Jagose, *Lesbian Utopics,* 1–24, for lucid commentaries on these issues.

47. Pope's translation reads as follows:

> No more the *Lesbian* Dames my Passion move,
> Once the dear Objects of my guilty Love;
> All other Loves are lost in only thine,
> Ah youth ungrateful to a Flame like mine!
>
> (ll. 17–20)

Nicholas Venette, *Conjugal Love; or, The Pleasures of the Marriage Bed* (London, 1750), describes the clitoris and Sappho this way:

> According to the opinion of some authors, there is a part above the nymphæ longer more or less than half a finger, called by anatomists clitoris; the which I may justly term the fury and rage of love; there Nature has placed the seat of pleasure and lust, as it has on the other hand in the glands of man; there it has placed those excessive ticklings, and there is lechery and lasciviousness established; for, in the action of love, the clitoris fills with spirits, and afterwards stiffens as a man's virge, which part it resembles. One may see its pipes, its nerves, and muscles: neither is there a gland or prepuce wanting; and if it was hollow through, one would say it was altogether like a man's member.
>
> This part lascivious women often abuse. The lesbian Sappho would never have acquired such indifferent reputation, if this part of hers had been less. (18–19; sig. B7ᵛ–B8)

48. The examples of Eleanor Butler and Sarah Ponsonby, the Ladies of Llangollen (see Mavor, *The Ladies*), and of Sarah Scott's autobiographical *A Description of Millenium Hall* (1762) are perhaps the best known. Faderman's *Surpassing the Love of Men* is the *locus classicus* for a (de-eroticizing) discussion of romantic friendship.

CHAPTER III

1. I use "sapphic" somewhat anachronistically in the title of this chapter and in the text that follows to suggest the emblematic evocations of Sappho in the constructedness of early modern understandings of female same-sex relations. It is particularly useful in underlining the continuity of those understandings and in anticipating the later historical moment in which it replaced, at least in more genteel social strata, the epithets "tribade," *"fricatrice,"* "rubster," "tommy," and so on. The use of "sapphic" as a descriptor for "lesbianism" does not become strictly historically appropriate until the later nineteenth century, at least in England; while the *OED* cites the first instance of this usage in 1890 by Billings's *National Medical Dictionary,* "sapphic" is likely to have been used in speech well before that date. It is ironically appropriate that "sapphic" should be first cited in a medical dictionary, since it was in the medical texts of the sixteenth and seventeenth centuries that Sappho was used to exemplify the tribadism of women who "abused" the clitoris.

2. Philips's works include a single volume of poems written for her friends, published in an unauthorized edition in the year of her death, and then reedited, expanded, and reprinted posthumously, perhaps by her friend and literary executor, Sir Charles Cotterell; a translation of Pierre Corneille's *Pompey* and a partial translation of *Horace* completed by Robert Denham; a volume of her letters to Sir Charles, dubbed Poliarchus in *précieuse* fashion, edited and published posthumously by him in 1705; and four letters to Berenice, an anonymous noblewoman, published with the *Familiar Letters* of John Wilmot, earl of Rochester, in 1697. In all, five editions of her work appeared after the unauthorized 1664 folio edition of her *Poems,* the final one being the 1710 octavo of her *Works.* The editor of the 1667 edition expanded the unauthorized 1664 quarto by including a letter Sir Charles had received from Philips before her death; an introduction; commendatory poems and eulogies by the earls of Orrery and Roscommon, Abraham Cowley, the anonymous Philo-Philippa, and others; some additional poems by Philips, including short translations from the French; and her *Pompey* and *Horace.* The editions of 1669, 1678, and 1710 are essentially reprints of the 1667 edition. The poems did not become available again until George Saintsbury edited them, using the 1678 edition; see his *Minor Poets of the Caroline Period,* 486–612. Modern editions of Philips are those of Catherine Cole Mambretti, "A Critical Edition of the Poetry of Katherine Philips," and Patrick Thomas, *The Collected Works of Katherine Philips, The Matchless Orinda,* 3 vols. Thomas's edition, the most comprehensive edition of Philips's work to date and originally a 1982 dissertation at the University College of Wales, includes the *Letters to Poliarchus* (1705), the letters to Berenice, as well as her translations and other newly discovered materials. An authoritative edition of Philips's complete works is in preparation by Elizabeth H. Hageman and Andrea Sununu for Oxford University Press, and I am editing Philips's poems for an edition under contract with Broadview Press. All citations of Philips's writing in this text refer to Thomas's three-volume edition, unless otherwise indicated. I have consulted copies of the 1664 and 1667 editions of Philips's poems at the Folger Shakespeare Library and at the University of Texas at Austin, Harry Ransom Humanities Research Center; I have also examined the

two primary manuscripts in Philips's hand at the National Library of Wales, Aberystwyth, (NLW MS 775 [A] and NLW MS 776 [B]), and manuscript poems in the hand of Sir Edward Dering (*HRC 151 Philips MS 14,937 [D]) and the published 1705 *Letters,* both at the University of Texas at Austin, Harry Ransom Humanities Research Center.

3. She made other important literary connections, influencing Andrew Marvell and having a number of her poems set to music by Henry Lawes (see Allan Pritchard, "Marvell's 'The Garden': A Restoration Poem?"; Philip Webster Souers, *The Matchless Orinda,* 57–79; and Thomas, *The Collected Works,* I:3). Also see Thomas, *The Collected Works,* I:23–39, on her reputation. Fidelis Morgan, *The Female Wits: Women Playwrights of the Restoration,* 3–11, esp. 3–4, quotes Keats's letter to John Hamilton Reynolds (September 21, 1817) distinguishing "one beautiful Mrs Philips" from other poets of her sex.

4. See Nancy Cotton, *Women Playwrights in England: 1363–1750,* 194–212.

5. She is typically described by female critics as having "wielded persistently her all too fluent pen" (Kathleen M. Lynch, *The Social Mode of Restoration Comedy,* 113–23, esp. 114); as having had friendships with women "florid in their intensity" (Morgan, *The Female Wits,* 6); or as having "wanted to take on, by cajolery rather than by assault, an artistic role generally reserved for men" (Hilda L. Smith, *Reason's Disciples: Seventeenth-Century English Feminists,* 152–56, esp. 154). More recently, the discomfort expressed by earlier critics resurfaces in, for example, Celia A. Easton, "Excusing the Breach of Nature's Laws: The Discourse of Denial and Disguise in Katherine Philips' Friendship Poetry," who describes Philips's poems as "combin[ing] commonplaces with the gushing of an enamored individual" and twice deprecates Orinda's articulations of passion as a "cooing and cooing and cooing" (esp. 11, 6, 8).

Other views of her work have included her role as a member of male literary circles, for the sake of her distinguished literary connections or for her literary influence (see, for example, Souers, *The Matchless Orinda,* 276–77; and Allan Pritchard and Patrick Thomas, "Orinda, Vaughan and Watkyns: Anglo-Welsh Literary Relationships During the Interregnum"), or as a minor example of *préciosité*—a fashionable style associated with a Parisian literary salon during the first half of the seventeenth century—or, conversely, as an example of "the growing influence of neoclassicism" (Jennifer R. Waller, "'My Hand a Needle Better Fits': Anne Bradstreet and Women Poets in the Renaissance," 441). With the scholarly recovery of women writers during the 1980s and '90s, she garnered a perfunctory place in anthologies of women writers (see, e.g., Sandra Gilbert and Susan Gubar, eds., *The Norton Anthology of Literature by Women,* 81–82; Moira Ferguson, ed., *First Feminists: British Women Writers, 1578–1799,* 102–13; Angeline Goreau, ed., *The Whole Duty of a Woman: Female Writers in Seventeenth-Century England,* 15–16, 193–205; and Katharine M. Rogers and William McCarthy, eds., *The Meridian Anthology of Early Women Writers,* 373–75. Exceptions are the thirteen poems by Philips and one commendatory poem by Philo-Philippa in *Kissing the Rod,* ed. Greer and others, 186–213; and the nineteen Philips poems edited by Elizabeth H. Hageman, "Katherine Philips: The Matchless Orinda."

6. See, for example, chapter 2, "Orinda and Her Daughters," in Marilyn L. Williamson, *Raising Their Voices: British Women Writers, 1650–1750,* 64–133.

7. Waller, "'My Hand a Needle . . . ,'" 444.

8. Faderman, *Surpassing the Love of Men,* 68–71.

9. Good examples are Hobby, "Katherine Philips," 183–204; and Arlene Stiebel, "Not Since Sappho: The Erotic in Poems of Katherine Philips and Aphra Behn." Disregarding the languages of transgressive sexualities in early modern England, Hobby anachronistically identifies Philips as "closeted," while Stiebel views the poetry of Philips and Behn through the lens of modern lesbian identities and twentieth-century sexualities. Other feminist critics are more subtle in their readings, but display discomfort with a female same-sex erotics at the same time as they acknowledge its possibilities. Carol Barash, *English Women's Poetry, 1649– 1714,* desiring to assimilate Philips into the tradition of the *femme forte,* emphasizes the political dimensions of Orinda's friendships; she attributes to Philips the need to "translate the potentially erotic passion of the relationship between *Orinda* and *Lucasia* into a culturally sanctioned honour which does not threaten marriage" (95). Elizabeth Susan Wahl, *Invisible Relations: Representations of Female Intimacy in the Age of Enlightenment,* situates Philips in a historical context that assumes the binaries of hetero-/homo-sexuality, which were not culturally stable until much later. In commenting that Philips "makes claims for female intimacy that cross the boundaries of the conventional but then refuses to confront the implications of such claims, returning instead to a rhetoric of platonic equilibrium and recoding her ideas in terms of transparency and 'innocence'" (156), Wahl attributes to Philips a quite modern, twentieth-century subjectivity and self-consciousness about normative sexualities.

10. See Susan Arlene Hardebeck, "'If Soules No Sexes Have . . . ': Women, Convention and Negotiation in the Poetry of Katherine Philips"; Jennifer Lange, "'Hearts Thus Intermixed Speak': Erotic 'Friendship' in the Poems of Katherine Philips"; and David Michael Robinson, "To Boldly Go Where No Man Has Gone Before: The Representation of Lesbianism in Mid-Seventeenth Century to Early Eighteenth-Century British and French Literature." The most illuminating of these analyses is Hardebeck's lucid and orderly approach using the Marxist perspective and terminology initially employed by Ann Rosalind Jones (in *The Currency of Eros: Women's Love Lyric in Europe, 1540–1620*) to explore early women's poetry. Hardebeck reads Philips's poetry through three "viewer positions": dominant/hegemonic, oppositional, and negotiated. The idea of "negotiation" yields the most interesting results since it captures quite neatly the ways in which Philips establishes and maintains the presence of her erotics through a partial agreement with the dominant ideology of chastity and marital duty (17–18). Lange sensitively and productively examines Philips's use, in conformity with contemporary male usage, of the metaphor of "mixing" souls to express her erotics. Robinson attempts to place Philips within continental, especially French, traditions of the ideology of friendship; he also theorizes his use of "lesbian" by asserting the need to demonstrate the continuity of sexual identities over time, an

admirable effort in many respects, but one not entirely successful in enriching our historical understanding.

11. I use "platonic" here to refer to the Platonic tradition of spiritualized *and* eroticized relations as it made its way from the classics into the Renaissance. See my discussions of Montaigne, Brathwait, and Digby below. Wahl, *Invisible Relations*, following Easton, "Excusing the Breach," reads Philips as "produc[ing] a poetic language that aspires to transcend the body even as the physicality of its tropes undermines that longing" and expressing a "desire to renounce carnal relations in favor of a spiritual union between souls" (143–44). As will become apparent, such a dichotomizing reading ignores the eroticized complexities of the male traditions within which Philips was writing.

12. *Préciosité*, the fashionable style associated with the literary salon at the Hôtel de Rambouillet, was originally characterized by "the pursuit of elegance and distinction in manners, style, and language, devising new and metaphorical expressions, avoiding low or barbarous words, and pursuing clearness and precision" (Sir Paul Harvey and J. E. Heseltine, eds., *The Oxford Companion to French Literature*, 568). These qualities lent themselves to excess and, eventually, to parody by those not associated with the salon. Thomas accepts the view of Philips as a *précieux* poet on the grounds that *préciosité* is a form of coterie poetry particularly appropriate to the English Interregnum (I:10). Despite Henrietta Maria's introduction of this French literary and intellectual fashion into England in the 1630s, however, the cavalier poets (and Philips) do not conform to the closed society that Odette de Mourgues finds necessary for *préciosité* to flourish: "What characterized English court lyricists (and the seventeenth-century Cavalier poets are a good illustration) is that they were more ready to absorb than to reject" (*Metaphysical, Baroque, and Précieux Poetry*, 102–42, esp. 141).

See Thomas (I:3, 10–12) on Philips's so-called society of friendship. Though Thomas is critical of earlier attempts to reconstruct this society, his own account of its nature is also speculative. It remains unclear, for instance, to what extent the persons included by Philips in her society at various times knew one another, whether or not they ever met as an organized group, or whether, instead, inclusion might not have been used by Philips as a means of flattering and drawing closer to herself those whose friendship she sought. The degree of slippage between the possibly fictive ideal attributed to Orinda by her friend Sir Edward Dering and the reality may have been considerable (see letter to Anne Owen [Lucasia], written shortly after Philips's death, eulogizing Orinda's ideal society [quoted by Thomas, I:11]). An apparently similar slippage occurs in Philips's use of classical names, both for herself and for others. She seems to have used these in her social life as well as in her poetry: almost all her surviving letters are signed Orinda, and Sir Edward Dering uses the names familiar from her poetry in his letters both to her and to their mutual acquaintances (Letterbook, 1661–1665 [Ohio Historical Society, Philips MS. 14932]). This suggests that, for Philips and perhaps for a few of her friends, there was some conflation between the literary personae she created and the actual persons they were meant to represent. I have attempted to retain the quality of this ambiguity in the discussion that follows.

13. On Cowley, see Bruce King, *Seventeenth-Century English Literature,* 144; and Nicholas Jose, *Ideas of the Restoration in English Literature,* 67–96.

14. Ruth Perry, *The Celebrated Mary Astell,* uses this phrase to describe Mary Astell's expression of her feelings toward women but to deny Astell's sexual interest in other women (141).

15. The genital definition of sexuality persists into the present and underlies the question still asked of lesbians, "What do you *do?*"—a question whose subtext is "What *can* you do (without a penis)?"

16. Faderman, *Surpassing the Love of Men,* 69–70; Hageman, "Katherine Philips," 572–73; and others more recently have also noted Philips's use of Donne.

17. Thomas, no. 59, I:153–56. The text of Philips's works used here is that established by Thomas; all further references in the text, as well as subsequent citations to Thomas, refer to his *Collected Works of Katherine Philips;* Saintsbury's 1905 *Minor Poets,* however, is still the most readily available.

18. In her dissertation, Lange singles out the language of "mixing" or "mingling" as a metaphor for the fusion desired and described by Philips and some of her male contemporaries; see note 10 above.

19. Thomas quotes Rosemary Freeman, *English Emblem Books,* 147, on the significance of the compasses in Donne as "an accepted emblem of constancy" (*Collected Works,* I:343).

20. Sir Richard Maitland, Arbuthnot, and others, *The Maitland Quarto Manuscript,* edited by W. A. Craigie, 160–62. See Jane Farnsworth, "Voicing Female Desire in 'Poem XLIX,'" for an attentive reading of this poem.

21. Farnsworth, "Voicing Female Desire," 69n. 18, provides a brief survey of some of the Renaissance mentions and uses of this myth from the *Metamorphoses.* It is my observation that Ovid's tale of Iphis and Ianthe had a much more pervasive influence on the disguisings and shape-changings in early modern writing than has as yet been recognized.

22. Andrea Alciati, *Emblemata: Lyons, 1550/Andrea Alciato,* 171–72. This Lyons edition was presumably the last over which Alciati exercised authorial control. Its format, organization, and detailed woodcuts were reproduced in successive editions throughout Europe. See introduction by John Manning and annotations by translator Betty I. Knott (ix–xxx).

23. Alciati, *Emblemata,* 171–72. Translation by Betty I. Knott.

24. Joachim Camerarius, *Symbola et Emblemata* [Nürnberg 1590 bis 1604], facs. rpt., 2 vols., 1:44. My translation.

25. See Faderman, *Surpassing the Love of Men,* 65–68, for some pertinent examples of earlier male friendship literature. An excerpt from Walter Dorke's small pamphlet *A tipe or figure of friendship . . .* (London, 1589 [2nd ed.]) provides additional insight into the vernacular discourse popularly circulated in England. Having given brief accounts of a series of familiar classical male couples, Dorke concludes his essay:

> To be ſhort, what was the reaſon that the[ſe] honourable Romanes, Scipio and Lælius ſo greatly loued; inſomuch that one houſe ſerued them both, one face, one

ioint ſtudie, one delight, one conſent in all things: not onely in priuate affaires, but alſo in publique, in trauailes, in voyages, in ſoiourning, at home and abroad all were alike common: was not this a laudable kind of Friendſhip? Yea, to make our ful period, (though Friendſhips praiſe be infinite) ſuch is the force therof, that mightie Kings haue deſired it, it is ſo glorious: famous Philoſopheres haue honoured it, it is ſo ſpecious: cruell tyrants haue been amazed at it, it is ſo victorious: al men in generall haue praiſed it, it is ſo precious: and yet few haue effectually at any time attained unto it, it is ſo miraculous. (sig. B2–B2ᵛ)

Laurens J. Mills's account in *One Soul in Bodies Twain: Friendship in Tudor Literature and Stuart Drama* (1937) of the continuity of classical ideas of male friendship through the Middle Ages and Renaissance still provides a standard and useful summary of the subject. Of the classical ideals represented in texts that addressed the topic during the late sixteenth and early seventeenth centuries were "the joining of two souls in one; community of joys and sorrows; friendship tends toward virtue; equality and likeness in manners are the conditions of friendship; friends delight in service; to wrong a friend is a foul deed; steadfast friends should be cherished; . . . value of confining friendship to a few persons; . . . a friend is another self; . . . friends keep no secrets from each other" (244). See Halperin, "How to Do," for a different view of this discourse of male friendship: "[P]recisely by banishing any hint of subordination on the part of one friend to the other, and thus any suggestion of hierarchy, the emphasis on the fusion of two souls into one actually distances such a love from erotic passion" (101). Halperin seems to me to ignore here the erotic dangers posed by these friendships and to which Bray calls our attention so effectively in "Homosexuality and the Signs of Male Friendship" and in Alan Bray and Michael Rey, "The Body of the Friend: Continuity and Change in Masculine Friendship in the Seventeenth Century."

26. Jeffrey Masten, *Textual Intercourse: Collaboration, Authorship, and Sexualities in Renaissance Drama*, 34–35. Masten's reading of the language of Florio's Montaigne is a finely nuanced account of the ways in which a disavowal of transgressive sexuality operates to confirm a more permissible erotics of love between equals.

27. Masten, *Textual Intercourse*, offers a range of possible translations for the Latin motto, including this one (30). He also notes that "individual" is here used in its earlier meaning of "indivisible" (28). See entries in the *OED* for additional examples of this usage, which is not only different from but opposite to modern usage.

28. Masten, *Textual Intercourse*, observes a striking difference—which he reads as part of a "shift" in the sex/gender system during this period—between the visual representations for "Acquaintance" used in the earlier editions of the 1630s and the 1641 edition bound with *The English Gentlewoman*. Woodcuts in the earlier editions depict "Acquaintance" as two men in full-body embrace, while the 1641 engraving substitutes two disembodied hands shaking (176n. 6). This change in representation is analogous to and supports my own observations of the suppression of explicit discourses of transgressive female sexuality that was taking place at the same time (see chapters 1 and 2). Further, Bray's account of the divergence of sodomy and friendship as discourses of a same-sex erotics, which this example

from the consecutive editions of Brathwait's book adumbrates, provides a perspective for male same-sex relations not unlike my own view of female erotics (see Bray, "Homosexuality and the Signs of Male Friendship").

29. Richard Brathwait, *The English Gentleman* [London, 1630], 233–304; sigs. Hh1–Qq4ᵛ.

30. The silence of Brathwait and others about the friendships of women may also result from a perceived danger to men from intimacy between women.

31. Sir Kenelm Digby, *Private Memoirs of Sir Kenelm Digby . . . /written by himself. . . with an introductory memoir [by Sir Nicholas Harris Nicolas]* (London, 1827), 6. These fictionalized memoirs were written in 1628, when Digby was twenty-five years old, and titled "Loose Fantasies"; their publisher in 1827 changed the title to *Private Memoirs* and provided a "Private Key" to explicate the classical and pastoral pseudonyms that contribute to the narrative's roman à clef–like characteristics.

32. Digby, *Private Memoirs*, 6–9.

33. The classical pseudonym Stelliana certainly plays on Lady Venetia's maiden name of Stanley, but it may also pay homage to Sidney's Stella, since Digby was an admirer of both Sidney and Spencer. Digby himself assumed the name Theagenes in the text of his memoirs.

34. Apart from other common interests, both Digby and Van Dyck were Catholic.

35. Zirka Zaremba Filipczak, "Reflections on Motifs in Van Dyck's Portraits," 62.

36. Filipczack, "Reflections," 63.

37. Filipczack, "Reflections," notes that "[t]hese portraits may actually be commemorations of a friendship at its high point, prior to the distancing resulting from the very marriage that the friendship had helped to promote" (64).

38. Bruce R. Smith, *Homosexual Desire in Shakespeare's England: A Cultural Poetics*, 33–42, provides an important account of the Renaissance heritage of the Aristotelian and Platonic traditions of male friendship via Cicero's *De Amicitia*, on the one hand, and Plutarch's "Of Love" (*Moralia* 767) and the pseudo-Lucian's "*Erotes*," on the other. As Smith points out, Aristotle, and Cicero after him, distinguish between *philia* (true friendship) and *eros* (sexual desire), whereas for Plato "male friendship and sexual attraction, far from being opposites, are two aspects of the same bond," and the "contest between marriage and male companionship" that we see in Montaigne derives finally through Plutarch's version of the Platonic tradition (37).

39. Earl Miner, *The Cavalier Mode from Jonson to Cotton*, 256–59. Miner uses the term "cavalier winter" to describe the exclusion of royalists, among whom were the cavalier poets, from social and political power during the Interregnum.

40. See Souers, *Matchless Orinda*, 79–92; and Thomas, *Collected Works*, I:1–22. "Upon the double murther of K. Charles, in answer to a libellous rime made by V.P." (1651), Philips's royalist reply to Vavasor Powell's poem attacking the memory of Charles I, seems to have become a useful tool in the hands of James Philips's political enemies, though he seems not to have attempted to restrain her expression of her sympathies. After the Restoration, her poems addressed to the

newly restored royal family not only reflect the change in atmosphere that meant that poets could once again address the court, but they also reflect her concern for her husband's political situation and their mutual need for patronage.

41. See, for example, "Orinda to Lucasia parting, October 1661. at London" (Thomas, *Collected Works*, no. 93, I:211–13).

42. Lucy Brashear, "The Forgotten Legacy of the 'Matchless Orinda,'" also observes this omission: "One looks vainly for topics that provided the foundation of her life—home, family responsibilities, and personal joys and frustrations"; but her conclusion, that "finding no literary precedent to direct her, *Orinda* refused to write about her own experiences," overlooks the important possibility that Philips was indeed writing about those experiences that "provided the foundation of her life" in writing about the emotional friendships that compensated for a less than absorbing domestic experience (72).

43. See "On Rosania's Apostacy, and Lucasia's Friendship" (Thomas, *Collected Works*, no. 68, I:176–77), and *"Injuria amici"* (Thomas, *Collected Works*, no. 38, I:123–25), probably also addressed to Rosania on the occasion of her marriage. Compare these with the more formal and perfunctory "Rosania's private marriage" (Thomas, *Collected Works*, no. 37, I:122–23).

44. Letters 1–12 to Sir Charles (Thomas, *Collected Works*, II:13–41) describe Philips's activities on behalf of his suit to Lucasia. Souers, *Matchless Orinda*, 123–27, 132, has identified the Calanthe of these letters as Anne Owen. Orinda's relationship with Sir Charles was one of mutual benefit: as he sought to advance her husband and her career, so she encouraged his courting of Lucasia, though she seems to have had the additional motive of wanting to keep Lucasia nearby. Philips refers to the Italian postscripts inquiring after Calanthe in Sir Charles's letters, which she answers in English, apologizing that she can read but not write Italian. The enterprise thus had a rather clandestine air because Calanthe often asked after, and even seems to have read, some of Sir Charles's correspondence.

45. Thomas identifies Berenice as Lady Elizabeth Ker (or Carre), one of the daughters of Robert Ker, first earl of Ancram (*Collected Works*, II:11n. 2), but his argument for doing so is not entirely convincing. Philips had addressed her in "To the Rt. Hono: the Lady E.C." (*Collected Works*, no. 45, I:132–36), which is, like the letters to Berenice, full of breathless admiration.

46. The letters to Berenice were originally published in T. Brown, ed., *Familiar Letters written by the late Earl of Rochester, with letters written by Mr. Thomas Otway and Mrs. K. Philips* (London, 1697), sigs. K7ᵛ–L8, esp. L4. See Thomas, *Collected Works*, II:12n. 4, for doubts about the dating of the last letter to Berenice. The erotic tone of the letters to Berenice is even more striking when compared with that in the letters to Sir Charles or in the one surviving letter to Lady Temple (Thomas, *Collected Works*, II:137–42), also aristocrats whose friendship and goodwill Philips was eager to propitiate but with whom she was clearly not intimate in the same way.

47. See "Pierre Corneille" in Harvey and Heseltine, eds., *Oxford Companion*, 170.

48. Thomas implies that *Pompey* is political allegory (*Collected Works*, Letter 39a,

II:113n. 17), while Jacqueline Pearson points out its contemporary relevance for Philips and her audience (*The Prostituted Muse: Images of Women and Women Dramatists 1642–1737*, 122). Jose observes that "the word 'restore' runs like a *leitmotif*" throughout the play, which was performed in 1663 (*Ideas of the Restoration*, 131).

49. Souers, *Matchless Orinda*, 148.

50. See also "To the Lady E. Boyl" (Thomas, *Collected Works*, no. 102, I:221–22), "To my Lady Ann Boyle's saying I look'd angrily upon her" (no. 85, I:201–2), and "To my Lady M. Cavendish, choosing the name of Policrite" (no. 95, I:213–14), all written between 1662 and 1664, after the defection of Lucasia, and all exhibiting Orinda's consciousness of the difficulties of friendship with social superiors. Ann Boyle was known as Valeria; Mary Cavendish, whose maiden name was Butler, was a daughter of the duke of Ormonde. This dispersal of Philips's poetic affections among several different women is telling in light of the philosophy she had expounded in "A Dialogue of Friendship multiplyed" (no. 97, I:215–16): "The purity of friendship's flame" requires "that the hearts so close do knit, / They no third partner can admit."

51. I distinguish here between the conduct books, memoirs, and other widely disseminated vernacular texts discussed above and the poetry and prose narratives more traditionally described as "literature" and referred to by Stephen Latt, "The Progress of Friendship: The Topoi for Society and the Ideal Experience in the Poetry and Prose of Seventeenth-Century England."

52. Latt, "Progress of Friendship," 74.

53. Latt, "Progress of Friendship," 187.

54. Latt, "Progress of Friendship," 184.

55. Reginald Heber, ed., *The Whole Works of the Right Rev. Jeremy Taylor*, 15 vols. (London, 1822), 11:299–335, esp. 331. Philips takes up this issue in "A Friend" (Thomas, *Collected Works*, no. 64, I:165–68): "If soules no sexes have, for men 't'exclude / Women from friendship's vast capacity, / Is a design injurious and rude, / Onely maintain'd by partiall tyranny."

56. Quoted in W. G. Hiscock, "*Friendship:* Francis Finch's Discourse and the Circle of the Matchless Orinda." See also Thomas, *Collected Works*, I:330–31. Philips wrote two poems in tribute to Finch: "Friendship: To the noble Palaemon on his incomparable discourse of Friendship" (Thomas, *Collected Works*, no. 12, I:83–84) and "Friendship" (no. 57, I:150–51).

57. Finch made very few copies of his discourse, wanting to keep it "from all but merciful eyes" (Hiscock, "*Friendship*," 466), only one of which seems to be extant. Hiscock remarks, with an evident awareness of the issues of sexuality raised by Finch, that the treatise "would seem to have been specifically set down for *the guidance* of Orinda and her Circle" (467; my emphasis).

58. Katherine Philips, *Poems* (London, 1667), sig. a1v–a2 (also Saintsbury, *Minor Poets*, 493).

59. Philips, *Poems*, sig. d1 (also Saintsbury, *Minor Poets*, 498). Philo-Philippa's

poem was one of the many verses and letters sent to Philips following the performance of *Pompey*. Philips's interest in Philo-Philippa no doubt contributed to
Sir Charles's decision to include the latter's verses in his edition: "One of them,
who pretends to be a woman, writes very well, but I cannot imagine who the
Author is, nor by any Inquiry I can make, have hitherto been able to discover. I
intend to keep that Copy by me, to shew it you when next we meet" (Thomas,
Collected Works, Letter 26, II:78).

60. Philips, *Poems,* sig. c1–c1ᵛ (also Saintsbury, *Minor Poets,* 496).

61. Delarivier Manley, *The Royal Mischief* (London, 1696), sig. A3ᵛ. Similar references in the prefatory material to plays by women, chiefly linking Orinda and
Astrea as precursors, continue through the 1690s into the beginning of the eighteenth century. See, for example, the commendatory poems to Catharine Trotter
that preface her plays *Agnes de Castro* (1696), *Fatal Friendship* (1698), and *The Unhappy Penitent* (1701).

62. See "Orinda and Astrea" in Cotton, *Women Playwrights,* 194–212; and Jane
Spencer, *The Rise of the Woman Novelist,* 22–33. While female writers continued
to admire the two divergent traditions fostered by the very different personal and
literary styles of Philips and Aphra Behn, male writers disparaged the flamboy-
ance of Astrea's behavior and writing.

63. Spencer also notes the persistent use of the comparison to Sappho, emphasizing its literary aspect (*Woman Novelist,* 27–32). Gerard Langbaine, *An Account of
the English Dramatick Poets,* (Oxford, 1691), sig. Cc2–Cc3ᵛ, provides an example
of the perpetuation of the literary strain of this compliment in the late seventeenth century.

64. John Duncombe, *The Feminiad* (London, 1754), sig. B2ᵛ, ll. 104–15.

65. Saintsbury, *Minor Poets,* 488.

66. See Ovid, *Heroïdes* ("Sappho to Phaon") 15.15–20; Horace, *Epistles,* 1.19.61,
and *Odes,* 2.13.24–25; and Longinus, *On the Sublime,* 10.2. The translation from
Ovid given here is Pope's 1707 version (*The Poems of Alexander Pope,* 29, ll. 17–18).

67. See Grierson, *Poems of John Donne* (1960), 110–12, for the complete text of
this poem.

68. See "Sappho" in Pierre Bayle, *An Historical and Critical Dictionary,* 4 vols.
(London, 1710), vol. 4, sig. Rrr3–Rrr4, esp. Rrr3. Bonnet, *Un choix sans équivoque,*
23–34, gives a history of Sappho and of the use of "tribade" in French literature
from the sixteenth through the nineteenth centuries. The term itself comes from
the Greek τριβείν, used to identify a woman who engaged with other women in
acts considered unnatural. The contemporary debate about Sappho's presumed
tribadism, which Bayle describes in his notes, continues in the twentieth century
as a discussion about her lesbianism. See Jacobson, *Ovid's "Heroïdes,"* 290–99;
Judith P. Hallett, "Sappho and Her Social Context: Sense and Sensuality"; and
Eva Stehle Stigers, "Romantic Sensuality, Poetic Sense: A Response to Hallett on
Sappho," for an exposition of the arguments concerning the nature of Sappho's
relations with women. "Lesbian" is of course a modern word, not in the *Oxford*

English Dictionary in its present, sexualized meaning, and in the Victorian *Century Cyclopedia* only as a prim "amatory" or "erotic."

69. A striking example of the use of pastoral conventions to convey an overtly male same-sex sexuality is that of Richard Barnfield (1574–1627), a member of the literary circle of Mary Herbert, countess of Pembroke, whose *The Affectionate Shepheard* (1594) in imitation of Virgil's second eclogue takes up the theme of the speaker's homoerotic love for Ganymede. Barnfield's poems use a pastoral setting and are sexually explicit in their playful, parodic use of convention. He developed this mode further the following year in the "Certaine Sonnets" appended to *Cynthia* (1595), a celebration of Queen Elizabeth I, in which he adapted the form of the sonnet sequence. See Bruce Smith, *Homosexual Desire,* 99–115, for an analysis of Barnfield's homoerotic poems, and *Richard Barnfield: The Complete Poems,* edited by George Klawitter, 11–58, for an account of Barnfield's life and social connections. While it is impossible to speculate—and there is no external evidence to encourage such speculation—whether Philips might have been aware of Barnfield's poetry, his early appropriation of the pastoral to voice a same-sex erotics for an all-male audience is a strong testament to the unique appropriateness of the pastoral to expressions of same-sex passion, whether explicitly phallic, as in Barnfield's case, or "chastely" erotic, as in the case of Philips.

Several male critics, among them Bruce Smith, *Homosexual Desire,* and Jonathan Goldberg, *Sodometries: Renaissance Texts, Modern Sexualities,* have noted the English Renaissance legacy of male homoerotic pastoral verse by Theocritus and Virgil in Spenser, Barnfield, and Marlowe; Stephen Whitworth, "The Name of the Ancients: Humanist Homoerotics and the Signs of Pastoral," engages their insights. Frederick Greene, "Subversions of Pastoral: Queer Theory and the Politics and Poetics of Elegy," offers a historical perspective from the Renaissance into the nineteenth century in which he argues a case for pastoral as a queer genre both because of its theme of male homoerotic desire and its form that is paradoxically communal yet solipsistic. That the pastoral also yielded opportunities for a richly expressive homoerotic discourse for women, and that Katherine Philips was the first English female poet to recognize them, is central to my argument here and in chapter 4.

70. See, for example, studies by Elizabeth H. Hageman, "Making a Good Impression: Early Texts of Poems and Letters by Katherine Philips, the 'Matchless Orinda'"; Hageman and Andrea Sununu, "'More Copies of it abroad than I could have imagin'd': Further Manuscript Texts of Katherine Philips, 'the Matchless Orinda'"; Claudia A. Limbert, "The Poetry of Katherine Philips: Holographs, Manuscripts, and Early Printed Texts"; and Ellen Moody, "Orinda, Rosania, Lucasia et aliae: Towards a New Edition of the Works of Katherine Philips."

71. Barash, *Women's Poetry,* esp. 55–100, emphasizes that female friendship in Philips's poetry carries a political valence as symbolic community-in-exile surrounding the absent body of the king. Comparing the manuscripts of the 1550s to the *Poems* of 1664—that is, during the Interregnum and following the Restoration—she observes that "[t]he manuscripts . . . suggest that Philips organized her poems differently for different audiences. . . . [T]he manuscripts' narratives . . .

cohere quite differently before and after the restoration of Charles II" (62–63). Elaborating on Barash's observation of the considerable differences in organization between manuscripts and printed texts, Wahl notes a "deliberate fracturing of Philips's narrative of her friendships with Rosania and Lucasia" (*Invisible Relations*, 164–65), which she attributes, anachronistically, to a consciousness of the threat of female same-sex bonds.

The manuscript book discussed here is National Library of Wales MS 775[A].

72. The issues surrounding the presumably unauthorized publication of the 1664 edition, which Philips repudiated, illuminate our ignorance of the complexities of the transition from manuscript to print culture and continue to vex scholars; see the recent, and opposed, analyses of Philips's possible complicity in the printing of her manuscript by Germaine Greer, "Editorial Conundra in the Texts of Katherine Philips," and *Slip-Shod Sibyls: Recognition, Rejection and the Woman Poet*, 147–72, and by Peter Beal, *In Praise of Scribes: Manuscripts and Their Makers in Seventeenth-Century England*, 147–91.

73. Margaret Cavendish, *The Convent of Pleasure: A Comedy*, in *Plays, never before printed* (London, 1668). All references are to the copy in the Folger Shakespeare Library and will be made in the text following citations.

74. Jeanne Addison Roberts, "Margaret Cavendish Plays with Shakespeare," offers a more sustained reading of the class and status issues to which Cavendish draws our attention in this play.

75. Note that this conversation anticipates the attempts of Crowne's Jupiter-disguised to seduce Calisto, discussed in my chapter 5, but with an absence of dramatic irony since the reader/audience of Cavendish's play is as yet unaware of the ploy involved.

76. The Folger Library copy of *The Convent of Pleasure*, and several other extant copies of the play, including the one at the University of Pennsylvania, contain a pasted-in printed line reading "VVritten by my Lord Duke" interpolated between the stage directions and the text in three places near the end of the play; the third and last of these interpolations appears just before the lines quoted above, at the opening of act 5, scene 2 (sig. N) between the stage direction (*"Enter Madam Mediator lamenting and crying with a Handkerchief in her hand"*) and Madam Mediator's first line, "O Gentlemen, that I never had been born. . . ." The significance of this pasted-in attribution of material to the duke of Newcastle has not been determined. My own examination of the points at which these pasted-in notices appear in *The Convent of Pleasure* and in a second play in the same volume, *The Bridals*, suggests that the duke's interpolations may appear at moments when a resolution is needed or to provide closure to a situation that has threatened to get out of hand. In the present example from *The Convent of Pleasure*, for instance, the scene presumably written by the duke may be read as reassuring the audience/reader of the boundaries between acceptable and transgressive female same-sex relations. My analysis of the duke's interpolations is speculative and provisional, pending further research.

77. This myth is the probable paradigm for a number of such sex-change narratives in early modern drama. These lines from Iphis' extended lament on her

passion for Ianthe are from the Sandys translation (*Ovid's Metamorphosis Englished by George Sandys*, 8th ed. [London, 1690]):

> What will become of me (she weeping said)
> Whom new, unknown, prodigious loves invade?
> If pitiful, the Gods should me have 'stroyed:
> Or else have giv'n what might have been injoy'd.
>
> . . . .
>
> Can Art convert a Virgin to a Boy?
> Or fit Ianthe for a maiden's joy?
> No, fix thy mind; compose thy fond desires:
> O quench these ill-advis'd and foolish fires.
>
> . . . .
>
> We both are Brides; but where is the Bride-groom?
>
> (sig. H₁₀ᵛ, H₁₁)

The myth provides opportunity both for the elaboration of transgressive passion and for its condemnation. Ironically, the passion is not destroyed but enabled by the god's intervention and an impossible passion is facilitated by the sex change. In this way, the same-sex passion of Iphis and Ianthe is affirmed as a possibility in human experience.

78. Ros Ballaster, *Seductive Forms: Women's Amatory Fiction from 1684–1740*, 75.

79. Ferguson, *First Feminists*, 147.

80. Ballaster, *Seductive Forms*, 76.

81. Ballaster, *Seductive Forms*, 76. Gilbert and Gubar, *The Norton Anthology of Literature by Women*, 94n. 1, also point out the pun in the last line.

82. I follow Delarivier Manley, *The New Atalantis (1709)*, edited by Rosalind Ballaster, p. vi, in using these dates for Manley's life. Scholars have not been able to determine her birth date more precisely than sometime between 1667 and 1671. I also rely on Ballaster's biographical introduction (pp. v–xix) for details of Manley's life.

83. See Tim Hitchcock, *English Sexualities, 1700–1800;* Hitchcock and Michèle Cohen, eds., *English Masculinities, 1660–1800;* and Randolph Trumbach, *Sex and the Gender Revolution: Heterosexuality and the Third Gender in Enlightenment London,* on the movement to a heteronormative ideology of binary sexualities in the later seventeenth and early eighteenth centuries. Hitchcock and Cohen, *English Masculinities,* 1–22, provide a very useful summary of recent historical research that addresses the nuances of this issue, particularly with respect to the social history of masculinity.

84. Manley's novels followed in the tradition of the popular French *chronique scandaleuse,* with which she was no doubt familiar (Ballaster in Manley, *New Atalantis,* vii).

85. Ballaster in Manley, *New Atalantis,* v. Manley also wrote *Queen Zara,* a satire that focuses specifically on Sarah Jennings, duchess of Marlborough, and Queen Anne's favorite.

86. Ballaster in Manley, *New Atalantis,* xiii.

87. Citations in the text refer to Delarivier Manley, *The New Atalantis (1709),* edited by Rosalind Ballaster. See also the facsimile edition, Patricia Köster, ed. *The Novels of Mary Delariviere Manley,* which includes an important "key" to the persons in the novels.

88. Bonnet, "Importance of Culture," notes that "[I]t is . . . striking that since the nineteenth century French lesbians have seldom used the word *lesbiennes* to refer to themselves, preferring the term *amitié* (friendship)" (162) and cites a number of prominent examples, including Natalie Clifford Barney's "Temple à l'Amitié" in her Paris garden. Manley's use of the French-derived "amity" should encourage us to look for additional instances in the early modern period, as in *The Maitland Quarto,* Poem XLIX.

89. Manley's account of the Cabal is a rich treasury of nonpornographic, but salacious, rhetoric of sexuality at the turn of the century. For example, in the passages that follow my selections, Manley makes it clear that those who have been "released from the imposing matrimonial fetters" are the "ornament" and governors of the Cabal; but she reserves her more serious satire of "the taste of the Cabal"— its "peculiar taste," its *"terra incognita"*—for particular individuals and for the female masculinity that informs their transvestism. These further descriptions suggest more recognizably transgressive behaviors than those of the passionate "amity" now associated with tribadism. For the purposes of my argument here, however, I have chosen not to pursue this tangential and complex issue.

90. Roger Thompson, *Unfit for Modest Ears: A Study of Pornographic, Obscene and Bawdy Works Written or Published in England in the Second Half of the Seventeenth Century,* reviews briefly the dissemination of Latin erotic texts and the popularity of Italian pornographic works in England before the Restoration and then goes on to describe the burgeoning importation of French pornography into England and translated into English that took place after 1655 and continued through the reign of Charles II (3–17).

91. The preponderance of studies still address female same-sex relations—"lesbianism"—in the nineteenth and twentieth centuries (e.g., Jane Rule, *Lesbian Images;* Estelle B. Freedman, Barbara Charlesworth Gelpi, Susan L. Johnson, and Kathleen M. Weston, eds., "Special Issue: The Lesbian Issue," *Signs 9,* no. 4 [summer 1984]; Bonnet, *Un choix;* Faderman, *Surpassing the Love of Men;* and Jeanette Foster, *Sex Variant Women in Literature,* 17–50); but an increasing number of studies survey the evidence, often written by men, for female same-sex erotics in earlier periods. Judith C. Brown's early study, in *Immodest Acts: The Life of a Lesbian Nun in Renaissance Italy,* is an extensively documented example of behavior. See also Ferguson, *First Feminists,* 31–36, for a survey of early women's writing on love and friendship; and Perry, *Celebrated Mary Astell,* esp. 120–48, for an account of late-seventeenth-century female attitudes toward sexuality.

Trumbach, "London's Sapphists," 111–36, explores some theoretical issues in the history of eighteenth-century England, while Brooten, *Love between Women,* emphasizes the active/passive dichotomies that obtained in the ancient world's understanding of sexualities and the ways in which those dichotomies were reinscribed throughout the Middle Ages. See Bruce Smith, *Homosexual Desire,* 41–53, for an excellent summary of the problems associated with modern attempts to interpret early modern English sodomy laws and the absence of their meaningful enforcement.

92. Bray, *Homosexuality in Renaissance England,* 67–68.

93. Bray and Rey, "The Body of the Friend," esp. 65, 77, 82.

94. Margaret R. Hunt, "The Sapphic Strain: English Lesbians in the Long Eighteenth Century," esp. 288, 290, 287.

95. Hunt, "Sapphic Strain," 285.

96. Bonnie Zimmerman, "What Has Never Been: An Overview of Lesbian Feminist Criticism," esp. 183–88. See also Catharine Stimpson, "Zero Degree Deviancy: The Lesbian Novel in English," and Rich, "Compulsory Heterosexuality and Lesbian Existence," 631–60. Rich's views have been the occasion of continuing discussion concerning their usefulness for historical scholarship: see Ann Ferguson, Jacquelyn N. Zita, and Kathryn Pyne Addelson, "On 'Compulsory Heterosexuality and Lesbian Existence': Defining the Issues."

97. In this respect, Faderman's perspective is like Carroll Smith-Rosenberg's de-eroticized reading of the language of nineteenth-century American women in her classic study, "The Female World of Love and Ritual: Relations between Women in Nineteenth-Century America." Zimmerman, "What Has Never Been," addresses the difficulties inherent in Faderman's definition, as does Martha Vicinus in "Sexuality and Power: A Review of Current Work in the History of Sexuality," esp. 147–51. Martin Bauml Duberman, "'I Am Not Contented': Female Masochism and Lesbianism in Early Twentieth-Century New England," esp. 83:n. 5, comments on the sometimes tenuous distinction between sensuality and sexuality made by Smith-Rosenberg.

98. The reason for this may perhaps be found in the strength of current tendencies to seek resolutions of ambiguity in biological or technological answers and so to affirm rather than to problematize sexual definition.

99. Marilyn R. Farwell, *Heterosexual Plots and Lesbian Narratives,* 19.

100. Zimmerman, "What Has Never Been," 186. While Zimmerman cautions critics to exercise judiciousness in reading texts by presumably heterosexual women, she points out that "if a text lends itself to a lesbian reading, then no amount of biographical 'proof' ought to be necessary to establish it as a lesbian text" (185). Further early elaborations of this view can be found in Barbara Smith's 1977 reading of Toni Morrison's *Sula* ("Toward a Black Feminist Criticism") and Jean E. Kennard's reader-response theory ("Ourself Behind Ourself: A Theory for Lesbian Readers").

101. Lillian Faderman, "Who Hid Lesbian History?," discusses the "techniques of bowdlerization, avoidance of the obvious" (115) used by biographers to avoid recognizing erotic relations between women, and Francis Doughty asks, "Why are there different standards of evidence in establishing heterosexuality as opposed to homosexuality?" ("Lesbian Biography, Biography of Lesbians," 123). Faderman and Doughty made this point in 1982; distressingly, evidentiary standards

for same-sex relations between women continue, in 2001, to be more stringent than they are for establishing male-female relations.

102. For the neglect and/or disparagement of Philips's poetry by some twentieth-century female critics, see, for example, Lynch, *Social Mode;* Morgan, *Female Wits;* and H. Smith, *Reason's Disciples.* Kennard's reader response theory is helpful in understanding those resisting readers who sense an unacceptable eroticism in Philips and "seek to affirm themselves by a denial of 'the other' rather than through a full recognition of it" ("Ourself," 658).

CHAPTER IV

1. I use "respectable" to describe women of the middling sort or of the aristocracy who had a social position to maintain for either economic or familial or religious reasons.

2. Jagose, *Lesbian Utopics,* 9.

3. Vicinus, "Lesbian History," 67, 72.

4. Castle, *Apparitional Lesbian,* esp. 1–20, 28–65, 107–49.

5. See Rich, "Compulsory Heterosexuality," and Stimpson, "Zero Degree Deviancy," as well as Zimmerman, "What Has Never Been," for the initial delineation of these critical stances.

6. Traub, Park, Simons, and I presented portions of our work in this field in a session on "Early Modern 'Lesbianisms': History, Theory, Representation" at Attending to Early Modern Women: A Symposium (Center for Renaissance and Baroque Studies, University of Maryland, April 1994). See Traub, "Psychomorphology"; Park, "Rediscovery of the Clitoris"; Simons, "Lesbian (In)visibility"; and Harriette Andreadis, "Sappho in Early Modern England: A Study in Sexual Reputation," for published versions of the materials presented at that conference. The work of Emma Donoghue, Theo van der Meer, and Randolph Trumbach has also enriched the study of sexual behaviors throughout Europe during this period. Patricia Crawford and Sara Mendelson's presentation of the legal materials in a case of female-female marriage provides a unique, if undertheorized, perspective on the connection between gender and sexuality ("Sexual Identities in Early Modern England: The Marriage of Two Women in 1680").

7. See chapter 2 for the role played by representations of Sappho as a cultural barometer of contemporary sexual understandings, as exemplar both of the heights of female literary achievement and of depraved, transgressive (heterosexual as well as same-sex female) sexuality.

8. See the now-classic studies of Faderman, *Surpassing the Love of Men,* and Smith-Rosenberg, "Female World," on female "romantic friendship" in the eighteenth and nineteenth centuries. Marylynne Diggs, "Romantic Friends or 'A Different Race of Creatures': The Representation of Lesbian Pathology in Nineteenth-Century America," furnishes a recent summary of the critical history of "romantic friendship" as it emerged from the relatively uncomplicated paradigm first proposed by Faderman and Smith-Rosenberg. Though Faderman and

Smith-Rosenberg were, in the '70s and '80s, loath to identify as sexual the erotics present in the texts they examine, their work does nevertheless identify the problems inherent in our retrospective attempts to comprehend the nature of sexuality and erotics for women in earlier periods. What were called "Boston marriages," which, as in the case of the Ladies of Llangollen, often also involved gender ambiguity, exemplify the difficulties posed to a modern understanding: these women were "respectable," yet their self-presentations and behaviors *read* like modern lesbianism. With the recovery and publication of the diaries of Anne Lister, it has become clear without a doubt that same-sex erotic behavior was in the later eighteenth and nineteenth centuries consciously enacted in ways that we understand as sexual. See the account of the Ladies of Llangollen by Mavor (*Ladies of Llangollen*), Whitbread's recent edition of the diaries of Anne Lister (*'I Know My Own Heart'*), and the essays of Liddington ("Anne Lister") and Anna Clark ("Anne Lister's Construction") exploring the nature of the sexuality presented in Lister's diaries.

9. Karla Jay, ed., *Lesbian Erotics,* 4.

10. Jane Garrity, "Encoding Bi-Location: Sylvia Townsend Warner and the Erotics of Dissimulation," 244.

11. Brooten, *Love between Women,* explores the notion of the "unnatural" (*para physin*) and its dependence on an active/passive distinction (i.e., necessitating a penetrator and a penetratee) for sexual behaviors during the early Christian period in the Roman world. The extent to which this distinction might have continued to operate in early modern Europe is examined by Roche, *Forbidden Friendships;* Halperin pursues the theoretical implications of this issue insofar as it is at stake in the eroticizing of hierarchy ("How to Do"); but further research is needed to determine the role that constructions of active/passive behaviors might have played in male-male relations in early modern England.

12. See collected poetry in these anthologies, among others: Robert W. Uphaus and Gretchen M. Foster, eds., *The "Other" Eighteenth Century: English Women of Letters 1660–1800;* Greer, Hastings, Medoff, and Sansone, *Kissing the Rod;* Roger Lonsdale, ed., *Eighteenth-Century Women Poets: An Oxford Anthology;* and Gilbert and Gubar, *Norton Anthology.*

13. During the Restoration, though, there were written female reimaginings of libertine poetry. See Warren Chernaik, *Sexual Freedom in Restoration Literature,* especially the chapter on Aphra Behn (160–213).

14. Berry, *Chastity,* 146. The recent work of Lawrence Manley on the growth of London (*Literature and Culture in Early Modern London*), of McKeon on the rise of domesticity ("Historicizing Patriarchy"), and of Valerie Wayne on the ideologies of marriage (intro. to *The Flower of Friendship: A Renaissance Dialogue Contesting Marriage by Edmund Tilney*) has enlarged our perspective on the complex interplay of these multiple social forces in early modern England.

15. Susanne Woods, intro. to *The Poems of Aemilia Lanyer,* xxxiii.

16. *Poems of Aemilia Lanyer,* 48.

17. Woods, intro. to *Poems of Aemilia Lanyer,* xxxvii.

18. Souers, *Matchless Orinda,* postulates that Philips had developed an actual "Society of Friendship" with herself at its center; however, as we have seen, Thomas, *Collected Works,* has questioned the existence of such a community apart from the verbal gestures of Philips and a few of her friends.

19. Ephelia continues to elude scholarly attempts to identify her, most recently by Maureen Mulvihill in the critical essay that accompanies her edition of Ephelia's *Female Poems on Several Occasions* in *Poems by Ephelia (c. 1679),* 3–88.

20. Citations in the text refer to *Poems by Ephelia (c. 1679).*

21. Jonathan Goldberg, *Women Writing: English Renaissance Examples,* explores how the erotics of class difference are played out in the writing of women. I have incorporated the perspective of his observations at many points in my own analyses of erotic ellipsis and the poetic vehicles through which it is expressed.

22. The tone here can be compared to that in Philips's letters to the unidentified gentlewoman Berenice, published in the same year as the volume of Ephelia's poems (T. Brown, ed., *Familiar Letters written by the late Earl of Rochester, with letters written by Mr. Thomas Otway and Mrs. K. Philips* [London, 1697]). It is tempting to speculate that Ephelia was familiar with these letters. Further, editions of Philips's poems continued to be current, the latest one having been published in 1678, the previous year.

23. A further echo of Philips, this time of her friendships with Sir Charles Cotterell and Sir Edward Dering, is seen in Ephelia's concern with the more abstract ethical and theoretical problems of friendship between women and men, as in her "To *Phylocles,* inviting him to Friendship." Again like Philips, Ephelia emphasizes sex difference and employs ideas of the sexlessness of the soul and platonic possibility.

24. Barash, *Poetry,* 149–52, esp. 150.

25. Another of Mary of Modena's waiting women was Sarah Jennings, later Sarah Churchill, duchess of Marlborough, who eventually became the very close companion of Queen Anne and was responsible for considerable scandal at court. See chapter 5.

26. According to Carol Shiner Wilson (intro. to *The Galesia Trilogy and Selected Manuscript Poems of Jane Barker*), currently available evidence suggests that Barker "was known at court but not necessarily an intimate there" (xxviii).

27. See Barash, *Poetry,* 152n. 10, for the likely candidates for editor and publisher of Killigrew's *Poems;* they are her father, Henry, her uncle William, or her brother Henry, with her father or brother the likeliest.

28. Anne Killigrew, *Poems* (London, 1686). Citations in the text refer to this edition.

29. Martha Rainbolt, "Their Ancient Claim: Sappho and Seventeenth and Eighteenth Century British Women's Poetry," discusses the availability of Sappho's texts during the seventeenth and eighteenth centuries and gives a thorough survey of the ways in which Sappho furnished "the foundation of a woman's legitimate right to the genre of lyric poetry" (111).

30. See Kristina Straub, "Indecent Liberties with a Poet: Audience and the Metaphor of Rape in Killigrew's 'Upon the saying that my Verses' and Pope's *Arbuthnot*," for an exploration of the feelings of violation and victimization expressed in the poem and for an analysis of the way in which Killigrew comes to terms with them by withdrawing from public space, a strategy contrasted with Philips's creation of a community of sympathetic individuals.

31. Barash, *Poetry*, 172. Barash also explores at length the ways in which Killigrew writes against various generic frames, most notably the kinds of strategies she employs by incorporating classical forms, as in the comparison between Killigrew's use of poetic speaker in "The Miseries of Man" and Virgil's in his first Eclogue (171).

32. Ann Messenger, *His & Hers: Essays in Restoration & 18th-Century Literature*, points out that this poem belongs to the familiar genre of the double tradition of Juvenal's tenth satire and Ecclesiastes' cry against vanity (25–29, esp. 25).

33. In 1903 Myra Reynolds wrote of Killigrew: "The thin volume of her published verse shows a vigor and a bitterness not to be looked for in a maid of honor. There is no hint of interest in nature, no tenderness, no lightness, almost no beauty or grace. The poems are marked by a crude virility" (intro. to *The Poems of Anne Countess of Winchelsea*, xxiii).

34. Killigrew, *Poems*, sig. M1ᵛ.

35. See Margaret Anne Doody, *The Daring Muse: Augustan Poetry Reconsidered*, 283; and Messenger, *His & Hers*, 29–36; Barash, *Poetry*, however, also relies on internal evidence in order to locate the poems: she describes them as "filled with stories and allusions that grow out of myth and ritual at the court of Mary of Modena" (154).

36. Messenger, *His & Hers*, 29 ff.

37. See Barash for another view: she concedes that these odes "are in many ways centred on what seems to be female emotional and erotic experience, and they develop—among other narratives—a story of a woman's courtship of another woman, based on the model of Katherine Philips's poetry"; yet she goes on to remark that "the beloved woman (if she is even that) is as often threatening as appealing. Therefore, it is not accurate, I think, to read these poems as evidence of Killigrew's homo-eroticism" (*Poetry*, 154n. 19). To argue for the erotic transgressiveness of these poems and for the self-contradictory complexity of their eroticism, as I do here, is not necessarily to argue (with Messenger) for an actively homoerotic experience in our terms. While Killigrew's emotional experience in these odes is affectively erotic toward other women, sometimes even taking pleasure in danger, precisely what this meant for her daily life we can never know.

38. For the erotic significance of the lute as used in early modern English poetry, see Sir Thomas Wyatt's poems "My lute awake" or "Blame not my lute." The lyre is of course inevitably associated with Sappho.

39. Heneage Finch was a nonjuror, that is, he was unwilling to take an oath to uphold the reign of William and Mary and therefore endured reprisals during their reign. See Reynolds, intro. to *Winchelsea*, xxvii–xxx; and Barbara

McGovern, *Anne Finch and Her Poetry,* 183–86, for fuller accounts of the Finches' years away from court.

40. Reynolds, *Winchelsea,* 122. Unless otherwise noted, references to the texts of Finch's poems are to this edition. Both McGovern, *Anne Finch,* and Barash, *Poetry,* have indicated that they are, separately, engaged in producing new editions of Finch's poems; these have not yet, to my knowledge, been published. The Reynolds edition collects the poems published by Finch as *Miscellany Poems, on Several Occasions* (London, 1713) as well as poems from additional manuscripts and from various published miscellanies; however, it does not include the later poems that make up the manuscript held by Wellesley College, a selection of which are published as an appendix by McGovern in *Anne Finch.*

41. Reynolds, *Winchelsea,* adds that confirmation of Behn's place of birth has been found in parish records (427).

42. See Barash, *Poetry,* 284–87, for a more complex reading of the poem than the one offered here. My own reading does not support Barash's contention that the details of this poem describe the more sympathetic perspective toward Behn that she attributes to Finch.

43. Reynolds, *Winchelsea,* 10. McGovern, *Anne Finch,* 126, also comments on this passage.

44. Reynolds, *Winchelsea,* 19–20. Finch is reputed to have been encouraged and supported in her writing by her husband and was said to have been happily married, against all probability at court at the time.

45. Reynolds identifies Ephelia as Lady Worsley (*Winchelsea,* xxxviii–xxxix).

46. McGovern, *Anne Finch,* 209–10.

47. McGovern, *Anne Finch,* 112. McGovern comments that the comforting described in this poem is "suggestive of the full range of emotional experiences the two women shared" (111). See her chapter on Finch's relations with other women, "Female Friendships and Women Writers" (108–27).

48. Coote, *Homosexual Verse,* 168–69.

49. I have consulted the copy in the Folger Shakespeare Library as well as a microfilm of the copy in the British Library. All quotations refer to this edition; signatures are given in the text.

50. Several critics remark on the autobiographical nature of Barker's verse, which both overlaps with and differs from the available record of her life. Barash, *Poetry,* cautions against reading Barker's poetry "as autobiographical in a strict sense. It is more helpful to think of both individual poems and the narratives traced among poems as Barker's attempts to make meaning of the events of her life" (181).

51. Barker would have encountered in her reading, as well as in her knowledge of the court, the existence of female sexual transgressors. She was quite skilled as an herbalist and healer and had read extensively in the Latin poets and in medical texts, among whose authors she mentions Bartholine (i.e., Thomas Bartholin) as "the first of all this Crew" ("A Farewell to POETRY, WITH A Long Digression on ANATOMY," sig. H3ᵛ). Her poem "On the Apothecary's Filing my Bills amongst

the Doctors" describes how her rejection by a suitor caused her to turn to medicine and recognizes male prejudice against women's involvement in the healing arts:

> The sturdy Gout, which all Male power withstands,
> Is overcome by my soft Female hands:
>
> . . . .
>
> Some Women-haters may be so uncivil,
> To say the Devil's cast out by the Devil;
>
> . . . .
>
> Had he been true, I'd liv'd in sottish ease;
> Ne'er study'd ought, but how to love and please:
>
> . . . .
>
> Fool that I was to sigh, weep, almost dye,
> Little fore-thinking of this present joy:
> Thus happy Brides shed tears they know not why.
> (sigs. C8ᵛ–D)

In chapter 2, I provide a description of the medical texts of Bartholin *père et fils.* See also Greer, Hastings, Medoff, and Sansone, *Kissing the Rod,* 366, for a brief account of women's relation to the healing arts.

52. See "TO MY Young Lover": "For nought can make a more preposterous show, / Than April Flowers stuck on St. Michael's Bow. / To consecrate thy first-born Sighs to me, / A superannuated Deity" (sig. E7); "TO MY Young Lover ON HIS VOW," "TO MY Young Lover. A SONG," "THE COMPLAINT," "A SONG in SCIPINA," and "A SONG. I. [The Heart you left, when you took mine]" also take up this theme.

53. "A SONG in SCIPINA," for example, concludes with a bitingly ironic comment on the unpleasant requirements for making a match: "For Beauty may as well survive / Her Climacterick Twenty-five, / As without Wealth to get or keep a Heart" (sig. F8ᵛ).

54. Pastoralism as a classic form had a sustained vogue with more or less consistency for more than a hundred years, but it was particularly attractive among royalists when the monarchy was in jeopardy and its supporters felt threatened.

55. See Wilson, intro. to *Galesia,* xxix, for an account of the recently discovered evidence about Barker's return from exile in France.

56. Anne Finch also wrote many pastoral poems and was admired as a precursor to the Romantics by Wordsworth and others in the nineteenth century; but more recent critics argue against this narrow categorizing of her landscape poetry.

57. Barash, *Poetry,* 190–91, esp. 190, compares Barker's feeling for her brother to Katherine Philips's description of Orinda's love for Lucasia, and remarks on Barker's speaker as loving her brother more than a lover. However, Barash reads both instances of poetic feeling as idealizing a "political partner."

58. The complete title of this novel is revealing because it picks up the strains of thought in her earlier poetry: *A Patch-Work Screen for the Ladies; or, Love and Virtue Recommended: In a Collection of Instructive Novels. Related After a Manner in-*

tirely New, and interspersed with Rural Poems, describing the Innocence of a Country-Life. During her sojourn in France following her departure from London, Barker turned to writing novels. We can see this change of genre anticipated in the poems in *Poetical Recreations* in which she asserts her intention to take leave of verse writing and in the poems that indicate an underlying unhappiness with her financial situation. The lack of recognition for her poetry in London and her lack of wealth encouraged her, I believe, to seek income from novel writing. However, she did not altogether stop writing poetry after 1688. That she had novels already in mind is,evident in some of the comments of her Cambridge friends in *Poetical Recreations* and in her references to Galesia, who appears in the title of two of her earlier novels. Wilson comments that "Barker's literary career exemplifies the shift from the genteel tradition of literary production to a market-driven literary scene, where writers increasingly sought to please popular tastes to earn a living by their pens" (intro. to *Galesia*, xxxii). Barker also continued to write privately circulated poetry. There are two unpublished manuscripts of Barker's poems: "A Collection of Poems Refering to the times, since the Kings accession to the Crown," dedicated to the Prince of Wales in 1700, in the British Library (BL, ADD. MS 21,621); and "Poems on several occasions in three parts: The first refering to the times. The second, are poems writ since the author was in France, or at least most of them. The third, are taken out of a miscellany heretofore printed, and writ by the same author" (ca. 1701), in the Magdalen College Library, Oxford (Magdalen MS 343). Part 1 of this second manuscript is "virtually identical" with the volume of poems held by the British Library; part 2 collects her poems written in exile in France, a selection from which is now available at the end of Wilson's edition of Barker's *The Galesia Trilogy;* and part 3 presents Barker's revised versions of the poems in *Poetical Recreations* (*Galesia*, xlv). I have been unable to consult these manuscripts and have relied on Wilson's selection.

59. Kathryn R. King, "The Unaccountable Wife and Other Tales of Female Desire in Jane Barker's *A Patch-Work Screen for the Ladies*," 160, 165. See King for a more completely developed analysis of this tale.

60. In the previous stanza, Marissa has described the joys of a solitary, contemplative life.

61. Uphaus and Foster, *"Other" Eighteenth Century.*

62. See note 7 above.

63. Lonsdale, *Women Poets,* 56.

64. Leapor's poems were published in two volumes along with her play, *The Unhappy Father. A Tragedy,* in volume 2 of Mary Leapor, *Poems upon Several Occasions,* 2 vols. (London, 1748–51). Citations in the text refer to this edition. Donna Landry, *The Muses of Resistance: Laboring-Class Women's Poetry in Britain, 1739–1796,* remarks that Leapor's poetic voice in the second volume is more "protofeminist" than in the earlier collection of poems (99). Landry also speculates on the degree to which the laboring-class poets she discusses, including Leapor, might have known their poetic predecessors. She concludes, conservatively, that while there is no firm evidence that these poets actually had *read* Philips or Behn or

Manley, their poems often take up themes and forms with which we are already familiar in their writings. Leapor, however, considered herself a student of Pope.

65. See Heber, *Jeremy Taylor,* 11:299–335.

66. David and Jonathan were of course a traditional example of idealized yet eroticized male friendship. Abraham Cowley (1618–1667), a contemporary and admirer of Katherine Philips, had written *Davideis,* a homoerotically charged paean to male friendship that locates erotic ellipsis in an impassioned platonic discourse: "O *ye blest One*! whose *Love* on *earth* became / So pure that still in *Heav'en* 'tis but the same! / There now ye sit, and with mixt souls embrace, / Gazing upon great *Loves* mysterious Face" (book 2, ll. 114–17 [Coote, *Homosexual Verse,* 168–69]).

67. Landry, *Muses of Resistance,* 85.

68. While Orinda's immediate legacy is for the most part poetic, her articulation of female community also established a positive climate for the theoretical formulations of Mary Astell (see *A Serious Proposal* [1694]) and the increasingly visible literary presence of an explicitly defined female community in mid-eighteenth-century women's writing, for example, in Sarah Fielding's text for girls, *The Governess, or Little Female Academy* (1749), and in Sarah Scott's *Millenium Hall,* a remarkable testament to the possibilities of female friendship, published in 1762, a brief sixteen years after Leapor's death.

Barash examines "the importance of women's community as a political trope": "For numerous women writers between Philips and [Anne] Finch [1661–1720], the guise of safe, domestic affiliations between women upholds the idea—and figuratively protects the body—of the exiled monarch" (329). This additional dimension complicates and reinforces my more personal and intimate readings by suggesting a politically "respectable" rationale for the impetus to female community.

CHAPTER V

1. See Bray, "Homosexuality and the Signs of Male Friendship," and Bray and Rey, "The Body of the Friend," for astute analyses of the ways in which physicality and friendship were integrated in relations between men.

2. There is some uncertainty about when the play was first performed at court because of evidentiary ambiguities. According to Eleanore Boswell, *The Restoration Court Stage (1660–1702) with a Particular Account of the Production of* Calisto, *Calisto* was performed at least twice, in February and April 1675, with many rehearsals starting probably in November 1674; altogether, there were as many as twenty or thirty performances including rehearsals. John Evelyn, in his diary, reports attendance at performances that are likely to have been rehearsals on December 15, and again on December 22, 1674. *Calisto* was published in 1675 as a quarto, probably for presentation to members of the court, but the prologue—called by Boswell "an allegorical, operatic induction" (189)—had apparently been printed separately some months before. See also Arthur Franklin White, *John*

Crowne: His Life and Dramatic Works, 77; and John Crowne, *The Dramatic Works of John Crowne, with Prefatory Memoir and Notes,* 236–38.

3. Boswell, *Court Stage,* 225, 177. She describes *Calisto* in the following terms: "It is not really a masque at all, but a play with an operatic induction and *intermedii.* In structure it closely resembles the Restoration opera. . . . [T]hese *intermedii* bring singers and dancers from the public stage into the production, so that it represents both amateur and professional talent. . . . *Calisto* practically marks the culmination of the Court stage" (177). She estimates that the cost of the production would have been well over £5,000 (excluding costumes, jewels, etc., provided by amateurs) as contrasted with the £2,000 average cost of a royal masque during the Jacobean period (226). There were fifty-three musical instruments, including thirty-three violins, and the Hall Theatre in Whitehall was completely refurbished, including an extension of the stage, an enlargement of orchestral space, and the movement of the frame of the picture-frame stage farther into the pit (200 ff.).

4. Crowne, *Dramatic Works,* 237.

5. Crowne, *Dramatic Works,* 227.

6. Crowne, *Dramatic Works,* 237.

7. Traub, "Perversion of 'Lesbian' Desire," 23–49, surveys selected interpretations of the Calisto myth, particularly in Italy and with special attention to Pier Francesco Cavalli's 1651 opera *La Calisto.* I am indebted to Traub for calling attention to Heywood and Crowne's versions of the myth.

8. I am very grateful to Steve Oberhelman for his valuable assistance in translating this passage. Craig Kallendorf provided additional suggestions. The social significance of the Latin concept of *"stuprum"* in the penultimate line of this passage is discussed at length by Craig A. Williams, *Roman Homosexuality: Ideologies of Masculinity in Classical Antiquity,* 96–124. While *"stuprum"* is translated here as "sexually violated," the history of ideas associated with its usage is much more complex than that translation would suggest. Traditional Roman ideologies, which continued to be reflected into early Christian times, used *"stuprum"* to describe infringements upon the sexual integrity of the freeborn, whether of males or of females. In this instance, as well as in others—for example, Danae and Ganymede—the objects of Jupiter's lustful conquests are freeborn or royal adults not considered available for sexual use in a system that mandated the subordinate status of sexual object choice. *"Stuprum"* was also defined in opposition to *"pudicitia,"* chastity; here, Calisto's is a Christianized "chastity" that does not preclude same-sex relations and whose violation is encouraged by the text of the emblem. This account of Jupiter's rape of Calisto, not only an exemplar of chastity but also the daughter of a king, is a striking illustration of the persistence of Roman ideologies into a sixteenth-century Christian context.

Theodora Jankowski, *Pure Resistance: Queer Virginity in Early Modern English Drama,* explores in detail the complex status of notions of chastity and virginity in early modern England; see especially 1–110.

9. Simons, "Lesbian (In)visibility," 98.

10. Jane Davidson Reid, ed., *Oxford Guide to Classical Mythology in the Arts, 1300–1990s*, 1:281–85, lists many versions of the Calisto myth in literature, music, and the visual arts, most of them between the early seventeenth to the mid-eighteenth century. Artistic interpretations of the myths were especially popular in Italy. From the first mention of Calisto by Dante (ca. 1321) to about 1719, seventy-one artists, writers, librettists, and composers throughout Europe produced interpretations of the Calisto myth. Of these, twenty-eight were Italian, six were English if we include Caxton's translation of Lefèvre, and the rest were either Dutch, German, or French. The Veronese and Parmigianino paintings described by Simons, inexplicably, are not mentioned in this catalogue, so we might reasonably speculate that Italian treatments may have made up almost half the total. And both operas were of course Italian: Pier Francesco Cavalli's *La Calisto* was performed in 1651–52 in Venice; Antonio Lotti and Alessandro Scarlatti's *Giove in Argo* [Jupiter in Argos], a "melodramma pastorale," was first performed in 1717 in Dresden. The best-known French treatments, by François Boucher and Jean-Honoré Fragonard, are later in the eighteenth century. It is reasonable, then, to infer that English knowledge of the Calisto myth may have been strongly influenced by Italian visual representations later in the seventeenth century when their reputation would have traveled north, but that English knowledge was initially created by the more widely available textual representations in Latin editions of the *Metamorphoses*.

Traub, "Perversion of 'Lesbian' Desire," notes that "two of the most popular scenes for visual illustration have been Diana and her nymphs bathing in their grotto, and Diana's discovery of Calisto's pregnancy and gesture of expulsion" (27). The primarily Italian provenance of these visual illustrations points to their production by a fundamentally un-English sensibility that was often derided by the English for its attitudes toward sexual desire and erotic pleasure. The Italian culture that produced lush visual representations of physical intimacies among Diana's nymphs was a culture in which, for instance, sexual relations between Florentine men and boys was demonstrably institutionalized as part of a pervasive and accepted social ethic; for extensive documentation and analysis of the conduct and integration of male same-sex behaviors into Florentine culture, see Roche, *Forbidden Friendships*. Even though the interpretations of the Calisto myth produced in Italy eventually gained currency in England, their overt, often spectacular physicality was conveyed by the English through a more oblique verbal means rather than visually reproduced, especially before the eighteenth century.

11. Simons, "Lesbian (In)visibility," 106.

12. Robert A. van Kluyve, ed., *Thomae Walsingham De Archana Deorum* (early 1400s), and Ovid, *P. Ovidii Nasonis Metamorphoſeon Libri XV. Interpretatione at Notis Illustravit Daniel Crispinus, Helvetius. . . .* Edited by Joh. Freind (Oxford, 1696).

13. Kathleen Wall, *The Callisto Myth from Ovid to Atwood: Initiation and Rape in Literature*, 26–46, provides detailed comparative readings of several of these English texts of the Calisto story. Though her readings are informed by a feminist sensibility, she does not include any acknowledgment of the homoerotic possibilities implicit in the structure of the myth.

14. Thomas Heywood, *Troia Britanica or, Great Britaines Troy* (London, 1609). A very brief prose summary of the rape of "The bright Califto" also appears in the first book of Heywood's *GYNAIKEION* (1624) in "An abſtract of all the Fables" in the *Metamorphoses* (sig. F).

15. Thomas Heywood, *The Escapes of Jupiter,* edited by Henry D. Janzen and G. R. Proudfoot (Oxford: Malone Society Reprints, Oxford University Press, 1978). The play was never published before this Malone Society Reprint, which is based on Heywood's autograph manuscript in the British Library, MS. Egerton 1994, fols. 74–95. The title *Calisto* also appears in the manuscript even though it refers only to the first act. Janzen describes the manuscript as foul papers for a play never produced and follows Alfred Harbage and Samuel Schoenbaum, *Annals of English Drama 975–1700,* 122, within the date limits of ca. 1620–41; however, Peter Davison, in his entry on Thomas Heywood in the *Dictionary of Literary Biography,* 62:101, lists the play as having been performed in London, at an unknown theater, in 1625, the date used here.

16. Heywood, *The Escapes of Jupiter.* All citations are to this edition; page numbers appear in the text. I have italicized speakers' names and slightly reformatted the selections for ease of reading.

17. Anthony Hamilton, *Memoirs of the life of Count de Grammont: containing, in particular, the amorous intrigues of the court of England in the reign of King Charles II* (London, 1714) and *Memoirs of the Count de Gramont: Containing the Amorous History of the English Court Under the Reign of Charles II,* edited by Henry Vizetelly, 2 vols. (London, [1713] 1889), 2:89.

18. Ros Ballaster, "'The Vices of Old Rome Revived': Representations of Female Same-Sex Desire in Seventeenth and Eighteenth Century England," 15.

19. David Roberts, *The Ladies: Female Patronage of Restoration Drama, 1660–1700,* 111. Roberts suggests several other passages in the main text of the play that make unexpected political reference to personalities at court. James Anderson Winn, *"When Beauty Fires the Blood": Love and the Arts in the Age of Dryden,* points out another sexual innuendo that remarks on royal behavior: "Lady Anne Fitzroy, who played Juno, was the King's illegitimate daughter by the Countess of Castlemaine, a fact that surely led to some wry faces at the point of Juno's first speech, a complaint about Jupiter's mistresses" (237).

20. Crowne, *Dramatic Works,* 268–69.

21. Edward Gregg, *Queen Anne,* 21.

22. Gregg, *Queen Anne,* 21.

23. Gregg, *Queen Anne,* 12.

24. Quoted in Gregg, *Queen Anne,* 33.

25. Thomas, *Collected Works,* Letter 13, II:43.

26. Gregg, *Queen Anne,* 28.

27. Mary and Anne were the daughters of the Protestant Anne Hyde, but James was now married to the Italian-Catholic Mary of Modena, which created bitter religious tensions within the royal family. See further biographical information in Carola Oman, *Mary of Modena.*

28. Gregg, *Queen Anne*, 50.

29. Susan S. Lanser, "Befriending the Body: Female Intimacies as Class Acts," develops a theoretical analysis of the class parameters of "sapphism" after the Restoration and through the eighteenth century.

30. Quoted in Gregg, *Queen Anne*, 302. See Frances Harris, *A Passion for Government: The Life of Sarah, Duchess of Marlborough*, for a detailed analysis of the duchess of Marlborough's life and personality. Harris notes that the duchess was herself of the class of middling county gentry and was always conscious of the disability of her sex in the corridors of power: she "never ceased to chafe against [her] sense of 'insignificance' as a woman in the world of affairs. . . . 'I am confydent I should have been the greatest Hero that ever was known in the Parliament Hous, if I had been so happy as to have been a Man'" (3).

31. Quoted in Gregg, *Queen Anne*, 292.

32. Quoted in Gregg, *Queen Anne*, 326.

33. Though the duchess of Marlborough was most threatened by the queen's relations with Abigail Masham, the woman who was closest to Queen Anne in her last years was Elizabeth Percy, duchess of Somerset and, according to Gregg, "[t]he most important of her personal attendants. . . . After the Duchess of Marlborough's dismissal, the Duchess of Somerset received Sarah's principal offices, groom of the stole and first lady of the bedchamber. . . . As the heiress of the eleventh and last Earl of Northumberland, one of the oldest aristocratic families in the country, she was . . . 'the best bred as well as the best born lady in England.' She was to remain the closest royal companion during the last years of the queen's life. . . . Despite Sarah's accusations that the queen displayed a 'passion' for Abigail, the last four years of the queen's life make it clear that, while she treated the Duchess of Somerset as a companion, she continued to regard Abigail as a servant" (*Queen Anne*, 330–32). But politically, Abigail Masham continued to be the Tory rival to the duchess of Somerset at court. Unfortunately, the letters between Queen Anne and the duchess of Somerset have been destroyed and we can only speculate about what they might have revealed.

34. Quoted in Ballaster, "'Vices of Old Rome,'" 29.

35. Quoted in Ballaster, "'Vices of Old Rome,'" 30. See also Gregg, *Queen Anne*, 295.

Bibliography

Abbott, Sidney, and Barbara Love. *Sappho Was a Right-on Woman: A Liberated View of Lesbianism.* New York: Stein and Day, 1972.

Africanus, Leo. *The History and Description of Africa,* 1600.

Alciati, Andrea. *Emblemes d'Alciat, en Latin et Francois vers pour vers. Augmentez de plusiers Emblemes en latin dudict Autheur, traduictz nouvellement en Francoys.* Translated by Barthélemy Aneau [Lyons, 1565]. Paris: De l'Imprimerie de Hierosme de Marnef & Guillaume Cauellat, 1574.

———. *Emblemata: Lyons, 1550/Andrea Alciato.* Translated by Betty I. Knott. Introduction by John Manning. Facsimile rpt. Aldershot: Scolar Press, 1996.

Alloula, Malek. *The Colonial Harem.* Translated by Myrna Godzich and Wlad Godzich, 1981. Minneapolis: University of Minnesota Press, 1986.

Amano, Iodoco. *Gynæceum, Sive Theatrum Mulierum.* Francoforti [Frankfurt]: Impensis Sigismundi Feyrabendij, 1586.

Andreadis, Harriette. "The Sapphic-Platonics of Katherine Philips, 1632–1664." *Signs: A Journal of Women in Culture and Society* 15, no. 1 (autumn 1989): 34–60.

———. "Sappho in Early Modern England: A Study in Sexual Reputation." In *Re-Reading Sappho: Reception and Transmission,* edited by Ellen Greene, 105–21. Berkeley: University of California Press, 1997.

———. "The Erotics of Female Friendship in Early Modern England." In *Women's Alliances in Early Modern England,* edited by Karen Robertson and Susan Frye, 241–58. Oxford: Oxford University Press, 1999.

———. "Theorizing Early Modern Lesbianisms: Invisible Borders, Ambiguous Demarcations." In *Virtual Gender: Fantasies of Subjectivity and Embodiment,* edited by Mary Ann O'Farrell and Lynne Vallone, 125–46. Ann Arbor: University of Michigan Press, 1999.

Aneau, Barthélemy. *Picta Poesis. / Ab authore denuò recognita. / VT PICTVRA POESIS ERIT.* Lvgdvni [Lyons]: Apud Ludouicum & Carolum Pesnot, 1564.

Anonymous. *Satan's Harvest Home [London, 1749] and Hell upon Earth: or the Town in an Uproar [London, 1729].* Facsimile rpt. New York: Garland Publishing, 1985.

Applegate, Joan. "'Orinda upon Little Hector': An Unrecorded Musical Setting by Henry Lawes." In *English Manuscript Studies 1100–1700,* edited by Peter Beal and Jeremy Griffiths, 272–80. London: British Library; Toronto: University of Toronto Press, 1993.

Apter, Emily. "Female Trouble in the Colonial Harem." *differences* 4, no. 1 (1992): 205–24.

Artemidorus. *The Interpretation of Dreams: Oneirocritica.* Translated by Robert J. White. Noyes Classical Studies. Park Ridge, N.J.: Noyes Press, 1975.

Astell, Mary. *A Serious Proposal to the Ladies.* London, 1694.

Athenaeus. *The Deipnosophists*. Translated by Charles Burton Gulick. 7 vols. Cambridge: Harvard University Press; London: William Heinemann, 1969.

Aughterson, Kate, ed. *Renaissance Woman: A Sourcebook*. London: Routledge, 1995.

Aurelianus, Caelius. *On Acute Diseases and On Chronic Diseases*. Translated by I. E. Drabkin. Chicago: University of Chicago Press, 1950.

Ballaster, Rosalind. *Seductive Forms: Women's Amatory Fiction from 1684–1740*. Oxford: Clarendon Press , 1992.

———. "'The Vices of Old Rome Revived': Representations of Female Same-Sex Desire in Seventeenth and Eighteenth Century England." In *Volcanoes and Pearl Divers: Essays in Lesbian Feminist Studies*, edited by Suzanne Raitt, 13–36. Binghamton, N.Y.: Harrington Park Press, 1995.

Barash, Carol. "The Political Origins of Anne Finch's Poetry." *Huntington Library Quarterly* 54 (autumn 1991): 327–51.

———. *English Women's Poetry, 1649–1714*. Oxford: Clarendon Press, 1996.

Barker, Francis. *The Tremulous Private Body: Essays on Subjection*. London: Methuen, 1984.

Barker, Jane. *Poetical Recreations: Consisting of Original Poems, Songs, Odes, &c. With several New Translations. In Two Parts. Part I. Occasionally Written by Mrs. Jane Barker. Part II. By several Gentlemen of the Universities, and Others*. London: Printed for Benjamin Crayle, 1688.

———. *The Galesia Trilogy and Selected Manuscript Poems of Jane Barker*. Edited by Carol Shiner Wilson. New York: Oxford University Press, 1997.

Barnfield, Richard. *Richard Barnfield: The Complete Poems*. Edited by George Klawitter. Selinsgrove/London: Sesquehanna University Press; Toronto: Associated University Presses, 1990.

Barnstone, Willis, trans. *Sappho: Lyrics in the Original Greek with Translations*. New York: New York University Press, 1965.

Bartholin, Caspar. *C. Bartholini Anatomicae institutiones corporis humani*. Oxford, 1633.

Bartholin, Thomas. *The Anatomical History of Thomas Bartholin*. London, 1653.

Baudoin, Jean. *Emblèmes divers, representez dans cent quarante figures en taille douce. [Les recueils d'emblèmes et les traités de physiognomie de la Bibiothèque Interuniversitaire de Lille*. Paris: Chez Jean Baptiste Loyson, 1659]. Facsimile rpt. Paris: Aux Amateurs de Livres, 1987.

Bauhin, Casper. *Theatrum Anatomicum*. Basel, 1605.

Bayle, Pierre. *An Historical and Critical Dictionary*. 4 vols. London, 1710.

———. *Historical and Critical Dictionary*. Edited and revised by Mr. Des-Maizeaux. 2nd ed. Vol. 5. London, 1738.

Beal, Peter. "Orinda to Silvander: A New Letter by Katherine Philips." In *English Manuscript Studies 1100–1700*, edited by Peter Beal and Jeremy Griffiths, 281–86. London: British Library; Toronto: University of Toronto Press, 1993.

———. *In Praise of Scribes: Manuscripts and Their Makers in Seventeenth-Century England*. Oxford: Clarendon Press, 1998.

Behn, Aphra. "To the Fair Clarinda, Who Made Love to Me, Imagined More than Woman (1688)." In *The Norton Anthology of Literature by Women*, edited by Sandra Gilbert and Susan Gubar, 94. New York: W. W. Norton, 1985.

Belsey, Catherine. *The Subject of Tragedy: Identity and Difference in Renaissance Drama.* London: Methuen, 1985.

Bennett, Judith M. "'Lesbian-Like' and the Social History of Lesbianisms." *Journal of the History of Sexuality* 9, nos. 1–2 (January–April 2000): 1–24.

Bennett, Judith M., and Amy M. Froide, eds. *Singlewomen in the European Past, 1250–1800.* Philadelphia: University of Pennsylvania Press, 1999.

Berry, Philippa. *Of Chastity and Power: Elizabethan Literature and the Unmarried Queen.* London: Routledge, 1989.

Blackmer, Corinne. "The Ecstacies of St. Theresa." In *En travesti: Women, Gender Subversion, Opera.* New York: Columbia University Press, ca. 1995.

Blackwood, Evelyn, ed. *The Many Faces of Homosexuality.* New York: Haworth Press; London: Harrington Park Press, 1986.

Blank, Paula. "Comparing Sappho to Philaenis: John Donne's 'Homopoetics.'" *PMLA* 110, no. 3 (May 1995): 358–68.

Bonnet, Marie-Jo. *Un choix sans équivoque: Recherches historiques sur les relations amoureuses entre les femmes XVIe–XXe siècle.* Paris: Editions Denoël, 1981.

———. "Sappho, or the Importance of Culture in the Language of Love: *Tribade, Lesbienne, Homosexuelle.*" In *Queerly Phrased: Language, Gender, and Sexuality,* edited by Anna Livia and Kira Hall, 147–66. New York: Oxford University Press, 1997.

Bordo, Susan. "The Cartesian Masculinization of Thought." *Signs* 11 (1986): 439–56.

Boswell, Eleanore. *The Restoration Court Stage (1660–1702) with a Particular Account of the Production of Calisto.* Cambridge: Harvard University Press, 1932.

Boswell, John. *Christianity, Social Tolerance, and Homosexuality: Gay People in Western Europe from the Beginning of the Christian Era to the Fourteenth Century.* Chicago: University of Chicago Press, 1980.

Bosworth, William. *The chast and lost lovers lively shadowed in the person of Arcadius and Antigone, Eramio and Amissa, Phaon and Sappho. . . .* London: L. Blaiklock, 1651.

Brashear, Lucy. "The Forgotten Legacy of the 'Matchless Orinda.'" *Anglo-Welsh Review,* no. 65 (1979): 68–76.

Brathwait, Richard. *The English Gentlewoman* [London, 1631]. Amsterdam: Theatrum Orbis Terrarum; New York: Da Capo Press, 1970.

———. *The English Gentleman* [London, 1630]. Amsterdam: Theatrum Orbis Terrarum; Norwood, N.J.: W. J. Johnson, 1975.

Bray, Alan. *Homosexuality in Renaissance England.* London: Gay Men's Press, 1982.

———. "Homosexuality and the Signs of Male Friendship in Elizabethan England." In *Queering the Renaissance,* edited by Jonathan Goldberg, 40–61. Durham, N.C.: Duke University Press, 1994.

Bray, Alan, and Michael Rey. "The Body of the Friend: Continuity and Change in Masculine Friendship in the Seventeenth Century." In *English Masculinities, 1660–1800,* edited by Tim Hitchcock and Michèle Cohen, 65–84. London: Longman, 1999.

Brooten, Bernadette. *Love between Women: Early Christian Responses to Female Homoeroticism.* Chicago: University of Chicago Press, 1996.

Brown, Judith C. *Immodest Acts: The Life of a Lesbian Nun in Renaissance Italy.* New York: Oxford University Press, 1986.

Brown, T., ed. *Familiar Letters written by the late Earl of Rochester, with letters written by Mr. Thomas Otway and Mrs. K. Philips.* London, 1697.

Burton, Robert. *The Anatomy of Melancholy.* Translated by Floyd Dell. Edited by Paul Jordan-Smith. New York: Tudor Publishing, 1927.

Busbecq, Ogier Ghislain de [Augerius Gislenius Busbequius]. *Works.* Batavorvm: Ex Officina Elzeveriana, 1633.

———. *The Four Epistles of A. G. Busbequius, Concerning His Embassy into Turkey.* 1st English ed. London: J. Taylor and J. Wyat, 1694.

———. *Travels into Turkey.* London, 1744.

Camerarius, Joachim. *Symbola et Emblemata (Nürnberg 1590 bis 1604).* Facsimile rpt. 2 vols. Graz, Austria: Akademische Druk-u. Verlagsanstalt, 1986, 1988.

Castle, Terry. *The Apparitional Lesbian: Female Homosexuality and Modern Culture.* New York: Columbia University Press, 1993.

Castro, Roderici à. *Medicus-Politicus: Sive de officiis medico-politicis tractatus, quatuor distinctus Libris. . . .* Hamburgi [Hamburg]: Ex Bibliopolio Frobeniano, 1614.

Cavendish, Margaret, duchess of Newcastle. *The Convent of Pleasure: A Comedy.* In *Plays, never before printed.* London: A. Maxwell, 1668.

Chernaik, Warren. *Sexual Freedom in Restoration Literature.* Cambridge: Cambridge University Press, 1995.

Clark, Alice. *Working Life of Women in the Seventeenth Century.* London, 1919.

Clark, Anna. "Anne Lister's Construction of Lesbian Identity." *Journal of the History of Sexuality* 7, no. 1 (July 1996): 23–50.

Colman, George, ed. *Poems by Eminent Ladies. Particularly Mrs. Barber, Mrs. Behn, etc. . . . To which is prefixed, A short ACCOUNT of each Writer* [London, 1755]. Vols. I, II. Dublin: Printed for Sarah Cotter, 1757.

Connor, Margarette Regina. "Heirs to 'Astrea's Vacant Throne': Behn's Influence on Trotter, Pix, Manley and Centlivre." Ph.D. diss., City University of New York, 1995.

Cook, Harold J. *The Decline of the Old Medical Regime in Stuart London.* Ithaca: Cornell University Press, 1986.

Coote, Stephen, ed. *The Penguin Book of Homosexual Verse.* Middlesex, Eng.: Penguin, 1983.

Cotton, Nancy. *Women Playwrights in England: 1363–1750.* Lewisburg, Pa.: Bucknell University Press, 1980.

Crawford, Patricia, and Sara Mendelson. "Sexual Identities in Early Modern England: The Marriage of Two Women in 1680." *Gender & History* 7, no. 3 (November 1995): 362–77.

Cressy, David. *Literacy and the Social Order.* Cambridge: Cambridge University Press, 1980.

Crooke, Helkiah. *Microcosmographia. A Description of the Body of Man.* 2nd ed. London: Thomas and Richard Cotes, 1631 [1615].

Crowne, John. *The Dramatic Works of John Crowne, with Prefatory Memoir and Notes.* Edited by James Maidment and W. H. Logan. Vol. 1. Edinburgh: William Patterson; London: H. Sotheran & Co., 1873.

Davis, Natalie Zemon. "Boundaries and the Sense of Self in Sixteenth Century France." In *Reconstructing Individualism: Autonomy, Individuality and the Self in Western Thought,* edited by Thomas C. Heller, Morton Sosna, and David E. Wellbery. Stanford: Stanford University Press, 1986.

Davison, Peter. "Thomas Heywood." In *Dictionary of Literary Biography,* edited by Fredson Bowers, 101–35. Detroit: Gale Research, 1987.

Debus, Allen G., ed. *Medicine in Seventeenth Century England.* Berkeley: University of California Press, 1974.

DeJean, Joan. *Fictions of Sappho, 1546–1937.* Chicago: University of Chicago Press, 1989.

Dekker, Rudolf M., and Lotte C. van de Pol. *The Tradition of Female Transvestism in Early Modern Europe.* New York: St. Martin's Press, 1989.

Delmas, Christian. *Mythologie et Mythe dans Le Théâtre Français (1650–1676).* Geneva: Librairie Droz S.A., 1985.

Dering, Sir Edward. Letterbook, 1661–1665. Ohio Historical Society, Philips MS. 14932.

Diemerbroeck, Ysbrand van. *The Anatomy of Human Bodies; Comprehending the most Modern Discoveries and Curiosities in that Art.* Edited and translated by William Salmon. London: Printed for W. Whitwood, 1694.

———. *Opera Omnia, Anatomica et Medica.* London, 1685.

Digby, Sir Kenelm. *Private Memoirs of Sir Kenelm Digby . . . /written by himself . . . with an introductory memoir [by Sir Nicholas Harris Nicolas].* London: Saunders & Otley, 1827.

Diggs, Marylynne. "Romantic Friends or 'A Different Race of Creatures': The Representation of Lesbian Pathology in Nineteenth-Century America." *Feminist Studies* 21, no. 2 (summer 1995): 317–40.

Donoghue, Emma. *Passions between Women: British Lesbian Culture 1668–1801.* London: Scarlet Press, 1993.

Doody, Margaret Anne. *The Daring Muse: Augustan Poetry Reconsidered.* Cambridge: Cambridge University Press, 1985.

D[orke], W[alter]. *A tipe or figure of friendship. VVherein is liuelie, and compendiouslie expressed, the right nature and propertie of a perfect and true friend. Also a conclusion at the end in the praise of friendship.* London: Thomas Orwin and Henry Kirkham, 1589.

Doughty, Francis. "Lesbian Biography, Biography of Lesbians." In *Lesbian Studies: Present and Future,* edited by Margaret Cruikshank, 122–27. Old Westbury, N.Y.: Feminist Press, 1982.

Dover, K. J. *Greek Homosexuality.* New York: Vintage Books, 1980 [1978].

Dowling, Linda. *Hellenism and Homosexuality in Victorian Oxford.* Ithaca, N.Y.: Cornell University Press, 1994.

Duberman, Martin Bauml. "'I Am Not Contented': Female Masochism and Lesbianism in Early Twentieth-Century New England." *Signs* 5, no. 4 (summer 1980): 825–41.

Duggan, Lisa. "The Trials of Alice Mitchell: Sensationalism, Sexology, and the Lesbian Subject in Turn-of-the-Century America." *Signs* 18, no. 4 (summer 1993): 791–811.

Duncombe, John. *The Feminiad.* London, 1754.

Easton, Celia A. "Excusing the Breach of Nature's Laws: The Discourse of Denial and Disguise in Katherine Philips' Friendship Poetry." *Restoration: Studies in English Literary Culture, 1660–1700* 14, no. 1 (1990): 1–14.

Eccles, Audrey. *Obstetrics and Gynaecology in Tudor and Stuart England.* Kent, Ohio: Kent State University Press, 1982.

Edwardes, David. *Introduction to Anatomy* [1542]. Edited by C. D. O'Malley and K. F. Russell. Stanford: Stanford University Press, 1961.

Edwards, Catharine. *The Politics of Immorality in Ancient Rome.* Cambridge, Eng.: Cambridge University Press, 1993.

Ephelia [pseud.]. *Poems by Ephelia (c. 1679).* Edited by Maureen Mulvihill. 2nd printing, revised ed. Delmar, N.Y.: Scholars' Facsimiles & Reprints, 1993.

Epstein, Julia. *Altered Conditions: Disease, Medicine, and Storytelling.* New York: Routledge, 1995.

Epstein, Julia, and Kristina Straub, eds. *Body Guards: The Cultural Politics of Gender Ambiguity.* New York: Routledge, 1991.

Erickson, Peter. *Patriarchal Structures in Shakespeare's Drama.* Berkeley: University of California Press, 1985.

Estienne, Henri [Henricus Stephanus]. *Carminum poetarum novem, lyricæ poesews* [*sic*] *principum fragmenta.* Paris, 1566.

Ezell, Margaret J. M. "The *Gentleman's Journal* and the Commercialization of Restoration Coterie Literary Practices." *Modern Philology* 89 (February 1992): 323–40.

———. "Reading Pseudonyms in Seventeenth-Century English Coterie Literature." *Essays in Literature* 21 (spring 1994): 14–25.

Faderman, Lillian. *Surpassing the Love of Men: Romantic Friendship and Love between Women from the Renaissance to the Present.* New York: William Morrow, 1981.

———. "Who Hid Lesbian History?" In *Lesbian Studies: Present and Future,* edited by Margaret Cruikshank, 115–21. Old Westbury, N.Y.: Feminist Press, 1982.

Fallopius, Gabriel. *Observationes Anatomicae.* Paris, 1562.

Farnsworth, Jane. "Voicing Female Desire in 'Poem XLIX.'" *SEL* 36, no. 1 (1996): 57–72.

Farwell, Marilyn R. "Heterosexual Plots and Lesbian Subtexts: Toward a Theory of Lesbian Narrative Space." In *Lesbian Texts and Contexts: Radical Revisions,* edited by Karla Jay and Joanne Glasgow, 91–103. New York: New York University Press, 1990.

———. *Heterosexual Plots and Lesbian Narratives.* New York: New York University Press, 1996.

Ferguson, Ann, Jacquelyn N. Zita, and Kathryn Pyne Addelson. "On 'Compulsory Heterosexuality and Lesbian Existence': Defining the Issues." In *Feminist Theory: A Critique of Ideology,* edited by Nannerl O. Keohane, Michelle Z.

Rosaldo, and Barbara C. Gelpi, 147–88. Chicago: University of Chicago Press, 1982.

Ferguson, Moira, ed. *First Feminists: British Women Writers, 1578–1799.* Bloomington: Indiana University Press, 1985.

Fielding, Sarah. *The Governess, or Little Female Academy* [1749]. Intro. by Mary Cadogan. London: Pandora Press, 1987.

Fien, John [Ioannis Fieni]. *De Flatibus Humanum Corpus.* Heidelbrgæ [Heidelberg], 1589.

Filipczak, Zirka Zaremba. "Reflections on Motifs in Van Dyck's Portraits." In *Anthony van Dyck,* edited by Arthur K. Wheelock Jr., Susan J. Barnes, and Julius S. Held. New York: Harry N. Abrams, 1990.

Fletcher, Anthony, ed. *Religion, Culture, and Society in Tudor England.* Cambridge: Cambridge University Press, 1994.

Florio, John. *A Worlde of Wordes, or Most copious, and exact Dictionarie in Italian and English.* London: Printed for Edw. Blount, 1598.

———. *Queen Anna's New World of Words, or Dictionarie of the Italian and English tongues....* London: Printed for Edw. Blount and William Barret, 1611.

Foeken, Ingrid. "A Ritual a Day Keeps the Therapist Away: The Merger Process in a New Perspective." In *Homosexuality, Which Homosexuality?,* edited by Dennis Altman, Carole Vance, Martha Vicinus, Jeffrey Weeks, and others, 83–95. London: GMP Publishers; Amsterdam: Schorer, 1989.

Fornaro, Sotera. "Immagini di Saffo." In *Rose di Pieria,* edited by Francesco De Martino, 137–161. Bari: Levante, 1991.

Foster, Jeanette. *Sex Variant Women in Literature* [1956]. Tallahassee, Fla.: Naiad Press, 1985.

Frantz, David O. *"Festum Voluptatis": A Study of Renaissance Erotica.* Columbus: Ohio State University Press, 1989.

Freedman, Estelle B., Barbara Charlesworth Gelpi, Susan L. Johnson, and Kathleen M. Weston, eds. "Special Issue: The Lesbian Issue." *Signs* 9, no. 4 (summer 1984).

Freeman, Rosemary. *English Emblem Books.* London: Chatto and Windus, 1948.

Gagnier, Regenia. *Subjectivities: A History of Self-Representation in Britain, 1832–1920.* New York: Oxford University Press, 1991.

Garrity, Jane. "Encoding Bi-Location: Sylvia Townsend Warner and the Erotics of Dissimulation." In *Lesbian Erotics,* edited by Karla Jay, 241–68. New York: New York University Press, 1995.

Gemert, Lia van. "Hiding Behind Words? Lesbianism in 17th-Century Dutch Poetry." *Thamyris: Mythmaking from Past to Present* 2, no. 1 (spring 1995): 11–44.

Gerard, Kent, and Gert Hekma, eds. *The Pursuit of Sodomy: Male Homosexuality in Renaissance and Enlightenment Europe.* New York: Harrington Park Press, 1989.

Gilbert, Sandra, and Susan Gubar, eds. *The Norton Anthology of Literature by Women.* New York: W. W. Norton, 1985.

Goldberg, Jonathan. *Sodometries: Renaissance Texts, Modern Sexualities.* Stanford: Stanford University Press, 1992.

———. *Women Writing: English Renaissance Examples.* Stanford: Stanford University Press, 1997.

Goreau, Angeline, ed. *The Whole Duty of a Woman: Female Writers in Seventeenth-Century England.* Garden City, N.Y.: Dial Press, 1987.

Gottfried, Robert S. *Doctors and Medicine in Medieval England 1340–1530.* Princeton: Princeton University Press, 1986.

Gowing, Laura. *Domestic Dangers: Women, Words, and Sex in Early Modern London.* Oxford: Clarendon Press, 1996.

Greene, Frederick. "Subversions of Pastoral: Queer Theory and the Politics and Poetics of Elegy." Ph.D. diss., University of California, Santa Barbara, 1997.

Greene, Richard. *Mary Leapor: A Study in Eighteenth-Century Women's Poetry.* Oxford: Clarendon Press, 1993.

Greenhut, Deborah S. *Feminine Rhetorical Culture: Tudor Adaptations of Ovid's Heroides.* New York: Peter Lang Publishing, 1988.

Greer, Germaine. *Slip-Shod Sibyls: Recognition, Rejection and the Woman Poet.* London: Viking, 1995.

———. "Editorial Conundra in the Texts of Katherine Philips." In *Editing Women: Papers Given at the Thirty-first Annual Conference on Editorial Problems, University of Toronto, 3–4 November 1995,* edited by Ann M. Hutchison, 79–98. Toronto: University of Toronto Press, ca. 1998.

Greer, Germaine, Susan Hastings, Jeslyn Medoff, and Melinda Sansone, eds. *Kissing the Rod: An Anthology of Seventeenth-Century Women's Verse.* New York: Farrar, Straus and Giroux, 1989.

Gregg, Edward. *Queen Anne.* London: Routledge & Kegan Paul, 1980.

Grierson, Herbert J. C., ed. *The Poems of John Donne.* 2 vols. Oxford: Clarendon Press, 1912.

———, ed. *The Poems of John Donne.* London: Oxford University Press, 1960.

Grose, Francis. *A Classical Dictionary of the Vulgar Tongue.* London: Hooper, 1796.

Gyraldus, Lilius Gregorius. *Opera Omnia, duobus Tomis Distincta.—Comment. Jo. Faes, ac animadvers. P. Colomesii illustrata, cura J. Jensii.* 2 vols. Leiden: Apud Hackium, Boutesteyn, Vivie, Vander AA, & Luchtmans, 1696.

Hageman, Elizabeth H. "Katherine Philips: The Matchless Orinda." In *Women Writers of the Renaissance and Reformation,* edited by Katharina M. Wilson, 566–608. Athens: University of Georgia Press, 1987.

———. "Making a Good Impression: Early Texts of Poems and Letters by Katherine Philips, the 'Matchless Orinda.'" *South Central Review* 11, no. 2 (summer 1994): 39–52.

———. "The 'false printed' Broadside of Katherine Philips's 'To the Queens Majesty on her Happy Arrival.'" *The Library,* 6th series, 17 (1995): 321–26.

Hageman, Elizabeth H., and Andrea Sununu. "New Manuscript Texts of Katherine Philips." In *English Manuscript Studies 1100–1700,* edited by Peter Beal and Jeremy Griffiths, 174–219. London: British Library; Toronto: University of Toronto Press, 1993.

———. "'More Copies of it abroad than I could have imagin'd': Further Manuscript Texts of Katherine Philips, 'the Matchless Orinda.'" In *English Manu-*

script Studies 1100–1700, edited by Peter Beal and Jeremy Griffiths, 127–69. London: British Library, 1995.

Haggerty, George E. "'Romantic Friendship' and Patriarchal Narrative in Sarah Scott's *Millenium Hall.*" *Genders,* no. 13 (spring 1992): 108–22.

———. *Unnatural Affections: Women and Fiction in the Later 18th Century.* Bloomington: Indiana University Press, 1998.

Hallett, Judith P. "Sappho and Her Social Context: Sense and Sensuality." *Signs: Journal of Women in Culture and Society* 4, no. 3 (spring 1979): 447–64.

———. "Female Homoeroticism and the Denial of Roman Reality in Latin Literature." *Yale Journal of Criticism* 3 (1989): 209–27.

Halperin, David M. *One Hundred Years of Homosexuality and Other Essays on Greek Love.* New York: Routledge, 1990.

———. "Forgetting Foucault: Acts, Identities, and the History of Sexuality." *representations,* no. 63 (1998): 93–120.

———. "How to Do the History of Male Homosexuality." *GLQ: A Journal of Lesbian and Gay Studies* 6, no. 1 (2000): 87–123.

Halperin, David M., Ann Pellegrini, Bernadette J. Brooten, and others. "The GLQ Forum: Lesbian Historiography Before the Name? on *Love between Women.*" *GLQ: A Journal of Lesbian and Gay Studies* 4, no. 4 (1998): 557–630.

Hamilton, Anthony. *Mémoires de la vie du comte de Grammont. English. Memoirs of the life of Count de Grammont: containing, in particular, the amorous intrigues of the court of England in the reign of King Charles II.* Translated by Mr. Boyer. London, 1714.

———. *Memoirs of the Count de Gramont: Containing the Amorous History of the English Court under the Reign of Charles II* [1713]. Edited by Henry Vizetelly. 2 vols. London: Vizetelly & Co., 1889.

Hammond, Paul. "Dryden's *Albion and Albanius:* the Apotheosis of Charles II." In *The Court Masque,* edited by David Lindley, 169–83. Manchester, N.H.: Manchester University Press, 1984.

Harbage, Alfred, and Samuel Schoenbaum. *Annals of English Drama.* Philadelphia: University of Pennsylvania Press, 1964.

Hardebeck, Susan Arlene. "'If Soules No Sexes Have . . .': Women, Convention and Negotiation in the Poetry of Katherine Philips." Ph.D. diss., Northern Illinois University, 1996.

Harris, Barbara J. "Women and Politics in Early Tudor England." *The Historical Journal* 33, no. 2 (1990): 259–81.

Harris, Frances. *A Passion for Government: The Life of Sarah, Duchess of Marlborough.* Oxford: Clarendon Press, 1991.

Harris, Jocelyn. "Sappho, Souls, and the Salic Law of Wit." In *Anticipations of the Enlightenment in England, France, and Germany,* edited by Alan C. Kors and Paul J. Korshin, 232–58. Philadelphia: University of Pennsylvania Press, 1987.

Harvey, Elizabeth D. "Ventriloquizing Sappho: Ovid, Donne, and the Erotics of the Feminine Voice." *Criticism* 31, no. 2 (1989): 115–38.

Harvey, Sir Paul, and J. E. Heseltine, eds. *The Oxford Companion to French Literature.* Oxford: Clarendon Press, 1959.

Harvey, William. *Lectures on the Whole of Anatomy.* Edited by C. D. O'Malley and K. F. Russell. Berkeley: University of California Press, 1961.

Heber, Reginald, ed. *The Whole Works of the Right Rev. Jeremy Taylor.* 15 vols. London, 1822.

Henkel, Arthur, and Albrecht Schöne. *Emblemata, Handbuch zur Sinnbildkunst des XVI. und XVII. Jahrhunderts.* Stuttgart: J. B. Metzlersche Verlagsbuchhandlung, 1967.

Herdt, Gilbert, ed. *Third Sex, Third Gender: Beyond Sexual Dimorphism in Culture and History.* New York: Zone Books, 1994.

Heywood, Thomas. *GYNAIKEION: or Nine Bookes of Various History Concerninge Women; Inscribed by ye names of ye Nine Muses.* London: Printed by Adam Islip, 1624.

———. *The generall History of VVomen, Containing the Lives of the most Holy and Prophane, the most Famous and Infamous in all ages, exactly described not only from Poeticall Fictions, but from the most Ancient, Modern, and Admired Historians, to our Times.* London: Printed for W. H., 1657.

———. *The Golden and Silver Ages. Two Plays by Thomas Heywood.* Intro. and notes by J. Payne Collier. London: Shakespeare Society, 1851.

———. *Troia Britanica or, Great Britaines Troy* [London, 1609]. Facsimile rpt. Amsterdam: Theatrum Orbis Terrarum; Norwood, N.J.: W. J. Johnson, 1974.

———. *The Escapes of Jupiter.* Edited by Henry D. Janzen and G. R. Proudfoot. Oxford: Malone Society Reprints, Oxford University Press, 1978.

Hinnant, Charles H. *The Poetry of Anne Finch: An Essay in Interpretation.* Newark: University of Delaware Press; Toronto: Associated University Presses, 1994.

Hiscock, W. G. "*Friendship:* Francis Finch's Discourse and the Circle of the Matchless Orinda." *Review of English Studies* 15, no. 60 (October 1939): 466–68.

Hitchcock, Tim. "Redefining Sex in Eighteenth Century England." *History Workshop Journal* 41 (1996): 73–90.

———. *English Sexualities, 1700–1800.* New York: St. Martin's Press, 1997.

Hitchcock, Tim, and Michèle Cohen, eds. *English Masculinities, 1660–1800.* London: Longman, 1999.

Hobby, Elaine. "Katherine Philips: Seventeenth-Century Lesbian Poet." In *What Lesbians Do in Books,* edited by Elaine Hobby and Chris White, 183–204. London: Women's Press, 1991.

Hobby, Elaine, Elspeth Graham, Hilary Hinds, and Helen Wilcox, eds. *Her Own Life: Autobiographical Writings by Seventeenth-Century Englishwomen.* New York: Routledge, 1989.

Holstun, James. "'Will you rent our ancient love asunder?' Lesbian Elegy in Donne, Marvell, and Milton." *ELH* 54, no. 4 (winter 1987): 835–67.

Howard, Edward. *Poems, and Essays: With a Paraphrase on Cicero's Lælius, or Of Friendship. Written in Heroick Verse. By a Gentleman of Quality.* 1st ed. London: Printed for W. Place, 1673.

Hunt, Margaret R. "The Sapphic Strain: English Lesbians in the Long Eighteenth Century." In *Singlewomen in the European Past, 1250–1800,* edited by Judith M. Bennett and Amy M. Froide, 270–96. Philadelphia: University of Pennsylvania Press, 1999.

Hutson, Lorna. *The Usurer's Daughter: Male Friendship and Fictions of Women in Sixteenth-Century England*. London: Routledge, 1994.

Hyatte, Reginald. *The Arts of Friendship: The Idealization of Friendship in Medieval and Early Renaissance Literature*. Vol. 50, Brill's Studies in Intellectual History. Leiden: E. J. Brill, 1994.

Jacobson, Howard. *Ovid's "Heroides."* Princeton: Princeton University Press, 1974.

Jagose, Annamarie. *Lesbian Utopics*. New York: Routledge, 1994.

Jankowski, Theodora A. "'Where there can be no cause of affection': Redefining Virgins, Their Desires, and Their Pleasures in John Lyly's *Gallathea*." In *Feminist Readings of Early Modern Culture: Emerging Subjects*, edited by Valerie Traub, M. Lindsay Kaplan, and Dympna Callaghan, 253–74. Cambridge: Cambridge University Press, 1996.

———. *Pure Resistance: Queer Virginity in Early Modern English Drama*. Philadelphia: University of Pennsylvania Press, 2000.

Jay, Karla, ed. *Lesbian Erotics*. New York: New York University Press, 1995.

Jeaffreson, John Cordy, ed. *Middlesex County Records*. 5 vols. London: Middlesex County Records Society, 1886.

Jones, Ann Rosalind. *The Currency of Eros: Women's Love Lyric in Europe, 1540–1620*. Bloomington: Indiana University Press, 1990.

Jose, Nicholas. *Ideas of the Restoration in English Literature*. Cambridge: Harvard University Press, 1984.

Katz, Jonathan Ned. *The Invention of Heterosexuality*. New York: Dutton, 1995.

Kegl, Rosemary. *The Rhetoric of Concealment: Figuring Gender and Class in Renaissance Literature*. Ithaca, N.Y.: Cornell University Press, 1994.

Kendall, Kathryn M. "Women in Lesotho and the (Western) Construction of Homophobia." In *Female Desires: Same-Sex Relations and Transgender Practices across Cultures*, edited by Evelyn Blackwood and Saskia E. Wieringa, 157–78. New York: Columbia University Press, 1999.

Kennard, Jean. "Ourself Behind Ourself: A Theory for Lesbian Readers." *Signs* 9, no. 4 (summer 1984): 647–62.

Kermode, Jennifer, and Garthine Walker, eds. *Women, Crime and the Courts in Early Modern England*. Chapel Hill: University of North Carolina Press; London: UCL Press, 1994.

Killigrew, Anne. *Poems*. London: Printed for Samuel Lowndes, 1686.

King, Bruce. *Seventeenth-Century English Literature*. New York: Schocken, 1982.

King, Elspeth. *The Hidden History of Glasgow's Women*. Edinburgh: Mainstream Publishing, 1993.

King, Kathryn R. "The Unaccountable Wife and Other Tales of Female Desire in Jane Barker's *A Patch-Work Screen for the Ladies*." *The Eighteenth Century* 35, no. 2 (1994): 155–72.

Klawitter, George. "Verse Letters to T.W. from John Donne: 'By You My Love Is Sent.'" In *Homosexuality in Renaissance and Enlightenment England: Literary Representations in Historical Context*, edited by Claude J. Summers. New York: Harrington Park Press, 1992.

Kluyve, Robert A. van, ed. *Thomae Walsingham De Archana Deorum* [early 1400s]. Durham, N.C.: Duke University Press, 1968.

Köster, Patricia, ed. *The Novels of Mary Delariviere Manley.* 2 vols. Gainesville, Fla.: Scholars' Facsimiles & Reprints, 1971.

Kowaleski-Wallace, Beth. "Milton's Daughters: The Education of Eighteenth-Century Women Writers." *Feminist Studies* 12 (1986): 275–93.

Krafft-Ebing, Richard von. *Psychopathia sexualis: a medico-forensic study* [1886]. New York: Putnam, 1965.

Kramnick, Jonathan Brody. "LGSN Review: The Lesbian Century." *LGSN: Lesbian and Gay Studies Newsletter* 22, no. 2 (summer 1995): 29–30.

Landry, Donna. *The Muses of Resistance: Laboring-Class Women's Poetry in Britain, 1739–1796.* Cambridge: Cambridge University Press, 1990.

Langbaine, Gerard. *An Account of the English Dramatick Poets* [1691]. Facsimile rpt. New York: Garland, 1973.

Lange, Jennifer. "'Hearts Thus Intermixed Speak': Erotic 'Friendship' in the Poems of Katherine Philips." Ph.D. diss., Bowling Green State University, 1995.

Lanser, Susan S. "Befriending the Body: Female Intimacies as Class Acts." *Eighteenth-Century Studies* 32, no. 2 (winter 1998): 179–87.

———. "Singular Politics: The Rise of the British Nation and the Production of the Old Maid." In *Singlewomen in the European Past, 1250–1800,* edited by Judith M. Bennett and Amy M. Froide, 297–323. Philadelphia: University of Pennsylvania Press, 1999.

Lanyer, Aemilia. *The Poems of Aemilia Lanyer.* Edited by Susanne Woods. New York: Oxford University Press, 1993.

Laqueur, Thomas. "Orgasm, Generation, and the Politics of Reproductive Biology." In *The Making of the Modern Body,* edited by Catherine Gallagher and Thomas Laqueur, 1–41. Berkeley: University of California Press, 1987.

———. "'Amor Veneris, vel Dulcedo Appeletur.'" In *Fragments for a History of the Human Body,* edited by Michael Feher and others, 93–130. New York: Zone Books, 1989.

———. *Making Sex: Body and Gender from the Greeks to Freud.* Cambridge: Harvard University Press, 1990.

Lardinois, André. "Lesbian Sappho and Sappho of Lesbos." In *From Sappho to De Sade: Moments in the History of Sexuality,* edited by Jan Bremmer, 15–35. London: Routledge, 1991.

Latt, Stephen. "The Progress of Friendship: The Topoi for Society and the Ideal Experience in the Poetry and Prose of Seventeenth-Century England." Ph.D. diss., University of California, Los Angeles, 1971.

Laurentius, Andreas. *Historia Anatomica Humani Corporis et singularum eius partium multis.* Paris, 1595.

Leapor, Mary. "'The Rural Maid's Reflexions' (poem)." *London Magazine* (1747): 45.

———. *Poems upon Several Occasions.* 2 vols. London, 1748–51.

Lemay, Helen Rodnite. "Masculinity and Femininity in Early Renaissance Treatises on Human Reproduction." *Clio Medica* 18 (1983): 21–31.

Lewalski, Barbara Kiefer. *Writing Women in Jacobean England.* Cambridge: Harvard University Press, 1993.

Liddington, Jill. "Anne Lister of Shibden Hall, Halifax (1791–1840): Her Diaries and the Historians." *History Workshop: A Journal of Socialist and Feminist Historians,* no. 35 (spring 1993): 45–77.

Limbert, Claudia A. "The Collected Works of Katherine Philips, the Matchless Orinda (book review): Vol. 1: The Poems." *Philological Quarterly* 70 (fall 1991): 503–5.

———. "Katherine Philips: Controlling a Life and Reputation." *South Atlantic Review* 56, no. 2 (1991): 27–42.

———. "The Poetry of Katherine Philips: Holographs, Manuscripts, and Early Printed Texts." *Philological Quarterly* 70 (spring 1991): 181–98.

Lonsdale, Roger, ed. *Eighteenth-Century Women Poets: An Oxford Anthology.* Oxford: Oxford University Press, 1990.

Lynch, Kathleen M. *The Social Mode of Restoration Comedy.* New York: Macmillan, 1926.

Lyons, John O. *The Invention of the Self: The Hinge of Consciousness in the Eighteenth Century.* Carbondale: Southern Illinois Press, 1978.

Macfarlane, Alan. *Marriage and Love in England: Modes of Reproduction 1300– 1840.* Oxford: Basil Blackwell, 1986.

Maclean, Ian. *Woman Triumphant: Feminism in French Literature, 1610–1652.* Oxford: Clarendon Press, 1977.

———. *The Renaissance Notion of Woman: A Study in the Fortunes of Scholasticism and Medical Science in European Intellectual Life.* Cambridge: Cambridge University Press, 1980.

Magner, Lois N. *A History of Medicine.* New York: Marcel Dekker, 1992.

Maines, Rachel P. *The Technology of Orgasm: "Hysteria," the Vibrator, and Women's Sexual Satisfaction.* Baltimore: Johns Hopkins University Press, 1999.

Maitland, Sir Richard, Arbuthnot, and others. *The Maitland Quarto Manuscript.* Edited by W. A. Craigie, The Scottish Text Society. Edinburgh: William Blackwood and Sons, 1920.

Malpighius, Marcellus. *Opera Omnia, seu Thesaurus Locupletissimus Botanico-Medico-Anatomicus, . . .* Lugduni Batavorum: Apud Petrum Vander, 1687.

Mambretti, Catherine Cole. "A Critical Edition of the Poetry of Katherine Philips." Ph.D. diss., University of Chicago, 1979.

Manley, Delarivier. *The Royal Mischief.* London, 1696.

———. *The New Atalantis* [1709]. Edited by Rosalind Ballaster. New York: Penguin, 1992.

Manley, Lawrence. *Literature and Culture in Early Modern London.* Cambridge: Cambridge University Press, 1995.

Marinda. *Poems and Translations upon Several Occasions.* London: Printed by J. Tonson, 1716.

Martial. *Epigrammes.* Translated by Michel de Marolles. Paris, 1655.

———. *Epigrams.* Translated by Walter C. A. Ker. 2 vols. Loeb Classical Library. Cambridge: Harvard University Press; London: William Heinemann, 1979.

Masten, Jeffrey. *Textual Intercourse: Collaboration, Authorship, and Sexualities in Renaissance Drama.* Cambridge: Cambridge University Press, 1997.

Mavor, Elizabeth. *The Ladies of Llangollen: A Study in Romantic Friendship.* Harmondsworth: Penguin Books, 1974.

McClean, Antonia. *Humanism and the Rise of Science in Tudor England.* New York: Neale Watson, 1972.

McGovern, Barbara. *Anne Finch and Her Poetry.* Athens: University of Georgia Press, 1992.

McIntosh, Mary. "The Homosexual Role." *Social Problems* 16 (1968): 182–92.

McKeon, Michael. "Historicizing Patriarchy: The Emergence of Gender Difference in England, 1660–1760." *Eighteenth-Century Studies* 28, no. 3 (1995): 295–322.

Meem, Deborah T. "Eliza Lynn Linton and the Rise of Lesbian Consciousness." *Journal of the History of Sexuality* 7, no. 4 (April 1997): 537–60.

Meer, Theo van der. "Tribades on Trial: Female Same-Sex Offenders in Late Eighteenth-Century Amsterdam." In *Forbidden History: The State, Society, and the Regulation of Sexuality in Modern Europe,* edited by John C. Fout, pp. 189–210. Chicago: University of Chicago Press, 1992.

———. "Sodomy and the Pursuit of a Third Sex in the Early Modern Period." In *Third Sex, Third Gender: Beyond Sexual Dimorphism in Culture and History,* edited by Gilbert Herdt, 137–88. New York: Zone Books, 1994.

Mermin, Dorothy. "Women Becoming Poets: Katherine Philips, Aphra Behn, Anne Finch." *ELH* 57 (summer 1990): 335–55.

Messenger, Ann. *His & Hers: Essays in Restoration & 18th-Century Literature.* Lexington: University Press of Kentucky, 1986.

Mills, Laurens J. *One Soul in Bodies Twain: Friendship in Tudor Literature and Stuart Drama.* Bloomington, Ind.: Principia Press, 1937.

Miner, Earl. *The Cavalier Mode from Jonson to Cotton.* Princeton: Princeton University Press, 1971.

Monck, Mary. *Marinda. Poems and Translations upon Several Occasions.* London: Printed by J. Tonson, 1716.

Montagu, Mary Wortley. *The Complete Letters of Lady Mary Wortley Montagu.* Edited by Robert Halsband. Vol. 1: 1708–1720. Oxford: Clarendon Press, 1967.

———. *Turkish Embassy Letters.* Athens: University of Georgia Press, 1993.

Montaigne, Michel de. *The Essayes of Michael Lord of Montaigne.* Translated by John Florio [1603]. Vol. 1. Edited by Desmond MacCarthy. London: J. M. Dent and Sons; New York: E. P. Dutton, 1928.

Montrose, Louis Adrian. "'Shaping Fantasies': Figurations of Gender and Power in Elizabethan Culture." In *Representing the English Renaissance,* edited by Stephen Greenblatt, 31–64. Berkeley: University of California Press, 1988.

Moody, Ellen. "Orinda, Rosania, Lucasia et aliae: Towards a New Edition of the Works of Katherine Philips." *Philological Quarterly* 66 (summer 1987): 325–54.

Moore, Lisa. "'Something More Tender Still Than Friendship': Romantic Friendship in Early-Nineteenth-Century England." *Feminist Studies* 18, no. 3 (1992): 499–520.

Morgan, Fidelis. *The Female Wits: Women Playwrights of the Restoration.* London: Virago Press, 1981.

Motteux, Peter Anthony, ed. *Gentleman's Journal; Or, the Monthly Miscellany. By Way of Letter to a Gentleman in the Country. Consisting of News, History, Philosophy, Poetry, Musick, Translations, &c.* Vols. 1–3. London, [January] 1692–[November] 1694.

Mourão, Manuela. "The Representation of Female Desire in Early Modern Pornographic Texts, 1660–1745." *Signs* 24, no. 3 (spring 1999): 593–602.

Mourges, Odette de. *Metaphysical, Baroque, and Précieux Poetry.* Oxford: Clarendon Press, 1953.

Mueller, Janel. "A Letter from Lesbos: Utopian Homoerotics in Donne's 'Sapho to Philaenis.'" Unpublished essay, 1989.

———. "Lesbian Erotics: The Utopian Trope of Donne's 'Sapho to Philaenis.'" In *Homosexuality in Renaissance and Enlightenment England: Literary Representations in Historical Context,* edited by Claude Summers, 103–34. New York: Harrington Park Press, 1992.

———. "Troping Utopia: Donne's Brief for Lesbianism in 'Sapho to Philaenis.'" In *Sexuality and Gender in Early Modern Europe: Institutions, Texts, Images,* edited by James Grantham Turner, 182–207. Cambridge: Cambridge University Press, 1993.

Mulvihill, Maureen E. "*The Collected Works of Katherine Philips, the Matchless Orinda* (book review): Vol. 1: The Poems." *Eighteenth Century Studies* 26 (winter 1992/93): 346–49.

Murray, S. O. *Social Theory, Homosexual Realities.* New York: Gay Academic Union, 1984.

Nagy, Gregory. "Phaethon, Sappho's Phaon, and the White Rock of Leukas." In *Harvard Studies in Classical Philology,* 137–77. Cambridge: Harvard University Press, 1973.

Newton, Esther. "The Mythic Mannish Lesbian: Radclyffe Hall and the New Woman." *Signs* 9, no. 4 (summer 1984): 557–75.

Nicolay, Nicolas de. *Nauigations into Turkie* [London, 1585]. Translated by T. Washington the younger. Facsimile rpt. No. 48 in The English Experience. Amsterdam: Theatrum Orbis Terrarum; New York: Da Capo Press, 1968.

Norbrook, David. "'This blushinge tribute of a borrowed muse': Robert Overton and His Overturning of the Poetic Canon." In *English Manuscript Studies 1100–1700,* edited by Peter Beal and Jeremy Griffiths, 220–66. London: British Library; Toronto: University of Toronto Press, 1993.

Norton, Rictor. *Mother Clap's Molly House: The Gay Subculture in England 1700–1830.* London: GMP Publishers, 1992.

O'Driscoll, Sally. "Outlaw Readings: Beyond Queer Theory." *Signs* 22, no. 1 (1996): 30–51.

Oman, Carola. *Mary of Modena.* Bungay, Suffolk: Hodder and Stoughton, 1962.

Ostovich, Helen. "'Unpossible to Resist': Lyly's *Gallathea* and the Erotic Imperative." Unpublished essay presentation. Newport, R.I.: Group for Early Modern Cultural Studies, 1998.

Ovid. *Epistolae Heroides. / With commentary by Antonius Volscus and Ubertinus Clericus. Sappho and Ibis. With commentary by Domitius.* Venice: Bonetus Locatellus for Octavianus Scotus, 1492.

———. *Heroides cum comment. Antonii Volsci et Ubertini Clerici Crescentinatis, Suppho et libellus in Ibin cum comment. Domitii Calderini.* Venezia: Johannes Tacuinus, 1499.

———. *The Heroycall Epistles of the Learned Poet Publius Ovidius Naso, In Englishe Verse: set out and translated by George Turbervile Gent.* . . . London: Henry Denham, 1567.

———. *Publii Ouidii Nasonis Heroidum epistolae.* London, 1583.

———. *Ovid's Heroicall Epistles. Englished by W.[Wye] S. [Saltonstall].* London: Printed by R.B. for Michael Sparke, 1636.

———. *Tristia.* Cambridge, 1638.

———. *Ovids Heroical Epistles.* Translated by John Sherburne. London: Printed for William Cooke, 1639.

———. *Ovid's Epistles Translated by Several Hands.* Preface by John Dryden. London: Printed for Jacob Tonson, 1680.

———. *Ovid's Metamorphosis Englished by George Sandys.* Translated by George Sandys. 8th ed. London: Printed for A. Roper, 1690.

———. *P. Ovidii Nasonis Metamorphoseon Libri XV. Interpretatione at Notis Illustravit Daniel Crispinus, Helvetius.* . . . Edited by Joh. Freind. Oxford: E Theatro Sheldoniano, 1696.

Paradin, M. Claudius. *The Heroicall Devises of M. Claudius Paradin Canon of Beauleu. Whereunto are added the Lord Gabriel Symeons and others* [London, 1591]. Introduction by John Doebler. Delmar, N.Y.: Scholars' Facsimiles & Reprints, 1984.

Paré, Ambroise. *The Works of Ambroise Paré.* London: Richard Cotes and William Dugard, 1649.

Park, Katharine. "The Rediscovery of the Clitoris: French Medicine and the Tribade, 1570–1620." In *The Body in Parts: Fantasies of Corporeality in Early Modern Europe,* edited by Carla Mazzio and David Hillman, 171–93. New York: Routledge, 1997.

Park, Katharine, and Lorraine Daston. "The Hermaphrodite and the Orders of Nature: Sexual Ambiguity in Early Modern France." *GLQ: A Journal of Lesbian and Gay Studies* 1, no. 4 (1994): 419–38.

Park, Katharine, and Robert A. Nye. "Destiny Is Anatomy. Review of *Making Sex* by Thomas Laqueur." *The New Republic* (February 18, 1991): 53–57.

Partridge, Eric. *Shakespeare's Bawdy.* London: Routledge, 1968.

Paster, Gail Kern. *The Body Embarrassed: Drama and the Disciplines of Shame in Early Modern England.* Ithaca, N.Y.: Cornell University Press, 1993.

Pearson, Jacqueline. *The Prostituted Muse: Images of Women and Women Dramatists 1642–1737.* New York: St. Martin's Press, 1988.

Peiss, Kathy, and Christina Simmons, eds. *Passion and Power: Sexuality in History.* Philadelphia: Temple University Press, 1989.

Perry, Ruth. *The Celebrated Mary Astell.* Chicago: University of Chicago Press, 1986.

Philips, Katherine. *Poems.* 2nd ed. London, 1667.

Pincombe, Michael. "*Sappho and Phao:* A Toy Made for Ladies." In *The Plays of*

John Lyly: Eros and Eliza, edited by Michael Pincombe, 52–78. New York: Manchester University Press, 1996.

———. "Lyly and Lesbianism: Mysteries of the Closet in *Sapho and Phao.*" In *Renaissance Configurations: Voices/Bodies/Spaces, 1580–1690,* edited by Gordon McMullan, 89–107. New York: St. Martin's Press, 1998.

Plomer, Henry R. *A Dictionary of the Booksellers and Printers Who Were at Work in England, Scotland and Ireland from 1641 to 1667.* Oxford: Bibliographical Society, 1968.

Pope, Alexander. *The Poems of Alexander Pope.* Edited by John Butt. New Haven: Yale University Press, 1963.

Porter, Roy. *English Society in the Eighteenth Century.* Pelican Social History of Great Britain. London: Pelican, 1982.

———. "Making Faces: Physiognomy and Fashion in Eighteenth-Century England." *Études Anglaises: Grande Bretagne, États-Unis* 38 (1985): 383–96.

———. *Disease, Medicine and Society in England 1550–1860.* London: Macmillan, 1987.

Pritchard, Allan. "Marvell's 'The Garden': A Restoration Poem?" *Studies in English Literature, 1500–1900* 23, no. 3 (1983): 371–88.

Pritchard, Allan, and Patrick Thomas. "Orinda, Vaughan and Watkyns: Anglo-Welsh Literary Relationships During the Interregnum." *Anglo-Welsh Review* 26, no. 57 (1976): 96–102.

Purkiss, Diane. *The Witch in History: Early Modern and Twentieth-Century Representations.* London: Routledge, 1996.

Quaife, G. R. *Wanton Wenches and Wayward Wives: Peasants and Illicit Sex in Early Seventeenth Century England.* New Brunswick, N.J.: Rutgers University Press, 1979.

Rainbolt, Martha. "Their Ancient Claim: Sappho and Seventeenth and Eighteenth Century British Women's Poetry." *Seventeenth Century* 12, no. 1 (spring 1997): 111–34.

Raynalde, Thomas. *The Birth of mankynde, otherwyse named the womans booke.* [London, 1552?].

Read, Alexander. *The Manuall of the Anatomy, or, Dissection of the Body of Man.* London, 1642.

Reid, Jane Davidson, ed. *Oxford Guide to Classical Mythology in the Arts, 1300–1990s.* 2 vols. New York: Oxford University Press, 1993.

Revard, Stella P. "The Sapphic Voice in Donne's 'Sapho to Philaenis.'" In *Renaissance Discourses of Desire,* edited by Claude J. Summers and Ted-Larry Pebworth, 63–76. Columbia: University of Missouri Press, 1993.

Reynolds, Myra, ed. *The Poems of Anne Countess of Winchelsea* [Chicago, 1903]. New York: AMS Press, 1974.

Rich, Adrienne. "Compulsory Heterosexuality and Lesbian Existence." *Signs* 5, no. 4 (summer 1980): 631–60.

Richlin, Amy, and Nancy Sorkin Rabinowitz, eds. *Feminist Theory and the Classics.* New York: Routledge, 1993.

Richter, G. M. A. *The Portraits of the Greeks.* Vol. 1. London: Phaidon Press, 1965.

Roberts, David. *The Ladies: Female Patronage of Restoration Drama, 1660–1700.* Oxford English Monographs. Oxford: Clarendon Press, 1989.

Roberts, Jeanne Addison. "Convents, Conventions, and Contraventions: *Love's Labor's Lost* and *The Convent of Pleasure.*" In *Shakespeare's Sweet Thunder: Essays on the Early Comedies,* edited by Michael J. Collins. Newark: University of Delaware Press, 1997.

———. "Margaret Cavendish Plays with Shakespeare." In *Renaissance Papers 1997,* edited by T. H. Howard-Hill and Philip Rollinson, 113–24. Columbia, S.C.: Camden House, 1997.

Robinson, David Michael. "To Boldly Go Where No Man Has Gone Before: The Representation of Lesbianism in Mid-Seventeenth Century to Early Eighteenth-Century British and French Literature." Ph.D. diss., University of California, Berkeley, 1998.

Robinson, Mary. *Sappho and Phaon: In a Series of Legitimate Sonnets* [1796]. Introduction by Terence Allen Hoagwood and Rebecca Jackson. Delmar, N.Y.: Scholars' Facsimiles & Reprints, 1995.

Roche, Michael. *Forbidden Friendships: Homosexuality and Male Culture in Renaissance Florence.* New York: Oxford University Press, 1996.

Rogers, Katharine M., ed. *Selected Poems of Anne Finch Countess of Winchelsea.* New York: Frederick Ungar Publishing, 1979.

Rogers, Katharine M., and William McCarthy, eds. *The Meridian Anthology of Early Women Writers.* New York: Penguin, 1987.

Rueff, Jacob. *The Expert Midwife.* London, 1637.

Ruggiero, Guido. *Binding Passions: Tales of Magic, Marriage, and Power at the End of the Renaissance.* New York: Oxford University Press, 1993.

Rule, Jane. *Lesbian Images.* New York: Pocket Books, 1976.

Sabino, Georgio. *Fabularum Ovidii Interpretation, Tradita in Academia Regiomontana.* Wittenberg: Clemens Schleich & Antonius Schöne, 1572.

Saintsbury, George, ed. *Minor Poets of the Caroline Period.* Oxford: Clarendon Press, 1905.

Scott, Sarah. *A Description of Millenium Hall* [1762]. Edited by Gary Kelly. Ontario: Broadview Press, 1995.

Scudéry, Madeleine de. *Les Femmes Illustres or the Heroick Harrangues of the Illustrious Women.* Translated by James Innes. Edinburgh: Printed by Thomas Brown, James Glen and John Weir Booksellers, 1681.

Sedgwick, Eve Kosofsky. *Epistemology of the Closet.* Berkeley: University of California Press, 1990.

Sharp, Jane. *The Midwives Book* [London, 1671]. New York: Garland Publishing, 1985.

Shifflett, Andrew. "'How many virtues must I hate': Katherine Philips and the Politics of Clemency." *Studies in Philology* 94 (winter 1997): 103–35.

Silvius, Jacob, ed. *In Hippocratis et Galeni Physiologiae Partem Anatomicam Isagoge. . . .* Paris, 1561.

Simons, Patricia. "Lesbian (In)visibility in Italian Renaissance Culture: Diana and Other Cases of *donna con donna.*" *Journal of Homosexuality* 27, nos. 1–2 (1994): 81–122.

Singer, Charles. *Evolution of Anatomy.* New York: Steven Austin and Sons, 1925.

Siraisi, Nancy G. *Medieval and Early Renaissance Medicine: An Introduction to Knowledge and Practice.* Chicago: University of Chicago Press, 1990.

Smith, Barbara. "Toward a Black Feminist Criticism." In *The New Feminist Criticism: Essays on Women, Literature, and Theory,* edited by Elaine Showalter, 168–85. New York: Pantheon, 1977.

Smith, Bruce R. *Homosexual Desire in Shakespeare's England: A Cultural Poetics.* Chicago: University of Chicago Press, 1991.

———. "Premodern Sexualities." *PMLA* 115, no. 3 (May 2000): 318–29.

Smith, Hilda. "Gynecology and Ideology in Seventeenth-Century England." In *Liberating Women's History: Theoretical and Critical Essays,* edited by Berenice A. Carroll, 97–114. Urbana: University of Illinois Press, 1976.

———. *Reason's Disciples: Seventeenth-Century English Feminists.* Urbana: University of Illinois Press, 1982.

Smith-Rosenberg, Carroll. "The Female World of Love and Ritual: Relations between Women in Nineteenth-Century America." *Signs: Journal of Women in Culture and Society* 1 (autumn 1975): 1–29.

Snyder, Jane McIntosh. *Lesbian Desire in the Lyrics of Sappho.* New York: Columbia University Press, 1997.

Souers, Philip Webster. *The Matchless Orinda.* Cambridge: Harvard University Press, 1931.

Southerne, Thomas. *Oroonoko.* Edited by Maximillian E. Novak and David Stuart Rodes. Lincoln: University of Nebraska Press, 1976.

Spachius, Israel. *Nomenclator Scriptorum Medicorum. Hoc est: Elenchus eorum, qui artem medicam suis scriptis illustrarunt. . . .* Francofurti [Frankfurt]: Impensis Nicolai Bassæi, 1591.

Spencer, Jane. *The Rise of the Woman Novelist.* Oxford: Basil Blackwell, 1986.

Stallybrass, Peter. "Patriarchal Territories: The Body Enclosed." In *Rewriting the Renaissance: The Discourses of Sexual Difference in Early Modern Europe,* edited by Maureen Quilligan, Margaret W. Ferguson, and Nancy J. Vickers, 123–42. Chicago: University of Chicago Press, 1986.

Stanton, Domna C. "The Fiction of Préciosité and the Fear of Women." *Yale French Studies* 62 (1981): 107–34.

Stehle, Eva. "Sappho's Gaze: Fantasies of a Goddess and Young Man." *differences* 2, no. 1 (1990): 88–125.

Stein, Judith Ellen. "The Iconography of Sappho, 1775–1875." Ph.D. diss., University of Pennsylvania, 1981.

Stewart, Alan. *Close Readers: Humanism and Sodomy in Early Modern England.* Princeton: Princeton University Press, 1997.

Stiebel, Arlene. "Not Since Sappho: The Erotic in Poems of Katherine Philips and Aphra Behn." In *Homosexuality in Renaissance and Enlightenment England: Literary Representations in Historical Context,* edited by Claude Summers, 153–71. New York: Haworth Press, 1992.

Stigers, Eva Stehle. "Romantic Sensuality, Poetic Sense: A Response to Hallett on Sappho." *Signs: Journal of Women in Culture and Society* 4, no. 3 (spring 1979): 465–71.

Stimpson, Catharine. "Zero Degree Deviancy: The Lesbian Novel in English." In *Writing and Sexual Difference,* edited by Elizabeth Abel, 243–59. Chicago: University of Chicago Press, 1982.

Straub, Kristina. "Indecent Liberties with a Poet: Audience and the Metaphor of Rape in Killigrew's 'Upon the saying that my Verses' and Pope's *Arbuthnot.*" *Tulsa Studies in Women's Literature* 6, no. 1 (1987): 27–45.

Summers, Claude J., ed. *Homosexuality in Renaissance and Enlightenment England: Literary Representations in Historical Context.* New York: Haworth Press, 1992.

Symonds, John Addington. *Studies in Sexual Inversion: Embodying "A Study in Greek Ethics" and "A Study in Modern Ethics"* [1928]. New York: AMS Press, 1975.

Taylor, Charles. *Sources of the Self: The Making of the Modern Identity.* Cambridge: Harvard University Press, 1989.

Terry, Jennifer. "Theorizing Deviant Historiography." *differences* 5 (1991): 55–74.

———. "Theorizing Deviant Historiography." In *Feminists Revision History,* edited by Ann-Louise Shapiro, 276–303. New Brunswick, N.J.: Rutgers University Press, 1994.

Thomas, Patrick. *The Collected Works of Katherine Philips, The Matchless Orinda.* 3 vols. Stump Cross, Eng.: Stump Cross Books, 1990.

Thompson, Roger. *Unfit for Modest Ears: A Study of Pornographic, Obscene and Bawdy Works Written or Published in England in the Second Half of the Seventeenth Century.* London: Macmillan Press, 1979.

Tinker, Nathan P. "John Grismond: Printer of the Unauthorized Edition of Katherine Philips's Poems (1664)." *English Language Notes* 34 (September 1996): 30–35.

Tomlinson, Sophie. " 'My Brain the Stage': Margaret Cavendish and the Fantasy of Female Performance." In *Women, Texts & Histories 1575–1760,* edited by Clare Brant and Diane Purkiss, 134–63. London: Routledge, 1992.

Traub, Valerie. "The Psychomorphology of the Clitoris." *GLQ: A Journal of Lesbian and Gay Studies* 2, nos. 1–2 (1995): 81–113.

———. "The Perversion of 'Lesbian' Desire." *History Workshop Journal,* no. 41 (1996): 23–49.

———. "The Rewards of Lesbian History." *Feminist Studies* 25, no. 2 (summer 1999): 363–94.

———. "Recent Studies in Homoeroticism." *English Literary Renaissance* 30, no. 2 (spring 2000): 284–329.

Trefousse, Rashelle F. "The Reputation of Katherine Philips." Ph.D. diss., City University of New York, 1990.

Trotter, Catharine. *Agnes de Castro.* London, 1696.

———. *Fatal Friendship.* London, 1698.

———. *The Unhappy Penitent.* London, 1701.

Trumbach, Randolph. "Sodomitical Subcultures, Sodomitical Roles, and the Gender Revolution of the Eighteenth Century: The Recent Historiography." *Eighteenth Century Life* 9, no. 3 (1985): 109–21.

———. "Sex, Gender, and Sexual Identity in Modern Culture: Male Sodomy and Female Prostitution in Enlightenment London." In *Forbidden History: The State, Society, and the Regulation of Sexuality in Modern Europe,* edited by John C. Fout, 89–106. Chicago: University of Chicago Press, 1992.

———. "London's Sapphists: From Three Sexes to Four Genders in the Making of Modern Culture." In *Third Sex, Third Gender: Beyond Sexual Dimorphism in Culture and History,* edited by Gilbert Herdt, 111–36. New York: Zone Books, 1994.

———. *Sex and the Gender Revolution: Heterosexuality and the Third Gender in Enlightenment London.* Vol. 1. Chicago: University of Chicago Press, 1998.

Uphaus, Robert W., and Gretchen M. Foster, eds. *The "Other" Eighteenth Century: English Women of Letters 1660–1800.* East Lansing, Mich.: Colleagues Press, 1991.

Venette, Nicholas. *Conjugal Love; or, The Pleasures of the Marriage Bed* [London, 1750]. Facsimile rpt. New York: Garland Publishing, 1984.

Verducci, Florence. *Ovid's Toyshop of the Heart: Epistulae Herodium.* Princeton: Princeton University Press, 1985.

Vicary, Thomas. *Profitable Treatise of the Anatomie of Mans Body* [1577]. Amsterdam: Da Capo Press, 1973.

Vicinus, Martha. "Sexuality and Power: A Review of Current Work in the History of Sexuality." *Feminist Studies* 8, no. 1 (spring 1982): 133–56.

———. "Distance and Desire: English Boarding-School Friendships." *Signs* 9 (summer 1984): 600–22.

———. "Lesbian History: All Theory and No Facts or All Facts and No Theory?" *Radical History Review* 60 (1994): 57–75.

Wagner, Peter. "The Discourse on Sex—or Sex as Discourse: Eighteenth-Century Medical and Paramedical Erotica." In *Sexual Underworlds of the Enlightenment,* edited by G. S. Rousseau and Roy Porter, 46–68. Chapel Hill: University of North Carolina Press, 1988.

Wahl, Elizabeth Susan. *Invisible Relations: Representations of Female Intimacy in the Age of Enlightenment.* Stanford: Stanford University Press, 1999.

Wall, Kathleen. *The Callisto Myth from Ovid to Atwood: Initiation and Rape in Literature.* Kingston: McGill-Queen's University Press, 1988.

Waller, Jennifer R. "'My Hand a Needle Better Fits': Anne Bradstreet and Women Poets in the Renaissance." *Dalhousie Review* 54 (autumn 1974): 436–50.

Wayne, Valerie, ed. *The Flower of Friendship: A Renaissance Dialogue Contesting Marriage by Edmund Tilney.* Ithaca, N.Y.: Cornell University Press, 1992.

Weeks, Jeffrey. *Sex, Politics, and Society: The Regulation of Sexuality Since 1800.* London: [n.p.], 1981.

Wheelock, Arthur K., Jr., Susan J. Barnes, and Julius S. Held. *Anthony van Dyck.* New York: Harry N. Abrams, 1990.

Whigham, Frank. "Encoding the Alimentary Tract: More on the Body in Renaissance Drama." *ELH* 55 (1988): 333–50.

Whitbread, Helena, ed. *"I Know My Own Heart": The Diaries of Anne Lister, 1791–1840.* New York: New York University Press, 1992.

White, Arthur Franklin. *John Crowne: His Life and Dramatic Works.* Cleveland: Western Reserve University Press, 1922.

Whitworth, Stephen. "The Name of the Ancients: Humanist Homoerotics and the Signs of Pastoral." Ph.D. diss., University of Michigan, 1995.

Wiesner, Merry E. *Women and Gender in Early Modern Europe.* Cambridge: Cambridge University Press, 1993.

Williams, Craig A. *Roman Homosexuality: Ideologies of Masculinity in Classical Antiquity.* New York: Oxford University Press, 1999.

Williamson, Marilyn L. *Raising Their Voices: British Women Writers, 1650–1750.* Detroit: Wayne State University Press, 1990.

Wilson, Lyn Hatherly. *Sappho's Sweetbitter Songs: Configurations of Female and Male in Ancient Greek Lyric.* London: Routledge, 1996.

Winn, James Anderson. *"When Beauty Fires the Blood": Love and the Arts in the Age of Dryden.* Ann Arbor: University of Michigan Press, 1992.

Woods, Susanne, ed. *The Poems of Aemilia Lanyer—Salve Deus Rex Judæorum.* New York: Oxford University Press, 1993.

Woodward, Carolyn. "'My Heart So Wrapt': Lesbian Disruptions in Eighteenth-Century Fiction." *Signs* 18, no. 4 (summer 1993): 838–65.

Wrightson, Keith. "'Sorts of People' in Tudor and Stuart England." In *The Middling Sort of People: Culture, Society and Politics in England, 1550–1800,* edited by Jonathan Barry and Christopher Brooks, 28–51. New York: St. Martin's Press, 1994.

Zimmerman, Bonnie. "What Has Never Been: An Overview of Lesbian Feminist Criticism." In *Feminist Literary Criticism,* edited by Gayle Greene and Coppelia Kahn, 177–210. London: Methuen, 1985.

Zwicker, Steven, and Derek Hirst. "High Summer at Nun Appleton, 1651: Andrew Marvell and Lord Fairfax's Occasions." *Historical Journal* 36, no. 2 (1993): 247–69.

Acknowledgments

Like others engaged in a lengthy and complex project, I owe debts of gratitude to many kind and generous individuals and to my home institution, without whose interest and help I would never have undertaken, let alone have completed, this book. I want to thank the English Department and the Center for Humanities Research (formerly the Interdisciplinary Group for Humanities Studies) at Texas A&M University for their continued support in granting course releases that provided time for research. A Texas A&M University Program to Enhance Scholarly and Creative Activities Grant provided invaluable research time at the Folger Shakespeare Library during the summer of 1998. Two English Department Undergraduate Research Opportunity Awards provided research assistance, and a Women's Studies Faculty Fellowship in the summer of 1995 helped me formulate the project. Apart from this material assistance, I have benefited enormously from the goodwill and intellectual camaraderie of the Texas A&M English Department during the past ten years.

I owe Larry Mitchell special and heartfelt thanks for his support during many years of far-ranging discussions. Marian Eide and Dennis Berthold, both of whom generously read my manuscript and made crucial suggestions, contributed immeasurably to its improvement. Steve Oberhelman and Craig Kallendorf repeatedly and with great good cheer provided translations from the Latin when I was befuddled. Jackson Boswell kept directing me to material of incalculable importance. Shawn Maurer and Margot Backus made this book possible with their warm encouragement and astute comments on my earlier efforts. I am grateful also to Jane Donawerth for first suggesting that I undertake this book.

It would be impossible to name the many other colleagues and friends who have helped sharpen my thinking. Suffice it to say that I am grateful to recall the numerous conversations, virtual and real, in which others kindly have shared their ideas. My two readers for the University of Chicago Press, Bruce R. Smith and an anonymous colleague, should, however, be singled out: my work is by far better for the care and attention they lavished on it. Douglas Mitchell, Robert Devens, Erin DeWitt, and the production team at the University of Chicago Press have made my final efforts a pleasure.

Friends to whom I am particularly grateful include R L Widmann, whose companionship has always enriched my time at the Folger. For tea and sympathy, I want to acknowledge my former colleague Harry P. Kroitor and Pru Merton and Jo Spiller (and the critters of Leonard Road, especially River, Breeze, and my namesake, André): they have kept me connected to the pleasures of the material world during the months of seclusion that intellectual work demands. At home, Teddy and Vita, and now Niko, have made certain to keep me cheerful.

This book is dedicated to my sister, Demetra Carrie Andreadis, a woman of uncommon courage and great passion, whose friendship was a rare gift.

Index

Barker, Jane (*continued*)
my Adopted Brother; on the nigh
approach of his Nuptials," 134; "To
Mr. HILL, on his Verses to the Dutchess
of YORK, when she was at Cambridge,"
134; "To my BROTHER, whilst he was
in France," 139–40; "To my Cousin
Mr. E. F. on his Excellent PAINTING,"
134; "*To My Friend* Exillus, *on his
perſuading me to Marry Old* Damon,"
135–36; "To my Reverend Friend
Mr. H——. on his Presenting me The
Reasonableness of Christianity, and
The History of King CHARLES the First,
&c.," 134; "TO MY Young Lover," 210n.
52; "The Unaccountable Wife," 142–43;
"A Virgin Life," 134–35
Barley-Breake, The, or a Warning for Wantons
(W. N.), 161
Barney, Natalie Clifford, 203n. 88
Barnfield, Richard, 200n. 69
Bartholin, Caspar, 42–43
Bartholin, Thomas, 42–43, 49, 209n. 51
Bassa, 45, 46
Bayle, Pierre, 81, 199n. 68
"Beauties of the Spring, The" (Leapor), 146
Behn, Aphra (Astrea), 88–90; Barker
contrasted with, 138; Brereton on, 145;
"The Disappointment," 16, 88; Ephelia
paying homage to, 108; explicit idea of
female same-sex relations in writings
of, xii, 16, 88, 102, 104, 152; and Finch,
125, 126, 127; and Howard, 188n. 38;
and Hoyle, 90; *Lycidas; or the Lover in
Fashion,* 88; and Mary of Modena's
court, 170; "On Her Loving Two
Equally," 16, 88; Philips linked with, 79–
80, 199nn. 61, 62; *Poems,* 188n. 38; social
status of, 84; "To the Fair Clarinda," 16,
88–90, 127; as unconstrained by social
propriety, 91; "The Willing Mistress," 88
Belle Assemblée, La (Haywood), 19
Belsey, Catherine, 2, 177n. 2
Berenice (Lady Elizabeth Ker), 73–74, 75,
197nn. 45, 46, 207n. 22
Berry, Philippa, 186n. 14
Blazing World, The (Cavendish), 84
Bonnet, Marie-Jo, 178n. 5, 203n. 88
Boston marriages, 206n. 8
Boswell, Eleanore, 153, 212n. 2, 213n. 3
Boswell, John, 180n. 20
Bosworth, William, 36

Boyle, Ann (Valeria), 74–75, 198n. 50
Boyle, Lady Elizabeth (Celimena), 74–75,
198n. 50
Brashear, Lucy, 197n. 42
Brathwait, Richard: *The English Gentleman,*
65–67, 67, 195nn. 27, 28; *The English
Gentlewoman,* 65, 67–68, 100
Bray, Alan, 52, 95–96, 180n. 19, 181n. 25, 195n.
28
Brereton, Jane, 144–45
Brooten, Bernadette, 10–11, 180n. 20, 203n.
91, 206n. 11
Brown, Judith C., 180n. 20, 203n. 91
Bulstrode, Cecilia, 46
Burton, Robert, 45
Busbecq, Ogier Ghislain de (Augerius
Gislenius Busbequius), 5–7, 179n. 10

Calderinus, Domitius (Domizio Calderino),
29–30
Calisto: in Aneau's *Picta Poesis,* 155–57, 156;
in Crowne's *Calisto,* 154–55; Heywood's
treatments of, 162–67; interpretations
of myth of, 214n. 10; in Ovid, 154;
textual representations of, 160–67;
in Titian's *Diana and Callisto,* 160;
visual representations of, 155–56; in
Volaterrani's edition of Ovid, 157–59, 159
Calisto, La (Cavalli), 214n. 10
Calisto: or the Chaste Nimph (Crowne): cost
of, 213n. 3; as de-eroticizing the relations
between the nymphs, 154–55, 167,
176; Diana in costume for, 150; first
performance of, 212n. 2; as hastily
composed, 152–53; and the Hobart affair,
167–70; hybridity of form of, 153, 213n. 3;
inappropriateness of, 153–54; as male-
authored manipulation of female
same-sex erotics, 152; as mediating
between contemporary discourses
of transgressiveness, 176; Ovid's myth
as basis of, 152, 154; references to
personalities at court, 215n. 19; and
representations of Calisto and Diana's
nymphs, 155
Camerarius, Joachim, 64
Carew, Thomas, 75
Castle, Terry, 11, 20–21, 49, 102, 178n. 5
Catlin, Zachary, 37
cavalier poets, 56, 57, 58, 59, 81, 110, 193n. 12
Cavalli, Pier Francesco, 214n. 10
Cavendish, Margaret, duchess of Newcastle,

Index 252